A ROOM WITH A WORLD VIEW

50 YEARS OF INTER-CONTINENTAL HOTELS AND ITS PEOPLE

1946 – 1996

INTER·CONTINENTAL

50 YEARS OF GLOBAL HOSPITALITY

A ROOM WITH

A WORLD VIEW

50 YEARS OF INTER-CONTINENTAL HOTELS AND ITS PEOPLE 1946–1996

TEXT BY JAMES E. POTTER

INTER·CONTINENTAL®

HOTELS AND RESORTS

WEIDENFELD & NICOLSON
LONDON

First published in Great Britain in 1996 by
George Weidenfeld & Nicolson Ltd

Copyright © Inter-Continental Hotels
Corporation 1996

Weidenfeld & Nicolson Ltd
The Orion Publishing Group
Orion House
5 Upper St Martin's Lane
London WC2H 9EA

A catalogue record for this book is available from
the British Library.

ISBN 0297 83578 5

Book design by Harry Green
Printed and bound in Italy

With sincere thanks to Inter-Continental's
50th Anniversary Committee for assisting
with the worldwide anniversary campaign:
Melanie Baker, Warren Bartle,
Richard Blamey, Didier Boidin,
Johnny Fattaleh, Karen Gill,
Wolfgang Grimm, Gerhard Mitrovits,
Tom Krooswijk, Paddy Pastore,
Fred G. Peelen, Michael Prager,
Hege Salvesen, Dagmar Woodward.

C O N T E N T S

FOREWORD

On April 4 1946 a dream was born – to bring high-quality hotel accommodation to each corner of the globe, so that the demands of a growing number of international travelers could be met. Fifty years on, the overwhelming evidence that the dream has come true stands before you in the shape of Inter-Continental Hotels and Resorts, a company acknowledged as one of the world's finest providers of luxury hospitality.

As chairman of that great organization it gives me enormous pleasure to introduce this history of Inter-Continental's first half-century. It is a book that will fascinate and intrigue, inform and amuse, standing as a testimony to the achievements and durability of a company that has seen its fair share of bad times in between the good.

Perhaps most importantly, it is a tribute to the people who have put Inter-Continental where it is today: our guests, of course; our owners, naturally; and also our staff, both past and present.

The decision to chronicle the history of the company was taken in 1993 by joint managing director Robert Collier to preserve a written legacy of the company's past for the enlightenment, and perhaps amusement, of those in the future. Retired executive James E. Potter was the natural choice to undertake such a project. Potter traveled to more than twenty countries to interview over one hundred past and present employees of Inter-Continental, Pan-American Airways and Grand Metropolitan, and the Saison Group.

This book charts the efforts and resolve of such people and the company they have helped to build, from the early days in Latin America through the various changes of ownership to our current rapid expansion.

With the first fifty years now behind us, of course, our task is to ensure that the next fifty are just as illustrious and successful. If the progress made in the future is similar to that of the past, then one thing is sure: our 100th-anniversary commemorative book will make equally fascinating reading.

Seiji Tsutsumi

SEIJI TSUTSUMI

Chairman and Chief Executive Officer

THE BEGINNING

"Anticipating the need for additional hotel accommodations, particularly clean, modern accommodations for travelers of modest means, your company immediately after V-J Day undertook to sponsor the development of such facilities in all Latin American countries.

A subsidiary, Intercontinental Hotels Corporation, was organized to assist local capital in the design and construction and ultimately the management and operation of individual hotels in important traffic centers.

Our government, of course, is eager to encourage business and tourist travel abroad. Foreign travel expenditures are an important and direct contribution to dollar purchasing power in other nations, and sound two-way international trade. The Export-Import Bank is cooperating in your company's progress. A credit in the amount of $25,000,000 has been extended to facilitate the financing of the individual hotel companies, in the form of long-term mortgages to be guaranteed by the several governments or central banks. Ownership and control in the new hotels are to be held by local investors. Intercontinental Hotels Corporation and other North American companies interested in furthering Latin American trade are also taking a small financial interest in the project."

Thus, Pan American World Airways, in its 19th Annual Report covering the year 1946, advised its 35,700 shareholders that it was diversifying into the hotel trade. The incorporation of International Hotels Corporation on April 4 1946 was the culmination of a series of discussions involving Pan Am's chairman and founder Juan T. Trippe and several U.S. government officials. Early in his first term in 1933 U.S. president Franklin D. Roosevelt had made a statement that American policy toward Latin America was henceforth to be based on "neighborly cooperation" coupled with mutual respect for borders, for independence, and for others' points of view; each nation must "grow by an advancement of civilization and social well-being, not by the acquisition of territory at the expense of any neighbor." Roosevelt foresaw the need and potential for inter-American trade as a means for improving the economies of all the nations in the hemisphere; the prevailing, though not always warranted, image of the United States as the "big stick"-carrying bully from the north had to go.

In furtherance of this "good neighbor" policy, by the late 1930s two inter-American conferences had taken place under the auspices of the revitalized Pan-American Union, and Roosevelt had established the Office of Inter-American Affairs with, in 1940, Nelson Rockefeller, aged thirty-two, as coordinator. (Rockefeller is reported to have defined "coordinator" as a man who can keep all the balls in the air without losing his own.) While the immediate challenges which he faced had to do with hemispheric unity in neutralizing German (i.e., pro-Hitler) and Italian influences in South America as a matter of national defense, the long-term goal was a vast increase in U.S. trade with the Latin nations so as to enrich and strengthen local economies, thereby creating a measure of prosperity for large numbers of people in each country and diminishing the comparative appeal of alternate European-dominated influences be they fascist or communist.

As World War II neared its end, Roosevelt secured Rockefeller's appointment as assistant secretary of state for Latin American affairs under former U.S. Steel executive Edward Stettinius Jr., the newly named secretary of state, and Juan Trippe's brother-in-law. In short order Roosevelt became convinced that the success of a policy to foster trade with Latin America would depend very much on widespread expansion of sea and air services and on the building of adequate hotel facilities in many locations. It is not certain who contacted whom first, but as early as 1944, Trippe was meeting with Rockefeller and Roosevelt to discuss the whole gamut of post-war Latin-American travel, transportation and tourism planning. It was incumbent upon Trippe, as the chief executive of the leading U.S. international air carrier operating in the region in an era of governmental regulation covering rates and fares, to cooperate whenever possible. Concurrently, the whole question of U.S. post-war air policy was under review in Washington. Pan Am was pressing to be designated as the principal, if not sole, U.S. flag carrier operating an earth-girdling route system. In opposition were a powerful group of legislators and bureaucrats who wanted to see competitors on most high-density routes. Trippe needed every friend he could muster. He suggested that Statler Hotels Corporation would be an ideal American firm to undertake the appropriate hotel development activities. Statler's chief executive, H. B. Callis, was contacted, promptly undertook a detailed study, and, in due course, concluded that the project would put too great a strain on Statler's limited personnel and financial resources, which were planned to be directed at U.S. growth (Los Angeles, Dallas, Hartford) and the refurbishing of existing hotels as soon as the war ended.

Juan Terry Trippe, Pan American World Airways founder and aviation visionary, who undertook to establish the Intercontinental chain of hotels in Latin America.

Trippe contacted other U.S. hotel groups and none was interested. He was again invited to Roosevelt's office and Pan Am was specifically requested to take the lead itself in a hotel development program involving 5,000 hotel rooms in some twenty countries south of the border. At a capital cost in those days of about $10,000 per room, this was a $50,000,000 project. Trippe explained that Pan Am, whose net profit for 1945 was foreseen to be no more than $3 million, could hardly be expected to assume such a huge undertaking.

Roosevelt was not to be refused and, on the spot, sought the advice and involvement of Jesse

Jones. Jones, a wealthy financier from Texas, had joined the government in the 1930s to head the Reconstruction Finance Corporation – a lending agency created to help finance the reopening of factories and other activities aimed at lifting the U.S. economy from the depths of the Great Depression. The RFC had also helped to finance the production of war equipment which was shipped to the United Kingdom and other friendly countries under the lend-lease program prior to America's direct involvement in World War II. By 1945 all government lending agencies had been consolidated under Jones' supervision. In short order it was determined that the U.S. Export-Import Bank, an entity which had been created to finance U.S. export sales, would be the appropriate vehicle for government assistance. Ex-im was administered in those days by the U.S. State Department, with which Pan Am hammered out an agreement. A $25,000,000 line of credit was to be made available to Pan Am under which U.S. dollar denominated loans could be made by Ex-im to designated hotel-owning companies, the proceeds of which would be used to purchase goods and services (including shipping) of U.S. origin. The loans would typically have a twenty-year repayment period with a two-year moratorium from the first draw down of funds, would carry an attractive below-market interest rate (4 percent was foreseen), and would be secured by a government or central bank guarantee from the host country, which would receive a mortgage on the property as security. The loans would

ABOVE: Pan American initiated the first overseas mail flight from Miami, Florida, to Managua in Nicaragua in 1930. This shows Miami's city commissioners and postmaster loading the first mail sack on to one of the airline's clippers. RIGHT: By 1946 Pan American operated twenty-four daily services from Florida to Havana, Cuba.

be for no more than 50 percent of the total project cost and could be prepaid without penalty. While the loans were outstanding the hotels would be managed by operators who were based in the United States.

With this impressive commitment from the U.S. government, Pan Am agreed to take up the challenge, reserving the right to assign the package to an existing U.S. company if an interested one could be found, a search which continued to prove fruitless.

Pan Am knew better than anyone that many hotels would have to be built if its vision of mass civilian international business and pleasure air travel was to become reality. The large transport aircraft developed during World War II would be adapted for commercial use, and sooner or later jet-engine technology could also be applied to civilian air travel. As early as 1941 Pan Am's annual

report had made its position clear: "Air transportation has the choice . . . the very clear choice . . . of becoming a luxury service to carry the well-to-do at high prices . . . or to carry the average man for what he can afford to pay. Pan American has chosen the latter course."

While recognizing the obvious connection between air travel and hotel development, Pan Am was somewhat reluctant to dilute its airline expansion efforts. At a time when the cost of one 200-room hotel was equivalent to the asking price for four of the latest model passenger aircraft, it took an extraordinary airline executive to consider diverting scarce assets to a program of hotel construction. Trippe was such a man.

By early 1946, Pan Am's principal commercial operations consisted of a daily flight to London; three times a week to Lisbon; twice to Leopoldville in Africa; twenty-four daily services to Havana from Florida; forty-six weekly services from Miami to San Juan, Puerto Rico; and a daily departure from Miami bound for Rio. This last trip took five days, with the same crew on each leg, overnighting en route at Pan Am guesthouses in San Juan, Port of Spain in Trinidad, and Belem and Recife in Brazil. Only a small fraction of international travelers utilized air transportation, and fares were high: in 1945 dollars New York City to London was $650; N.Y.C. to San Juan, $115; Miami to Havana (a distance about the same as New York to Washington), $55.

With the hotel subsidiary a reality, and while the Pan Am legal department took care of drafting corporate by-laws, authorizing the opening of a bank account, adopting a corporate seal, collecting $1,000 from Pan American for the purchase of 100 percent of International Hotels Corporation's shares, electing a board of directors (two from the legal department staff, a Pan Am vice president and treasurer), and increasing the authorized shares to 150,000, a search was mounted for a professional management team to lead the fledgling company. Juan Trippe at the time served as a director of New York's Hotel Waldorf-Astoria Corporation and was a good friend of its chief executive, Lucius Boomer. Boomer, at sixty-seven years of age, had an impressive hotelkeeping career behind him as developer and chief executive of the McAlpin Hotel on 34th Street at Herald Square (then New York's retail hub). He had introduced such U.S. hotel business "firsts" as the six-day work week, a floor reserved exclusively for women guests, a floor with Spanish-speaking clerks and maids to cater to guests from Latin America (which might not seem a novelty in New York today, but was unheard of in the 1920s), and the employment of women as front desk receptionists and clerks. Over the years he had been chairman and/or president of the hotel owning companies of the Waldorf-Astoria (on Fifth Avenue at 34th Street, as well as the "new" Waldorf which opened in 1931 on Park Avenue); the Bellevue Stratford, the premier hotel in Philadelphia; Washington's Willard; the Windsor in Montreal; the Sherry Netherland facing New York's Central Park; and the Lennox in Boston. A deal was struck with the Waldorf to provide Boomer's services to Pan Am and he was elected chairman. Concurrently the Waldorf leased rooms 575, 577, 579, and 581 to International for use as corporate offices, at an annual rent of $8,000.

With arguably America's most famous hotelier at the helm of his new hotel company, Trippe sought an individual with financial savvy, connections in the transport industry, friends in Washington and experience in business organization to become president. The choice was Wallace Whittaker, who had served for eighteen years as general manager (the equivalent of a 1990s division president) of General Motors Corporation's Inland Division. Early in World War II he had been sought out by the U.S. Air Force Service Command as an efficiency expert in the solving of organizational problems, and was commissioned as a colonel. In Europe he organized the Service Command Transportation Division of the Ninth Air Force, where he not only headed the planning for the division but also directed the procurement of personnel and equipment.

Pan Am would exercise control over the hotel company through a board of directors consisting of Boomer, Whittaker, two airline officers, Howard Dean and Erwin Balluder (who had many years' airline experience throughout South and Central America), Arrigo Righi, a South America specialist from the Pan Am legal department, and Henry Friendly, Pan Am's general counsel. Additionally the controller and assistant treasurer's positions were assigned as part-time jobs to Pan Am comptroller John Woodbridge and Oscar Balz, a Panagra financial officer with special expertise in foreign exchange. Eugene Voit, a well-known New York hotel man of the time, served as vice president for several months.

The board's earliest actions included a delegation of authority to the company's officers to approve capital expenditures up to a value of $1,000 and annual salaries up to $5,000. The company was authorized to borrow $25,000 from Pan Am to provide operating cash; the interest rate was 3.5 percent. Pan Am's Cooperative Retirement Income Plan, a contributory pension scheme, was extended to cover International's employees. By the end of 1946, draft standard operating and management and technical services agreements (TSAs) had been developed and approved. Fact-finding trips to several key cities, initially Guatemala City, Mexico City, Rio de Janeiro (Brazil), Montevideo (Uruguay), Buenos Aires (Argentina), Merida (Mexico) and Bogota (Colombia) were authorized and carried out by one or more officers.

By the spring of 1947, the board had concluded that the company's name did not adequately reflect the intention to develop in many countries around the world. "Intercontinental" sounded more expansive and worldwide than "International". The new name was in place in time to appear in 1946's "Wings Over the World," for many years the title under which Pan Am's annual reports were issued. 1947's corporate budget (all expenditures . . . no income was foreseen) totaled $342,230, to be financed by additional share purchases by the parent company.

The initial contacts in Latin America were often facilitated by local Pan Am station managers who as a general rule had excellent connections with government officials and leading business-men in their cities. Intercontinental (which soon became known as IHC) found that governments were mostly delighted with the notion of a new hotel, and particularly with low-cost long-term financing, and frequently offered duty-free concessions on machinery, construction materials and equipment to be imported to build and furnish the hotel. They were less inclined to guarantee the Ex-im loans and finding local partners who were willing to risk the required equity capital was proving difficult.

On the whole, the history of investing in hotels has not been a particularly rosy one. Capital must be tied up for two to three years during the design and construction phases and typically a new hotel takes three years to establish itself in the marketplace and start turning a profit. Thus investors seldom see any return for up to six years . . . rather dismal when compared with simply putting one's cash in a bank. But in the long run those properties which are successful have frequently paid 15 and 20 per-

OVERLEAF: The first of a fleet of Pan American stratocruisers flying between New York and London landed at London airport in 1949. INSET: Passengers board a Pan American air liner in Miami.

cent dividends once they are mature and even higher returns as the debt capital is retired. The most successful hotel investors are those who own the property surrounding a hotel and capitalize on the appreciation in land values which almost always accrues from proximity to the center of activity which most hotels become. There is also an intangible, perhaps emotional, value which some community leaders derive from owning a hotel and which motivates them to invest despite the prospect of slow returns.

One of IHC's earliest contacts was with Alberto Dodero, an Argentine shipping magnate who had an ambition to build and own the most up-to-date and best hotel in each of the two metropolises which face each other across the hundred-mile stretches of the Rio de la Plata: Buenos Aires in Argentina and Montevideo in Uruguay. Dodero, the owner of Argentine Navigation Line, had acquired a site near the railroad station and passenger ship terminal which years later became the site of the Buenos Aires Sheraton. He was also in the process of acquiring an uncompleted twenty-two-story office block facing Montevideo's principal square, the Plaza Independencia, in the center of the city, which he planned to complete as a hotel. He was a well-known international entrepreneur and social figure in Europe and America, and maintained a grand estate on Long Island's north shore not far from New York City. He had assisted Aristotle Onassis, then a Buenos Aires-based manufacturer of very expensive hand-rolled gold-wrapped cigarettes containing rose leaves and sold mostly to fashionable women (the international opera diva Claudia Muzio was a particular fan), in acquiring his first ship: a partially sunken tanker in the Montevideo harbor which Onassis purchased for practically nothing, floated, refitted and sold for a huge profit. In 1947 Dodero was trying to sell the transatlantic part of his empire to Onassis. Argentine president Juan Peron was anxious to see the sale go ahead so that the foreign funds would flow back to Argentina, and so it was arranged for his wife Evita to travel with Dodero to Onassis' yacht in the Mediterranean to lend her charms to the sales pitch; Onassis decided not to buy.

IHC and Dodero fairly quickly negotiated a lease to cover the Montevideo hotel, which was to be called the Victoria Plaza and was expected to be completed in two to three years. The rent would be 5.7 percent of an estimated 6 million pesos capital cost and IHC would invest 750,000 pesos to provide the hotel furnishings and fixtures. Construction started and stopped and dragged on for five years during which the capital cost rose several times, the border between Uruguay and Argentina was at one point closed, and the continued devaluation of the currency and imposition of exchange controls by Argentina made it more and more difficult for Dodero to continue funding the project. Eventually IHC agreed to finance the purchase of the hotel's china, glass, silver and linen (known as the "operating equipment" in hotel parlance) and agreed to give a lien on the furnishings to the bank which had provided the mortgage financing.

On June 26 1947 Lucius Boomer was killed in an air crash while vacationing in Homar, Norway.

In mid-1947, Sylvester J. Roll was transferred from Pan Am to Intercontinental to work full time on hotel development activities in Latin America. "Spec," as he was known ("with a name like Sylvester, you've got to have a nickname," his wife Barbara explains), was a member of the first graduating class of Georgetown University's Foreign Service School and had been hired by the State Department direct from the university and posted to Stockholm, where he quickly concluded that one could not get ahead in the service unless one was financially independent. Accordingly, he joined an international bank with offices in Paris and Mexico and lost his job in the 1929 crash. Then it was back to government service and a posting as commercial attaché at the U.S. embassy in Bogota, Colombia. In 1932, with Hoover's defeat by Roosevelt in the U.S. elections, all non-career foreign service officers were expected to be replaced. Enter Juan Trippe, who hired Roll to undertake an extraordinary project in Colombia.

Colombia is a country for which air travel might have been invented. Its central part is mountainous; high in the Andes, pleasant days and cool, even cold, nights are the rule in the capital which is close to the equator but at an elevation of 8,500 feet. There were no highways capable of truck travel east and west across the country, or from the mountain cities of Bogota, Medellin and Cali to the steamy Caribbean coastal ports of Barranquilla and Cartagena. Transport was via a combination of river, rail and road. An enterprising Austrian, Peter Paul von Bauer, had recognized that air service was the ideal means of facilitating travel in Colombia and had acquired a small airline SCADTA (Colombo-German Aerial Transport Company), which was already a successful operator by 1931. In a transaction so confidential that neither the U.S. nor Colombian governments were fully aware of it, Pan Am had acquired control of SCADTA. (One sentence in the 1931 annual report alluded to an investment of a substantial interest in SCADTA.) After Hitler had taken over in Germany, the United States began to be concerned about German influence in South America; especially worrying was the notion of an apparently German-owned airline with Luftwaffe-trained pilots regularly flying very close to the Panama Canal, a shipping channel of extreme strategic importance to the United States and Europe as transit for goods between the Atlantic and Pacific. A conscious program of "delousing," as it was called, was undertaken by the U.S. government and, by extension, U.S. companies doing business in South America, particularly in Argentina, Chile, Peru, and Colombia, to neutralize German (and later Italian) influence. Roll, who was fluent in Spanish and German, had been sent by Pan Am to Colombia under a technical assistance program as one of a team to help train SCADTA staff in the latest airline operational procedures including such mundane tasks as selling tickets, unloading baggage and controlling reservations in the main stations of Bogota and Barranquilla. His real job was to get friendly with all the German nationals and Colombians of German descent, who were in key jobs with the airline, particularly pilots, in order to identify those with pro-Hitler attitudes. When the public announcement was finally made that Pan Am in fact owned SCADTA, some eighty-five German personnel identified by Roll and his team were terminated and replaced by staff secretly recruited in the United States and brought into Colombia the day before aboard a strato-cruiser, a four-engine aircraft making its first flight to South America. Politics required Roll to be transferred out of Colombia and he was put in charge of Pan Am's southern Caribbean operation, based in Caracas, Venezuela. He spent three war years in Buenos Aires, a junction point for Pan Am and its affiliates – Panair do Brasil (with services from Europe) and Panagra (serving the west coast of South America). It was a regular routine to examine the addresses on the airmail from Germany in order to identify individuals who appeared to have close contacts, and perhaps sympathies, with the Germans. This information was passed to the security services of friendly countries. After the war Roll had been sent to Stockholm to establish a network of general sales agents for Pan Am in Scandinavia.

Roll moved to Bogota and quickly became Intercontinental's full-time man south of the border. He called on the relationships developed during his postings there and in Caracas and within a year had likely candidates for forming hotel companies in these two cities and in Maracaibo, Venezuela's oil capital.

Boomer's loss left a credibility gap in the facade: there was no real hotel expertise in the executive suite. Enter Byron Calhoun, appointed vice president a month after Boomer's death. A self-made man who at fourteen had taken his first job in a hotel, Calhoun had worked his way to the top over a thirty-five year career in leading hotels, principally in the Middle West heartland of the United States. While serving as assistant to Barney Ellis, owner of the Muehlbach Hotel in Kansas City, Calhoun was approached by the owners of the Radisson Hotel in Minneapolis with an offer to become general manager. He expressed interest, but insisted on an attractively priced option to acquire a substantial shareholding as part of the deal. He got it, the hotel's fortunes improved, he made the acquisition, and by 1947 his holdings had made him a millionaire. In those many years his natural inquisitiveness and intellect had given him a detailed knowledge of virtually every aspect of the physical, managerial, and human relations principles of successful hotelkeeping as practiced in the United States. While at the Radisson his concern at the rate of employee turnover had led to his engagement of a University of Chicago professor to analyze the problem. His discovery, years ahead of its time for the industry, was that employees only perform at their best when they feel the security of knowing precisely what their jobs consist of, and why each element of their work is necessary. Training was the key, and management's responsibility was to assure structured programs of indoctrination – a far cry from the haphazard methods in use in those days.

Calhoun's first priority with IHC was to assess the anticipated needs of the likely user of their hotels, the medium-income business traveler. The basic unit, of course, is the guest room; in the forthcoming days of air travel one-bedroom suites designed for extended stays and trunks full of clothing would become obsolete. The new traveler would need basic comforts: cleanliness, a good bed, reliable hot water and potable water, a private bathroom, fast laundry and valet service, safe food, telephone and wire service provided in the guest's own language, all at a price which he and his company could afford. IHC's corporate offices, having outgrown the Waldorf, were relocated to 41 East 42nd Street where additional space had been leased in which to create a model room. Walls were moved in and out, ceilings raised and lowered, closets enlarged and contracted, floor coverings laid and ripped up, furniture sat and slept on, until an optimum design was agreed

Maracaibo in Venezuela, site of one of Intercontinental's first hotels.

upon. One of the basic designs was for a so-called studio-type room containing a bed, a sofa convertible for sleeping use when/if the room might be required for two guests, a lounge chair, a desk/dresser combination, ample space for setting up a room service table, a built-in radio and music system, a full-length mirror and ample lighting with at least one fixture controlled from a switch at the door. Potential hotel owners could be shown this product while they were visiting the

head office; in the absence of any real hotel under the IHC banner, it was the only physical indication as to what this new hotel chain was about.

Byron Calhoun had developed, and patented, a design for a "sofa bed" which consisted of a top quality upholstered box spring, and mattress with fitted cover, mounted on casters and built into a frame consisting of upholstered arms at each end and a wooden compartment at the back, against which upholstered cushions could lean when the furniture was used as a sofa. The compartment provided storage space for bed pillows during the day. To convert for sleeping, the seat of the sofa was pulled 6 to 8 inches out into the room from under the wooden compartment, the mattress cover removed to reveal a premade single bed and the pillows removed from the compartment to be replaced with the sofa back cushions. It was intended to manufacture and install this piece of furniture in about 50 percent of the guest rooms in hotels built by IHC. To avoid any conflict of interest, Calhoun assigned his design ownership rights to IHC; these rights were subsequently sold to the Englander Company, a furniture maker which later produced the item for several Intercontinental hotels, revising the hardware from time to time.

Prior to joining Intercontinental Calhoun had made a fact-finding tour to South America with some other U.S. hoteliers. He had visited Rio, Buenos Aires, Santiago and Lima and knew the standard of accommodation offered in these capitals. Gregarious and outgoing, he easily made friendships with hotel owners and managers although he spoke not a word of Spanish or Portuguese. He convinced IHC's board that there was a real opportunity to sell IHC's management services to owners of existing hotels which met a certain standard, if the company could not afford to buy the hotels outright. It should be noted that the idea of leasing had been generally shunned because the civil code of most Latin countries, based on the laws of Napoleon, gives extraordinary rights of tenancy to lessees; it was unlikely that a property owner would turn over his hotel to a foreign company under terms whereby the tenant/operator could have occupancy for a limitless term. Hence management contracts became the acceptable vehicle for foreign operators to enter the Latin hotel market.

Calhoun made approaches in several cities, but without much success. Each owner wanted to see something more than good intentions, the apparent backing of Pan Am, and a sheaf of model contracts.

Caracas sits in a "bowl" surrounded by peaks at an altitude of 3,000 feet, yet is only six miles from the Caribbean, and boasts a climate of "perpetual spring." A group of local businessmen and land developers headed by Gustavo San Roman had acquired a coffee plantation halfway up a mountainside overlooking the city center and was redeveloping the land as a high class-residential district, "Las Mercedes." As an anchor for the project, a new hotel seemed ideal. Venezuela was a newly booming nation, thanks to the discovery of large petroleum reserves in the west of the country. Major infrastructural projects were being planned. Hotel accommodation was scarce and equity funds could be found . . . an ideal combination to take to the Ex-im Bank and utilize the Pan Am/IHC credit. In Bogota, the government had made a piece of land on the edge of the city center available to the Armed Forces Retirement Fund as an endowment. Roll convinced the generals that building a hotel on one edge of the land would be a good investment in its own right while also enhancing the value of the remaining portions of the site. Again, an Ex-im loan looked attractive. And in Maracaibo local civic leaders and the oil companies were desperate to see a hotel built as soon as possible and obtained a site on the shore of Lake Maracaibo; finance would be no problem in Venezuela's "oil town." But things moved slowly, negotiations dragged on and government officials changed, often requiring IHC to restart, and repeat, negotiations of matters which had been thought to have been settled.

Back in New York, Peter Grimm had been engaged as supervising manager of hotel operations. Grimm had been in the hotel business all his life, growing up in a family-owned hotel in Budapest, and serving apprenticeships in hotels throughout Europe, while becoming fluent in most continental languages. A period spent with General Motors in Spain and Hungary had exposed him to U.S. business methods. Emigrating to the United States, he began a hotel career which would include the New Yorker and Park Central hotels in New York, the Willard in Washington and eventually, as managing director, the Drake in Philadelphia and the Town House in New York.

Whittaker, Calhoun and Grimm were traveling all over the world meeting property owners, embassy commercial officers, and Pan Am local managers and had found expressions of interest for projects in Amsterdam, Rome, Frankfurt, Copenhagen, Paris, Lisbon, Dakar, Istanbul, Johannesburg, Abadan, Beirut, Teheran, Bahrain, Manila, Bangkok, and Tokyo. The annual expenditure budget foreseen for 1949 was half a million dollars.

The Ex-im credit had yet to be utilized and a project for Mexico had been turned down by the bank. The Victoria Plaza construction had stopped once again. And Pan Am was having second thoughts about being in the hotel business.

Just before Christmas 1948, Roll returned to New York with signed purchasing, technical service and management agreements for a 400-room hotel — the Tequendama — in Bogota, together with the various Colombian government assurances and concessions needed to successfully conclude a $4,000,000 Ex-im loan agreement. It turned out that these signed and sealed commitments with the Colombian government and armed forces saved Intercontinental from an early end: the Pan Am board had already set December 31 1948 as the date for terminating support for the hotel company, a decision which was now to be reversed.

In 1949, the agreements and financing for the Tamanaco (400 rooms) in Caracas and Del Lago (initially 150 rooms) in Maracaibo were concluded. And with a future assured, on May 1 Intercontinental assumed operation of its first hotel, the eighty-five room Grande in Belem, Brazil. The city was a Pan Am crossroads for services to South America and Africa, and had been a major base in World War II. The Pan-Am owned city-block-sized property was a true historic relic, built at the turn of the century. Each of the four floors had a single telephone which was under the supervision of a phone attendant who would run to summon guests from their rooms when a call arrived. The hotel's "laundry" was in a pool in the building's colonial-style central courtyard, where twenty laundresses washed by hand. The hotel had its own ice plant. Rooms were cooled by window air conditioners as was the bar. A very popular sidewalk café gave the place a vaguely European feeling, despite the heat and humidity which go with an ocean-front city one degree south of the equator. The hotel's losses were turned to profit in the first year, and this was doubled in the second year of IHC operations. The property was to remain an IHC responsibility for seventeen years, during which time it served as the first general manager posting for several young men who went on to important careers with the company, while the city became increasingly unimportant as an international trading port.

LATIN AMERICA

An intensified negotiation with the owners of the Hotel Carrera in Santiago, Chile, had finally produced an agreement to manage this 400-room hotel with effect from January 1950. Although the hotel was a grand dame among South American establishments, it was losing a great deal of money. Under a side agreement the owners had the right to cancel IHC's management if the hotel's earnings did not reach 16 million Chilean pesos within two years. This may have seemed like a major gamble for IHC, but Calhoun and Grimm were convinced that up-to-date management, accounting and control systems could make a real difference. During the years when the sale of alcoholic beverages was constitutionally prohibited in the United States, hotelkeepers had had to learn to make a profit from selling rooms and food without high-profit-margin wine and liquor sales. Rigorous systems of food and payroll control had been developed which provided management with almost daily cost information. Guest bookkeeping and receivables controls which involved daily balancing of accounts and up-to-the-minute availability of machine-produced guest bills had been introduced to improve guest service and employee productivity. Many of these innovations had been perfected and introduced by a firm of public accountants founded by three Hungarian immigrants, the Horwath brothers and Louis Toth. Typically they would not only perform the standard audit of a hotel's accounts, but also provide a "resident auditor" who was seconded to the hotel and who managed its accounts department. Horwath and Horwath, with offices in all principal U.S. cities, had been the auditors for the Waldorf and had been engaged for Intercontinental. IHC turned to them for assistance in installing a totally new accounts system for the Carrera. Horwath assigned one of its senior auditors, Guillermo (William in English) Busquets.

Bill Busquets had been born and raised in Cuba. He worked for many years with the Singer Sewing Machine Company as a salesman, traveling to remote parts of the countryside on horseback, and later as chief accountant and subsequently manager of the Havana store supervising a thirty-person staff. Armed with a masters degree in business administration from Havana University, he moved to the United States looking for better opportunities in accountancy, his chosen profession. After two years as a semi-senior auditor for Arthur Young and Company, he moved to Horwath, where better prospects seemed to be available.

During Busquets' assignment in Santiago he totally overhauled the accounting and control system, personally training Chileans to do their jobs in a new way. When one office clerk complained that she was being assigned too much for a day's work, he sat down, put a watch on the desk, accomplished the complete task himself in two hours and then challenged her to do it in four; it worked. He converted the books to the *Uniform System of Accounts for Hotels*, a standard codification of accounts which had been developed for the American Hotel Association largely by Horwath and Harris, Kerr, Forster (another accounting firm serving clients in the hotel and hospitality industries), and monthly financial statements were produced in a format which facilitated comparisons with the results of other hotels. Long queues of up to twenty guests at the check-out counter were eliminated when the European "Main-Courant" system (whereunder guest charges were accumulated on huge sheets of paper, one column for each room, and then written by hand or typed onto an individual guest bill only when the guest checked out) was replaced with a daily invoicing system, later mechanized, which produced up-to-date bills on call. The introduction of food and beverage cost control systems and the training of kitchen and storeroom personnel resulted in a reduction of the food and beverage cost from 70 percent to 42 percent of sales. (An attractive Chilena, hired as a cashier when the "gringos" arrived to restructure the management, became Señora Busquets within a year.)

Change was not limited to the back of the house. The door to the dining room was changed from its former way-off-the-beaten-track cul-de-sac to a highly visible location and redesigned to be attractive and welcoming. A medium-priced restaurant was redesigned as a coffee shop and decorated with burnished copper, recognizing Chile's chief export. Tony Vaughan, a Cornell University alumnus who had served for a short period as Grimm's assistant,

Pan Am consumer advertising carried references to Intercontinental properties in the early 1950s.

became general manager and under his direction the remodeled facilities were aggressively marketed. By the end of 1951 the Carrera was earning a net of 24 million (local currency), 50 percent more than the contract cancellation threshold.

By mid-year 1950, a management agreement had been negotiated covering the 220-room Hotel Del Prado (and its small beachside dependency, Pradomar) in Barranquilla, the main sea/river

Intercontinental in July 1951: the Tamanaco (right), Tequendama (above left) and the Victoria Plaza completed and awaiting the installation of furniture and equipment. The main picture shows the colonial-style Hotel El Prado in Barranquilla when Intercontinental first assumed operation in 1950.

port on Colombia's Caribbean coast. The hotel was owned principally by the Obregon family who had had a minority shareholding in SCADTA and was gaining majority control of the renamed Avianca from Pan Am. In time, IHC eventually acquired more than 90 percent of the shares of this hotel, financing the purchase with surplus Colombian pesos from Pan Am. The colonial-style building with whitewashed walls, arched loggia outdoor corridors, red tile roofs, black and white checkerboard tile walkways and a lush tropical garden and pool (where up to 5,000 people could be accommodated during the annual carnival festivities) had been a landmark of the city for many years and the social center of the high-class Prado residential area. Here too, IHC's early operational changes led to improved profitability.

In September of 1950, Bill Busquets joined IHC full time as general auditor responsible for all hotel accounting.

Construction was under way in 1952 on the Bogota, Caracas, Maracaibo and, with fits and starts, Montevideo properties, with Ex-im loans of $4,000,000 and $2,337,000 in place for Bogota and Caracas. To design these hotels, IHC had engaged the Chicago-based architecture firm Holabird, Root, and Burgee. Holabird, which had been founded in 1882, employed some 300 partners and staff, and had made somewhat of a specialty of hotel architecture, designing and supervising the building of twenty-four hotels, among them the Stevens (later the Conrad Hilton, at 3,000 rooms the world's largest at the time), Palmer House and Sherman in Chicago, the Muehlbach in Kansas City and the Statlers in Washington and Los Angeles. Senior architect Richard Smith was assigned by Holabird to the IHC projects.

Dick Smith had joined Holabird after completing studies at Ohio State University, where he was an all-American varsity football player. At the next table in the office sat William Tabler, a recent Harvard graduate. The two were sent to work on the Washington Statler, the first new large hotel started in the United States since the onset of the Great Depression. Bill was the site representative and Dick coordinated with the Statler people in their New York office. World War II temporarily detached both architects from Holabird, for service in the U.S. Navy: Dick in the Seabees in the South Pacific and Bill in Pearl Harbor, assigned to the admiral in charge of the Seabees. Shortly after Byron Calhoun's arrival in New York, he had put together a group of investors (among them some Pan Am officers) to acquire the Weylin Hotel, a commercial mid-priced property on Madison at 54th Street. Dick Smith had been assigned by Holabird to work with Calhoun on the changes which he proposed to make, and the two became friends.

While IHC looked to Holabird and Smith to supervise the hotels' design, locally qualified firms were naturally required to be the architects of record in each case. Smith worked temporarily in these firms' offices giving design guidance and personally involved himself in the layout of spaces within the hotel envelope. Tabler, who was working full time on Statler projects, had developed a set of standard space allocations based on existing, well-designed profitable properties in the Statler group and elsewhere in the United States; they were shared with Smith, and later became the basis for IHC's first set of architectural standards.

IHC's standard management contract of the time provided for a fixed annual fee denominated in U.S. dollars, and an incentive fee calculated at 20 to 25 percent of the hotel's gross operating profit (GOP), a widely understood hybrid term under the *Uniform System of Accounts*, which included all operating income and expenses over which hotel management had control. The GOP was the total profit from the business before deductions for property taxes, property insurance, building and contents depreciation, interest on borrowings and income taxes on the profits of the hotel owner. In addition, each hotel reimbursed IHC for a pro-rata share of the cost of corporate advertising and for the cost of reservations offices in certain locations. A commission of about 6 percent was charged on purchases made for the hotel by IHC's (actually Pan Am's) central procurement department. Given that most countries in Latin America had some form of currency remittance control, prior assurances from the Finance Ministry or Central Bank always had to be obtained to assure that dollars could be remitted abroad to service debt, to import essential spare parts and other goods not produced locally and to pay IHC's fees and reimbursables. Often this element was the most difficult to negotiate of all the various aspects of a successful deal. Two separate projects in Buenos Aires, one the purchase of an existing hotel, the other a new-build, were aborted at a late stage for failure to secure such approvals.

In 1951, IHC purchased the 270-room Reforma Hotel, a well-established top-quality establishment in the heart of the Zona Rosa on the Paseo de la Reforma in Mexico City, for 16,500,000 Mexican pesos. The funds were borrowed from Pan Am in Mexico on a ninety-day basis, with the intention of refinancing the acquisition with a local mortgage loan, a goal which was never achieved. An additional Ps.2,000,000 bank borrowing, guaranteed by Pan Am, was arranged to cover the costs of remodeling and expanding the hotel's food and beverage facilities. The Reforma boasted a luxurious and fashionable nightclub, and its Chanticler Restaurant was among Mexico's finest, enjoying an international reputation as a favorite of the Hollywood set who were regular visitors. From the roof garden in those days, on a clear day, one could see Popocatapetl.

As 1952 drew to a close, Dick Smith had joined IHC to take charge of engineering matters, and the company looked forward to the opening, at last, of the Victoria Plaza, with Harley Watson (Vaughan's assistant in Santiago) as general manager. Alberto Dodero had succeeded in selling his trans-Atlantic shipping company, and Peron's government had shortly thereafter nationalized it and acquired Dodero's other shipping interests. Dodero had gone to Peron in 1950 and asked that a portion of the proceeds of his sales to the government be made available in foreign exchange for remittance to Montevideo to enable completion of the hotel. Peron denied the request, leading Dodero to sell his New York home for $250,000, which he invested in the hotel. By early 1952 the building had been completed and was being furnished when a fire broke out in the port warehouse where the hotel's imported kitchen equipment (value $150,000) was waiting customs clearance and caused yet another delay while the whole order was remanufactured and shipped. Dodero did not live to see the hotel completed.

Popocatapetl near Mexico City. In fine weather the volcano was visible from the roof garden of the Reforma Hotel in the heart of the city's Zona Rosa.

To the north, the railway freight car carrying the heavy imported boiler from the Colombian coast to the Tequendama in Bogota spread the rails while rounding a bend high above a deep canyon in the Andes. The boiler was last seen bounding down the steep hillside to oblivion. And in Caracas it was discovered that the plumbers had failed to provide connections from the risers to the bathtubs in the guest rooms of the Tamanaco.

In other parts of the world IHC executives continued to talk and negotiate. Agreements were concluded for a 1,000-room hotel in Tokyo, over Calhoun's objection that the market could probably not support more than 750 rooms at the time. Proposals were developed for a ten-year lease on the Hotel Continental in Paris, with the rent to be based on the prior two years' earnings, and for acquisition of the Carlton (Frankfurt), the Nassauerhof (Wiesbaden), and Atlantic (Hamburg). None of these projects was ever brought to completion.

Intercontinental was to more than double its size in 1953. On January 1, a lease on the Princess Hotel in Bermuda took effect. The Victoria Plaza finally opened in Montevideo, to be followed by Bogota's Hotel Tequendama, the Del Lago in Maracaibo, and the Tamanaco in Caracas. Staffing these properties presented a major challenge. Calhoun ideally had wished to hire general managers with a combination of traditional European and U.S. experience: a firm hands-on knowledge of how a hotel functions partnered with an understanding of the latest management methods. In Ernst Etter he found such an individual.

Ernesto (as he was known during his South American days) Etter was born and raised in a small country town in Switzerland. After a two-and-a-half-year formal apprenticeship in Basel, he worked in several hotels and restaurants in Zurich and Berne, and in Antwerp, Belgium. He attempted to obtain experience at the Savoy in London, as a busboy, but was deported after three days since no work permit had been issued. The non-materializing of a promised job in Geneva led him to apply successfully – by mail – for a position at the Alvear Palace in Buenos Aires which had been advertised in a hotel trade publication. Taking charge of a money-losing restaurant and banqueting department, he installed a rudimentary food cost system which brought to light large-scale pilferage by cooks. The situation was remedied and good profits followed. His new grill room, designed by Jansen of Paris, attracted Messrs. Whittaker and Calhoun on one of their early visits searching for hotel deals. Upon his return to the United States Calhoun had offered Etter a food and beverage manager's position at the Radisson, but Etter's secretary intercepted and destroyed the letter, a fact not known to Etter until many years later. With Peron's regime strengthening its control over Argentina, the economy began to falter, unions became obstructionist, and Etter opted to leave, traveling to California where he had a brother in the brewery business. A contract with Gene Eppley (an owner of some ninety mid-sized hotels), whom he had met at the Alvear, led to a position at the club of the Santa Barbara Biltmore. Calhoun visited the club with a group of other hotelmen, renewed his acquaintance with Etter and recommended him to his friend and mentor, Barney Ellis, at the Muehlbach, who in turn hired Etter as executive assistant manager. It was from this position that

Ribbon cutting on May 15 1953 at the Hotel Tequendama, Bogota, Colombia, the first new hotel to be developed, designed and constructed completely under Intercontinental supervision. Left to right: Peter Grimm – general manager hotel operations, Intercontinental; Harry Bowrie – assistant manager, Tequendama; Dr. Jorge Esguerra Lopez – president, Hotel San Diego S.A., the hotel-owning company; Byron Calhoun – vice president, Intercontinental; Wallace Whittaker – president, Intercontinental; Erwin Balluder – vice president, Pan Am; Ernst Etter – general manager, Tequendama; Richard Smith – chief engineer, Intercontinental; Sylvester Roll – assistant to president of Intercontinental.

Calhoun engaged him for IHC in 1952. He was first sent on an interim assignment to the Princess, where he found a hotel with no hot water and the boiler totally corroded, but with a chief engineer who dined every evening dressed in a dinner suit and ordered off the à la carte menu in the hotel's top restaurant. Etter's establishment of an officers' dining room produced the engineer's and housekeeper's resignations. With a new housekeeper from New York, and what fabrics could be found locally, the hotel was cleaned from top to bottom and four bedrooms redecorated as sample rooms on which to base the major rehabilitation the owner had promised.

With four months remaining before the scheduled opening day of the Tequendama (the word means "open door" in the local Chibcha dialect), Etter arrived in Bogota and on his first day was guest at a press reception at the home of Dr. Jorge Esguerra Lopez, chairman of the hotel owning company. Among the hors d'oeuvres was a crunchy delicacy which turned out to be the roasted back halves of very large ants, which Etter quickly learned was an essential dish at any top party in Bogota. Dr. Lopez was known as "Chispas" ("sparks" in English); and the hotel's club-like bar would be named Chispas in his honor.

The 400-room hotel, the continent's largest, was an instant landmark. It featured baseboard heating for cold nights and, uniquely, had water storage facilities for thirty-six hours' estimated needs; during the dry season city water supplies were often interrupted for up to fourteen hours a day. The Salon Rojo (Red Room) was one of the largest banquet and reception venues in South America. The Salon Esmeralda featured European cuisine and a dance orchestra, and the Coffee Shop, a North-American style restaurant with counter and simple menu, was staffed with waitresses in "typical" Indian-style dress. Many in Bogota took offense at these "costumes," so Etter quickly imported standard U.S. white-dress-with-pastel-apron-and-cap waitress outfits, and the room began to fill up not only at mealtimes, but throughout the day with ladies and men ordering between-meal Colombian coffees and pastries.

A retired army major, Alvaro Roldan, was engaged as public and press relations director, a position not previously known in Colombia. It was important to assure positive publicity for the hotel in the face of local hoteliers' complaints that the Tequendama would steal all of their business, and to quickly establish reputations for the hotel's restaurants and catering facilities in the market.

The ribbon was cut on May 17 by Dr. Lopez, with all of IHC's senior management in attendance, and the inaugural banquet was attended by the president of Colombia, Roberto Urdaneta

Relaxing by the Hotel Del Lago pool on a sunny day in Maracaibo.

Arbedez. The first hotel designed wholly under IHC direction was open — seven years after the company's inauguration.

The Del Lago was a much more modest property than the Tequendama. It opened on August 14 with 150 rooms facing Lake Maracaibo and was fully occupied almost from its first day by business travelers involved in Venezuela's surging oil industry, which was centered in the city. Fred Gee, an American who was engaged as general manager shortly after the opening (the first incumbent had been an immediate failure and was terminated almost at once by Calhoun) had been employed by American Hotels Corporation, a U.S.-based hotel management company which had expanded into the Caribbean and was seeking opportunities in South America. He had been general manager of the Hotel Jaragua in Santo Domingo and had been in charge of the hotel group Nelson Rockefeller had established in Venezuela which included the Hotel Avila in Caracas. Gee joked that the Del Lago's air conditioning system must have been designed for Lake Erie, not Lake Maracaibo. It was hard pressed to cope with daily temperatures frequently hovering near 100 °F (38 °C) and humidity above 80 percent. A large pipe extended out into the lake through which water was pumped for cooling. Unfortunately, fish and turtles frequently made their way into the pipe jamming the compressors and shutting down the air conditioning, which then had to be cleaned out and restarted. Eventually, a new 10-inch piping line was built which extended almost to the ocean and drew water through strainers from a cement-block-walled "pool" in the lake, thereby keeping out the animals and sludge.

Almost from the first month it was clear that more rooms were needed. The first enlargement of sixty rooms was "designed" by Gee and Mario Belloso, the owning company manager, with sketches on the back of cocktail napkins in the hotel's Mara Bar. It was financed completely with bank over-drafts, which were repaid in two years. The late 1950s were to be heady years in Maracaibo.

The Tamanaco in Caracas had a "soft opening" of its 400 rooms in mid-November, followed by an official ceremonial inauguration on December 2. General manager René Lambert was a French national who had spent several years in charge of the Plaza Athénée in Paris. When the Plaza and its sister hotel the George V had been reopened after World War II, Lambert had proposed to the owner that each hotel should iden- tify a specific clientele at which to direct its promotional activities. George V, then managed by Max Blouet, would concentrate on the U.S. market, while the Plaza Athénée would target the United Kingdom and South America. At the time, strict exchange controls severely limited the amount of currency British

OVERLEAF: A 1954 advertisement featuring the newly opened Hotel Tamanaco (inset left) in Venezuela and (inset right) the hotel building (1971). The main picture shows the view from the hotel.

travelers could take out of the country, making this a somewhat problematic market for the Plaza. Panair do Brasil had its Paris office in the Plaza and Lambert had been able to secure a free ticket to visit South America on a sales promotion tour. Accordingly, in 1947, he visited Rio, Montev- ideo, Buenos Aires, Santiago and Lima. In 1949, Byron Calhoun visited Paris to interview poten- tial managers for IHC. Lambert organized a meeting of various Parisian hoteliers to meet him, and the next day an offer to manage the Carrera was made to Lambert. Having recently turned down an opportunity to manage the Ritz Carlton in Montreal (which had been acquired by the Plaza's owner), Lambert was not tempted with a similar secondary city like Santiago.

Two years later, however, he did accept a two-year contract to manage the Copacabana Palace in Rio, then the capital of Brazil. It was here that he became friendly with Peter Grimm, who was a frequent visitor and who, in early 1953, recruited him to open the Tamanaco. En route to Caracas, Lambert stopped in Bogota where he helped organize that hotel's front office.

The V-shaped Tamanaco featured tiered garden terraces fronting the suites at the ends of each floor, a lobby which was open to large terraces, an indoor/outdoor bar and restaurant which flowed into the gardens, and a free-form swimming pool and recreation area enclosed by a ring of cabanas – all designed to maximize the views of the city below and the surrounding mountain- peaks, and emphasize outdoor living while taking advantage of Caracas' nearly ideal climate. All

of the restaurant facilities were adjacent to and served from a central kitchen, an efficiency-driven feature which whenever possible was to become standard in most properties designed by IHC.

The official opening date was set to coincide with the anniversary of the ascendancy to power of the current dictator, General Marco Perez-Jimenez, and was to be marked with a series of events including the opening of the spectacular Caracas-to-the-coast highway and a new armed forces social club. Xavier Cougat's orchestra had been engaged for several weeks together with the singer Abbie Lane. Many of the decisions, however, had been taken by the government and included a guest list totaling some 2,000 for a dinner followed by a Copacabana-style show imported from New York. The general arrived at 21:30 and, having nibbled at the other events during the day, was not feeling hungry. Therefore (with a nod to Hofmannsthal's *Ariadne*) the program was revised on the spot; the musical spectacular was moved up from its 23:00 scheduled time, and the dinner postponed until later. The famished guests finally sat down to dinner at midnight.

During the pre-opening training period many of the staff were served in the restaurant so as to give practice to the waiters, captains and busboys. When this most pleasant experience was discontinued and the staff cafeteria opened, there was a near-strike – it seems that a benefit, once extended, is assumed to be permanent – a lesson which had to be learned more than once in the years ahead.

The openings of the Tamanaco and Tequendama hotels were honored with the issuance of new stamps by the postal authorities of Venezuela (above) and Colombia (top). In later years Curaçao, El Salvador, and Indonesia produced similar issues to commemorate IHC openings.

A week after the opening, diplomats and other delegates to an inter-American conference filled the hotel. Even with 100 percent occupancy, things appeared to be going well until a laundry attendant, nursing a running disagreement with his department head, "neglected" for one day to properly mark the clothing received from the guests, with the result that after washing and finishing nothing could be identified and returned to its owner. Peter Grimm, who was in the hotel, suggested that the disaster be turned into a party: put the clothes on long banquet tables, invite the guests to find their garments, and open a small bar. Cooler heads prevailed and a hopefully low-key tuxedo, stockings, dress shirt, petticoat, underwear, and gown "cafeteria" was set up in the ballroom accompanied by appropriate personal apologies from senior staff members. Most of the guests took it with good spirits. However, the word had gotten out and several press photographers who were covering the conference managed to take photos of the laundry debacle. A young Canadian assistant manager overreacted, insisting that the negatives be surrendered, failing which he "detained" the group in a banquet room pending instructions from his boss. Lambert, in the midst of a conference with Grimm, was interrupted by an outraged telephone call from Caracas' most influential publisher, demanding that his men be freed from Tamanaco incarceration at once. The subsequent mending of fences gave Lambert an opportunity to meet personally every press person in the city, and with most he became fast friends. A benefit from all of this: *Time* magazine carried a lighthearted report of the event in its worldwide editions; if there is truth in the maxim that "any publicity is good publicity," then the Tamanaco and IHC had scored a major coup.

In September, Whittaker was named chairman, Calhoun, president, and Roll and Balz, vice presidents of IHC. With nine hotels under its control, three of them brand-new and built to IHC's specifications, Pan Am wanted to see IHC profits, and quickly. Trippe continued to fume at Whittaker's perceived extravagance. With 2,600 real rooms to show off, there was no excuse to continue the model room, hotel-development picture-gallery office on 42nd Street. The lease was surrendered without penalty and IHC moved into an office block across the East River in Long Island City, which housed Pan Am's accounting, reservations, purchasing, and other support departments. A single suite of offices was found on the 59th floor of the Chrysler Building, in which Pan Am's executive offices occupied parts of five floors, to provide modest but prestigious accommodations for IHC senior executives. Belts were ordered to be tightened and new hotel projects to be pursued with increased vigor. Shortly, contracts were signed for Curaçao and El Salvador.

Ever more restrictive travel regulations had threatened to totally stop the flow of business and pleasure traffic between Argentina, the main source market, and Uruguay. The Doderos (Alberto's sons) wanted a readjustment to IHC's contract to help stop the hotel's flow of red ink. A task force headed by Grimm developed an emergency operating plan which would produce a break-even operation at occupancies as low as 37 percent. A concession was negotiated with the government whereby visitors from Argentina, paying in Argentine pesos, could receive a 45 percent discount on their room bills, with the Uruguayan government reimbursing for a portion of the discount.

Agreements and contracts for a new hotel in Ecuador were ready for signature. The local capital was committed with Quito's leading radio and newspaper owner as principal shareholder. On the day before the scheduled closing, his radio station broadcast a Spanish version of Orson Welles' famous adaptation of H.G. Wells' *War of the Worlds*. As had been the case in the United States, there was a certain amount of general panic; in Quito, however, mobs gathered in front of the station, violence erupted, and both station and newspaper buildings were destroyed. It would take ten years before another attempt was made to build a modern hotel.

1954 brought IHC's first incentive compensation scheme. On a trial basis, Carrera general manager Tony Vaughan, in Santiago, would be paid an amount equal to 3 percent of IHC's incentive management fee, a fee which only accrued after the hotel's owners had earned a certain return; Vaughan could earn an additional 2 percent of the fee if the food and beverage departmental profit exceeded 23 percent of revenue.

Throughout the 1950s star performers were an attraction at the Hotel Tamanaco in Caracas. They included (top left) Josephine Baker and Nat King Cole shown at hotel's poolside and (above) Ava Gardner photographed with a member of the local press.

Both the Tequendama and Tamanaco were taking time to get established and there was danger that insufficient funds would be generated to meet the first payments due on the U.S. Ex-im loans. IHC agreed to temporarily defer the payments of its fees and to guarantee short-term local bank borrowings by the owning companies. Additionally, the Tamanaco was suffering from chronically high 70 percent to 80 percent food costs. Busquets was summoned and a system of daily physical

Intercontinental's first general managers' conference, Chrysler Building, New York City, 1954. Front: Peter Grimm – vice president; Pete Sutherland – El Prado Hotel, Barranquilla; Byron Calhoun – president; Charles Bowers – Reforma, Mexico City; Oscar Balz – vice president. Rear: Fred Gee – Del Lago, Maracaibo; Tony Vaughan – Carrera, Santiago; Ernst Etter – Tequendama, Bogota; Phil Payne – Grande, Belem; Harley Watson – Victoria Plaza, Montevideo; René Lambert – Tamanaco, Caracas; Walter Root – director of sales.

inventories instituted by Lambert soon pinpointed the sources of the losses. One of the basic goals of any internal control system is to create an atmosphere in which the employee who is tempted to cheat realizes that such a choice is likely to result in immediate detection.

The Tamanaco sent each of its department heads out into the city at least once a month to visit the offices of leading businessmen armed with a script of introduction, a query as to how the hotel could be of better service to them, and a request that the client contact him personally for whatever his needs might be. These "sales blitzes" invariably resulted in immediate increases in restaurant bookings and cemented relations in the community.

In the United Kingdom, negotiations were undertaken and terminated without success on deals for the Mount Royal, Grosvenor House and May Fair hotels in London. Sales and booking representation agreements were reached with the Plaza and Continental Hotels in Buenos Aires and the Gran Hotel Bolivar and Country Club de Lima in Peru, whereby IHC provided reservations booking services at its other hotels and its central reservations office in New York. Discussions were begun aimed at establishing a system for Pan Am and Panagra sales offices in key cities to also accept bookings for all of the hotels in the group.

In 1954 the airplane replaced the surface vessel as the principal medium for overseas travel. Pan Am had played a pioneering role: to Latin America in 1929, to Alaska in 1932, across the Pacific to Manila and Hong Kong in 1936, across the Atlantic to Europe in 1939, to Africa in 1939, Australia in 1940, and around the world in 1947. With the introduction of larger aircraft, Pan Am had promoted "Rainbow" tourist-class service at substantially reduced fares to Honolulu and on most trans-Atlantic routes during 1952 and 1953. Twenty-eight percent of all travelers going overseas to and from the continental United States, whether by sea or air, did so on Pan Am's Clipper fleet. The era of international mass travel was dawning.

In 1954 Intercontinental recorded its first, admittedly small, profit. By this time Pan Am had invested more than $4,540,000 in stock purchases and advances and had guaranteed outsider loans to IHC of another $243,000. IHC's balance sheet featured a deferred development cost charge of $2,320,000 representing the costs of keeping the company in existence through the end of 1953.

In 1955 IHC succeeded in structuring the acquisition of a lease on the Hotel Nacional in Havana, Cuba. The venerable property was owned by the Cuban government and generally considered to be one of the top ten hotels in the world. IHC would own 47 percent, American Securities Corporation (later United Fruit Corp) 35 percent, and Cuban interests the remaining 18 percent of a new Cuban corporation which was to purchase an option covering the thirty-four-year unexpired term of a lease which had belonged to the Kirkeby Hotel group, a U.S. company specializing in resort operations. IHC would in turn enter into a management agreement with the new Cuban corporation. It was made clear by the landlord that the hotel's casino was to be subleased to a group prese-lected by the government on terms to be negotiated with government participation. The designated operator was an organization headed by Meyer Lansky, a Florida entrepreneur and financier who was subsequently reputed to have had close connections with organized crime. The agreed contract pro-

"Spec" Roll (left) is met on the tarmac at Santiago, Chile, by Pete Sutherland, general manager of the Hotel Carrera.

vided for a large minimum rent, against a percentage of gross win, and a subvention of a large por-tion of the hotel's entertainment and advertising budgets. Without selling a room or a meal, the hotel was guaranteed a profit so long as the casino turnover continued at its then current level. Built in a colonial style, the 550-room hotel featured lush tropical gardens, two pools – one in the sun, one in the shade for those who wanted to wear their designer beach clothes but not get tanned – a luxurious "boite" style nightclub, and a very exclusive Cabana Club, one of the most expensive and fashionable in Cuba. Tony Vaughan was transferred from the Carrera as general manager.

Replacing Vaughan in Santiago was John P. Sutherland. "Pete," as he was known, was a Texan who had worked in the United States and across the border in Mexico and had had his career interrupted by a military tour as a twice decorated Marine fighter pilot in Korea, prior to being engaged as general manager at the Del Prado in Barranquilla.

Pan Am and IHC had launched a special "off season" promotion package for Bermuda based on discounted rates at the Princess. The health of Bermuda's tourist industry had been assured for many years by strict control on the number of rooms in the market and adherence to published rates. For one hotel to undercut the others, by offering special rates to one group of customers car-ried by the leading U.S. air carrier, was considered by the Bermuda Trade Development Board to be a predatory and unfair trade practice. Discussion continued for months; concurrently the owner of the Princess was finding reasons for delaying the rooms' remodeling program, which had been committed when the IHC lease was negotiated. Conditions deteriorated and IHC terminated the lease for cause.

With a commitment to invest $269,000,000 in equipment and spare parts, Pan Am in 1955 announced it had placed orders for forty-eight pure jet aircraft from Boeing (B–707s) and Douglas (DC–8s) with delivery foreseen to commence late in 1958. Each plane would be able to carry up to 150 tourist-class passengers at 575 miles an hour non-stop across the Atlantic and to most Latin American destinations, and at a lower operating cost per passenger mile than piston aircraft. With this massive new airlift capacity on the horizon, the hotel shortage in many Pan Am destinations loomed as critical. As a senior airline officer put it, "you either build more hotels or fly fewer jets."

President Calhoun was a dynamic businessman and a stern taskmaster. An impeccably dressed bulldog of a figure, he could dominate any meeting, despite his relatively short stature. Most of the general managers were in awe, if not downright frightened, of him. He knew the hotel business backwards and forwards; there is no doubt that his relentless, driving energy was the most important single factor in establishing IHC's credibility and rapid ascendancy to a preeminent position in the hotel business in Latin America. Once the Colombian and Venezuelan properties were running smoothly and generating profits, he turned many operating responsibilities over to Grimm, while concentrating his own efforts on deal-making and troubleshooting. In 1956 he arranged the transfer of Levon Keenan from her position as resident auditor (provided by Harris, Kerr, Forster) at the Weylin Hotel, to IHC as his assistant. Keenan, a Cornell University graduate, came from a family of hotel owners in the U.S. Middle West; Calhoun began to rely on her analyses of the hotels' monthly reports to keep him up to date on the course of business – a function which she was later to perform for two more presidents.

By the end of 1956, Calhoun could, and did, boast of 90 percent occupancies in Bogota, Caracas, and Maracaibo. In less than three years the number of air passengers arriving in Bogota had more than doubled, and the Tequendama, with 500 Colombians employed, was generating $4.2 million in local purchases of goods and services and "earning more money than the Waldorf."

Roger Lewis, a former under secretary of the air force was hired by Trippe in 1956 as Pan Am executive vice president – development and defense projects; in other words, he was in charge of all of the airline's non-air transport activities. In addition to Intercontinental, these included technical assistance programs for aid in establishing airlines in such foreign nations as Turkey, Thailand, Pakistan, and Afghanistan; U.S. government contracts for planning and operating the guided missile range facilities at Cape Canaveral, Florida, and down range stations in the Atlantic and Caribbean; base management for military test sites in the Pacific; and airport management in Liberia and certain Pacific islands. After an extensive period of familiarization with IHC, Lewis concluded that the level of rapid worldwide growth which Pan Am required could not be achieved by the existing group of senior officers dividing their time between operations and development, and set about creating a hotel development staff within the airline. Assigning Latin America to Calhoun and Roll, he arranged for the heads of Pan Am's Atlantic and Pacific divisions each to engage a full-time officer to work on-site in his area, receiving guidance from, and reporting their progress back to, the IHC board. Harold Gray, executive vice president for the Atlantic division, and an IHC director, hired M. Lee Dayton to pursue hotel projects in Europe and the Middle East. Dayton had just retired from government service as an administrator for the Marshall Plan, the U.S.-financed European recovery program which was helping to reconstruct the economies of several war-ravaged nations. During World War II he had been attached to the American Red Cross and was among the first civilians to arrive after the Allied invasions of Italy and France to set up humanitarian programs in the liberated areas while gathering intelligence about lingering enemy activities and influences. His Marshall Plan activities had given him a comprehensive knowledge of the current economic conditions in Italy and Turkey, and he had been involved from the government side with Conrad Hilton's attempts to develop hotels in Rome and Istanbul. While civilian relief supplies of coal, wheat, flour, and medicines were being sent to Italy, Dayton was under pressure to locate or establish some sort of distribution system. He selected the only two organizations which at the time had the infrastructure to do the job: in the north, the Roman Catholic Church; and in the south and Sicily, the Mafia.

In Dayton's first briefing after joining Pan Am, Juan Trippe gave him a list of priority cities which began with Baghdad, Beirut, New Delhi, Teheran, and Ankara. Except for Vienna, Europe was way down the list, since in most continental capitals there was existing hotel inventory, albeit in small to medium-sized properties.

Najib Salha, a successful Lebanese businessman who had built a sizable fortune as a negotiator in Saudi Arabian government dealings with foreign companies, had acquired a prime hotel site on the Beirut waterfront and was assembling a group of investors and bank financing. Dayton was able to negotiate a management agreement for the property – to be named the Phoenicia Inter-continental – and obtained IHC approval for a $200,000 equity investment. Edward D. Stone, a leading American architect, was introduced to Salha and engaged to complete the design with IHC input from Dick Smith and Joe Salerno, a creative design architect who had joined Smith's staff and worked extensively on the Curaçao project. Salha had earlier engaged André Ham-burger, a Swiss hotel consultant who had previously managed the King David Hotel in Jerusalem, and whom IHC was subsequently to hire as general manager for Montevideo.

Meanwhile, Calhoun had concluded negotiations for a major new hotel and casino in San Juan, Puerto Rico, and, as a partial quid pro quo, had committed to a project for a 170-room property in Ponce, Puerto Rico's second and somewhat remote city on the south coast of the island. IHC would lease both hotels, and pay a rent of $66^2/3$ percent of the gross annual operating profit. As partial secu-rity for the debt capital, IHC would commit to a guaranteed minimum rent in each case. Additionally, IHC would subscribe to 15 percent to 20 percent of the hotel's equity, and as tenant would provide the working capital and the operating equipment. This sort of arrangement (minus the minimum) was similar to the structure which was concurrently being used by Hilton International Corporation which had been created in 1948, had a flagship hotel, the Caribe Hilton in San Juan, and was active in hotel development in Europe and Egypt. Grimm secured an IHC lease for a 130-room beach resort at Varadero, some eighty miles east of Havana, Cuba. Roll had concluded agreements in Guatemala City for a hotel to be called the Tikal Intercontinental and had a serious letter of intent for San José, Costa Rica, but neither of these projects ever materialized. Roll also made arrangements to acquire the Jaragua and Embajador hotels from the government of the Dominican Republic for $9 million under terms which would permit the purchase price to be paid largely from future earnings.

THE CARIBBEAN

During these early years all of IHC's hotel operating staff were of necessity hired from "outside" the company. Each general manager came from a unique background, no two very much alike. They received briefings from Calhoun and Grimm, and later regular visits from both, but there was no common thread in the way each managed his property . . . except for the accounting and control systems installed by Bill Busquets and a small staff whom he had trained and who assisted in hotel openings and in troubleshooting. Pan Am's internal audit group under corporate policy was required to review the operations of all company-controlled subsidiaries, but in IHC's case this meant only the 100 percent owned Mexico City, Dominican, Belem, and later majority owned Barranquilla, properties. Busquets and his staff filled the void, and early on developed an accounting manual in both Spanish and English. Organizationally, the hotel chief accountants were reporting functionally directly to Busquets, hopefully assuring consistency in financial reporting from the several hotels and a modicum of corporate control over local expenditure. After reviewing the results of the trial incentive compensation scheme which had been introduced at the Carrera, Busquets was asked to prepare a results-oriented plan which could be applied uniformly throughout the group. The resulting plan permitted general managers to earn 1.4 percent of the annual GOP with an additional 0.6 percent to be paid if food and beverage departmental profit was at least 25 percent of sales, and remained in effect for five years. During the years of 80 percent and higher occupancies, at least three hotel general managers were receiving taxable local currency bonuses which put their earnings at two to three times the amounts being earned by the corporation's officers. The food and beverage threshold unfortunately led one or two managers to think exclusively in percentage terms. Thus there was a temptation for a large social function, which had to be offered at a relatively high cost in order to secure the booking, to be passed by because of its possible negative effect on the magic 25 percent, even though it would have added several thousand dollars to the hotel's bottom line.

In 1957, Roger Lewis convinced Robert Smith to join the hotel development team as his deputy and a Pan Am assistant vice president. With a "speed up" degree from the University of Chicago, and a medical disqualification for military service, he had been hired by the airline in 1942 in a special junior executive training program. Within six months he was posted to Brownsville, Texas, and later to Mexico City, the first of many Central America locations in which he would work over the next fourteen years. Trippe had a plan to create a group of affiliated airlines, in which Pan Am was usually a minority shareholder, in Salvador, Panama, Nicaragua, and Costa Rica. Over the years Smith successfully shepherded the growth and assured the survival of these regional carriers, which faced severe competition from government-affiliated

Intercontinental advertising in the United States emphasized the "local flavor" and consistent standards of its hotels.

Local flavor,
American comfort...

INTERCONTINENTAL *style!*

From Cuba to Chile . . . from Mexico to Brazil, INTERCONTINENTAL HOTELS extend their special welcome to travelers on business or pleasure. Beautiful hotels in spectacular scenic settings, each offers the distinctive atmosphere of its own country—yet all assure the same high INTERCONTINENTAL standards: gracious hospitality, swift multi-lingual service, modern comfortable accommodations, excellent food, fine entertainment, and air conditioning where climate requires. Many have large swimming pools; all have their own smart shops, and are located close to business and transportation centers.

Intercontinental Hotel guests . . . whether on business or pleasure . . . will enjoy the music, intriguing native foods, and breath-taking scenery that are a part of life in exciting Latin America.

HOTEL CARRERA
Santiago, Chile

HOTEL DEL LAGO
Maracaibo, Venezuela

HOTEL GRANDE
Belém, Pará, Brasil

HOTEL NACIONAL DE CUBA
Havana, Cuba

REFORMA INTERCONTINENTAL
Mexico City, Mexico

HOTEL TAMANACO
Caracas, Venezuela

HOTEL TEQUENDAMA
Bogotá, Colombia

HOTEL VICTORIA PLAZA
Montevideo, Uruguay

INTERCONTINENTAL HOTELS

For the complete story . . . see your travel agent or send for our illustrated brochure
INTERCONTINENTAL HOTELS, Chrysler Building, New York—Roper Building, Miami

OPENING SOON—
FOUR NEW INTERCONTINENTAL HOTELS: | SALVADOR INTERCONTINENTAL, El Salvador • EL CURACAO, Curacao, N. W. I.
PHENICIA INTERCONTINENTAL, Beirut, Lebanon • SAN JUAN INTERCONTINENTAL, Puerto Rico

TACA airlines in the same countries. Trippe and Wilbur Morrison, the airline's senior officer in charge of Latin America, eventually gave Smith full rein and as its chief executive in the 1950s he was able to build LACSA, the Costa Rican carrier, into a financially sound and competitive airline.

The Nacional in Havana was planning a multimillion dollar refurbishing project, to include guest-room air conditioning and an overall upgrading of furnishings. Warren Pine, Pan Am's man in Havana, who also controlled the affiliated Cubana de Aviacion national carrier, had arranged a package of local bank and insurance company financing for the project; the lenders expected a guarantee from IHC. Although the Nacional was then the principal source of IHC's cash flow, Bob Smith felt that Cuba was not all that secure. He was able to convince Parker and Company, Pan Am's (and IHC's) worldwide insurance brokers to provide the guarantee, which they were able to protect with a back guarantee from the U.S. Agency for International Development (AID).

In August of 1957, Wallace Whittaker would reach retirement age. He had reduced his activities to largely ceremonial matters, and Calhoun had become chief executive officer in practice if not in fact. Two months later, just back from an exhausting trip to Panama where he had been negotiating to take over the management of the El Panama Hotel, Calhoun contracted a virulent strain of pneumonia and, within days, died. Peter Grimm was elected president, Roger Lewis became chairman, and Robert Ferguson, Pan Am's treasurer, joined the IHC board. Shortly thereafter, Balz retired, to be replaced by Charles Nielsen as IHC treasurer, and Richard Deichler was hired from American Airlines, where he had been vice president in charge of marketing, as executive vice president.

The Curaçao Intercontinental was a unique architectural creation built into and on top of a waterfront battlement guarding the entrance to the Curaçao harbor. Joe Salerno had played the leading role in a very imaginative design. A group of local and Venezuelan businessmen had arranged the financing for this

The Curaçao Intercontinental opened in 1957 and was featured in one of the company's 1958 advertisements, which also promoted the San Juan and El Salvador hotels and introduced IHC's new Mercator-style logo.

125-room hotel and had secured an exclusive casino license for the property. IHC hired an established operator, who had wide experience in Caribbean gaming facilities and a reputation of legitimacy in an industry known for shady dealings, for this and the Dominican casinos. The casino was built on a floor below the swimming pool deck and had porthole-style windows opening into the pool below the water's surface. The opening festivities featured a fashion parade of several French models who had been exhibiting in Caracas, a grand ball, and an enormous buffet supper which was consumed down to the last crumb by the 300 invited guests. Curaçao was not a major tourist destination except for duty-free purchases – then a novelty – and the hotel struggled from its opening day. IHC learned that the basic overhead, both local and corporate, required for its typical style of operation was too great for a stand-alone property of less than 200 rooms, except at occupancies in the 90 percent range.

In a change from the past practice of hiring local architects, IHC chose Bill Tabler to design the hotel in El Salvador. Located on the side of an extinct volcano in a pleasant residential neighborhood, the hotel structure had to be able to withstand the shock of earthquakes which occurred with some regularity. Mario di Genova was assigned as opening general manager of the 200-room El Salvador Intercontinental. Di Genova, born and educated in France, had moved with his parents to a ranch in Colombia. His father eventually sent him to the United States (lest he become a Latin "playboy"?) where he secured a job as front office rack clerk and later receptionist at New York's Taft Hotel, at the time one of the most popular and profitable hotels in the city. He was accepted by Hilton Hotels for their highly respected executive manager's course at the Waldorf Astoria and was assigned to the Plaza. As a U.S. resident he was subject to military service and was drafted for service in Korea, after which he became a U.S. citizen. He returned to Colombia and the ranch for a short time and then took a position in a hotel in Cali, where he met Ernst Etter. He joined the Tequendama in charge of the front office and uniformed services departments (Etter says that in his total experience no front office ever functioned better than under Mario in Bogota) and in two years he was executive assistant manager. Already tapped to open El Salvador, he took charge for a short time in Mexico City during a leave of absence by the incumbent, and served for eight months as acting general manager of the Nacional in Havana when Tony Vaughan suffered a heart attack.

For Christmas 1958 the Tamanaco in Caracas produced its own top-quality greeting cards in its printing shop.

After Bogota, Mexico and Havana, San Salvador was a very quiet place. Di Genova brought a certain measure of style to this relatively provincial corner of Central America: a chef from Quebec's Château Frontenac, food festivals from France, and Latin entertainers from the international circuit. But occupancies seldom exceeded 50 percent and the owning company was in serious financial difficulty. To improve the first year's earnings, and thereby the rent being paid by IHC, the unusual costs related to establishing the hotel in its early months (other than preopening) were deferred as "start-up expenses."

San Juan opened in a mini-boom when no rooms were to be had in the city during four months of the year. The preopening budget had been overspent, and construction cost overruns were met by last minute cutbacks in furniture and furnishing costs. The general manager, faced with shortages of what he believed to be essential equipment and supplies, went ahead and committed to various expenditures beyond the scope of certain budgets, resulting in friction between the owners and IHC from the opening day. Under strict Puerto Rican casino control regulations IHC, as tenant of the hotel, was required to operate the casino, the largest on the island, for its own

account, and it was this department which funded the rest of the hotel operation during the first year. As an adjunct to the casino, the hotel operated the Tropicoro, a show room where entertainers like Eartha Kitt, Harry Belafonte, Marlene Dietrich (with Burt Bacharach as her accompanist), and Paul Anka appeared for one- or two-week runs during the high season winter months.

In 1957, the company inaugurated its junior executive training (JET) program, a fast track management plan for university graduates. R. Kane Rufe and Richard Squier, with Cornell Hotel School degrees and military service behind them, were among the first four in the program and were sent to the Del Lago in Maracaibo where Fred Gee put them through an intensive

immersion schedule working in a wide range of jobs in every department of the hotel. Upon completion Rufe was sent to work as assistant manager in charge of the front office in San Juan, and Squier was selected to be administrative assistant to executive vice president Dick Deichler at the head office. In San Juan the major airlines had introduced a special deeply discounted night coach fare which was a huge success bringing planes full of guests to the island at five and six o'clock in the morning. Because check-out was not until noon, these guests had to be kept waiting for rooms; many went direct to the beach for four or five hours, after changing in the ballroom area washrooms, and suffered from serious sunburns. A certain percentage of guests did not check out as

The La Vega area of the Dominican Republic. The Embajador became an Intercontinental in 1957 in what was then Ciudad Trujillo.

OPPOSITE: A corporate advertising campaign promoted the delights of foreign travel combined with American-style comfort and featured the Del Lago.

scheduled, and an island-wide hotel overbooking emergency developed. Kane on several occasions chartered aircraft to ferry surplus guests to the Embajador in the Dominican Republic. Soon it was necessary to require guests to sign a formal declaration at check-in confirming their check-out date and their agreement to leave as scheduled.

Calhoun and Grimm had scheduled occasional meetings of the general managers in the early 1950s. In 1958, with sixteen hotels in operation, a major company-wide meeting brought together all of the managers and most of the corporate executives and department heads at the Embajador in what was then Ciudad Trujillo, Dominican Republic. It was the occasion for a presentation by Deichler of a new advertising campaign featuring full-color original artwork and the recently adopted Mercator-style logo. Bill Busquets and Charlie Nielson introduced a new structured annual budgeting and cash planning system, which provided for regular quarterly updates.

During the second half of 1957, the military dictators of Colombia and Venezuela were overthrown and eventually replaced with civilian governments. Business in the hotels was adversely affected for several months, particularly in Caracas where the Tamanaco had been a favorite of the exiled leader. There were some minor military incursions and attempts to "settle old scores" but no serious damage to the property.

Intercontinental's first group management conference at the El Embajador Intercontinental, Ciudad Trujillo, Dominican Republic in 1958. Left to right: Frank Irving – director of operations; Fred Gee – Del Lago, Maracaibo; Harley Watson – El San Juan IC, Puerto Rico; Pete Sutherland – Carrera, Santiago; Ed Dowling – director of purchasing; Ernst Etter – Tequendama, Bogota; Tom Mueller – Jaragua; Phil Payne – Grande, Belem; Charles Bowers – Reforma, Mexico City; Walter Root – director of sales; Hector Cruz – sales manager; William McKinnon – Curaçao; Klaus Winkler – El Prado, Barranquilla; André Hamburger – Victoria Plaza, Montevideo; Sylvester Roll – vice president, development; Peter Grimm – president; Andrew Diddell – advertising agency account manager; Richard Deichler – executive vice president; William Land – Nacional, Havana; Leo De Franco – Varadero Oasis, Cuba; William Busquets – general auditor; Charles Nielsen – treasurer; Peter Balas – director, food and beverage; Mario di Genova – El Salvador IC, San Salvador; Don Aymar – director of personnel; René Lambert – Tamanaco, Caracas; Curt Peyer – El Embajador IC, Dominican Republic.

be happy-go-luxury with
all the comforts of home

Psychoses, neuroses and plain old-fashioned nervous tension just don't stand a chance when the "Intercontinental Treatment" starts rolling. Even people who've had it right up to here get a new lease on life the minute they set foot in an Intercontinental hotel.

Ego need a booster shot? You'll get it here in double doses. Sit back and enjoy regal accommodations, sumptuous meals, solicitous service.

Have a suppressed desire to be an explorer? With 15 hotels in 11 fascinating foreign lands, an Intercontinental vacation lets you make like a modern Marco Polo. In fact, discovering the fun of swimming, sailing, sight-seeing, shopping, or simply "siesta-ing" in the tropics beats anything that footloose Venetian ever dreamed of!

Just name your vacation fantasy and we'll turn it into fact. What about the fee? Our rates are actually so low you can't afford to stay home.

In short, with our Double Delight Vacation—the flavor of foreign travel plus all the comforts of American-style hotels—you can't go wrong. Not when you *stay* at an Intercontinental Hotel! So call your travel agent right now—or write Intercontinental Hotels, Chrysler Building, New York 17.

Live it up—loaf it up at the Hotel del Lago in Maracaibo, Venezuela.

INTERCONTINENTAL HOTELS

The World's Largest Group of International Hotels

Bob Smith, in his first personal effort to develop a hotel, had come up with a serious property dealer who was offering a ninety-nine-year lease on an entire city block at Portman Square in London for a reasonable up-front premium and a nominal annual rental. The property would accommodate a hotel of up to 800 rooms, which would be the largest, most modern in the United Kingdom, and support Pan Am's needs in what was rapidly becoming its number one destination. Full financing was available, with some sort of guarantee from Pan Am as sole-owner-to-be. An architectural study was prepared by Salerno and the proposal presented to Lewis and Trippe for review. Trippe did not want to be in real estate or to own hotels outright, did not want guarantees for IHC projects cluttering up Pan Am's balance sheet, and was inclined to believe the opinion of rival London bankers that a site on the "wrong" north side of Oxford Street would never be suitable for a first-class property, and the deal was killed.

Ten years later apartment blocks were to be built on the site, one of which was converted during construction to become the Portman Inter-Continental.

Lewis had a brief to develop a worldwide hotel chain, but relatively limited funds. The original Ex-im credit had expired after granting only two loans totaling less than $7,000,000. The then current mentality in Washington lumped Ex-im loans with foreign aid, and certain politicians were railing against the notion of U.S. taxes going to finance luxury hotels. Pan Am had agreed in principle that IHC should make token catalytic investments of up to, say, 30 percent of the equity in new hotel projects, but Trippe insisted that the funding ought somehow to be generated in the host country. A possible source of finance might be funds which had been building up in countries to whom the United States was providing commodity aid. Surplus U.S. agricultural products were being sold to certain needy and developing countries around the world, with payment being made to the United States in the respective countries' local currencies. These "Cooley" funds (named after the congressman who had authored the enabling legislation) could be made available as loans to U.S. companies doing business in the recipient countries, to be used to make investments in private enterprise activities. Trippe was convinced that this would be an ideal source for IHC investment capital, particularly in Asia.

During the summer of 1958, Lewis organized a survey team to scout out hotel development opportunities along Pan Am's "round the world" route. Included in the team was an engineer from Bechtel Corporation with experience in estimating construction costs. Bechtel was a rapidly growing, privately owned American firm of engineers and construction general contractors with experience in heavy construction projects in many, particularly developing, countries around the world. Steve Bechtel, its founder, was friendly with Trippe and readily agreed to set up a section within his organization to specialize in hotel construction. Completing the group were Lee Dayton, an architect, and Charles Trippe, one of Juan's sons on summer recess from Harvard Business School. They visited Vienna, Istanbul, Teheran, Karachi, Delhi, Rangoon, and Bangkok, searching out sites, meeting government authorities, researching construction methods and available resources, gathering demographic data, analyzing international (and domestic) travel patterns and growth potential, and preparing architectural sketches for each destination.

In Washington, Juan Trippe and Harold Gray believed Pan Am lobbying had neutralized political opposition to Ex-im loans for hotel construction and so advised the development officers. Dayton, drawing on the connections made in Turkey during his Marshall Plan days, had inter-

The Emerald Buddha Temple in the Royal Grand Palace, Bangkok, Thailand. The city was on Pan Am's "round the world" route and one of the potential development sites investigated by IHC in 1958.

ested its government in a hotel for Istanbul, and possibly Ankara. An appointment was arranged for a Turkish minister in charge of finance matters to visit the president of Ex-im in Washington. Fortunately, the minister spoke very little English, as the Ex-im president was outspokenly inhospitable, and greeted the visitors with banging of fists, raised voice, and criticism of Pan Am and its officers using a colorful selection of words more suited to an alleyway than the diplomatic corridors of the nation. Dayton abruptly aborted the meeting after openly criticizing the official for his rude behavior, embarrassing to the minister and reflecting poorly on the United States. Behind the scenes a "blue ribbon" commission headed by the chairman of Inland Steel Corporation had been formed to study Ex-im's position and to make recommendations. The commission's report gave a lengthy reasoned argument: the Ex-im bank's function was principally to finance exports for projects of real importance in developing and friendly nations and in so doing to create jobs in the United States and to further U.S. interests abroad. In certain countries, the ability to cater to international business travelers was an essential infrastructural activity without which other trade and economic progress would be difficult to generate. All of the funds lent would flow back to the United States at once, and the foreign currency subsequently generated in the beneficiary nations through growth in international trade would create further funds for their development as well as enable the repayment of the loans. What may seem to be "luxury" in a country newly developing or recovering from war is an ordinary acceptable standard for traveling businessmen, congressmen, diplomats or tourists. Shortly, the Ex-im loan window was reopened to IHC, although not with the 1945-style line of credit; each project would have to stand on its own and each application be subject to strict commercial scrutiny. It was understood that IHC would be required to operate the hotel when it was completed.

The Phoenicia Intercontinental had been redesigned, and Bechtel brought in to guide the construction side of the project. Their revised cost estimates revealed shortfalls in the financing. This time IHC was successful in securing Ex-im participation.

After assuming the president's role, Peter Grimm engaged an operations director, Frank Irving, to look after some of Grimm's former tasks. Two Hungarian-Americans very close to Grimm – John Horwath, the brother in charge of Horwath's Chicago office, and John Sherry, a New York attorney with a specialized practice catering to the hotel trade (the Waldorf Astoria was an important client) – had recommended that IHC interview Peter Balas, a food and beverage specialist currently working in Hilton's Buffalo Statler. Calhoun and Grimm met him, and he was hired, reporting to Irving, as food and beverage coordinator. Balas, still in his twenties, had been born in Chicago (on April Fool's Day!) and grew up living in the Edgewater Beach Hotel where his father, a surgeon, maintained an office and served as the hotel doctor. Balas attended schools in Hungary and the United States and later studied at Culver Military Academy. After service with the U.S. Marines in Korea – at one point he was in charge of a communications group on MacArthur's flagship during the Inchon invasion – he attended the École Hôtelière at Lausanne, working between semesters at the Plaza Athénée in Paris. A short apprenticeship at London's Claridge's – where he met Kane Rufe, then being demobbed from the U.S. air force – was followed by a return to the United States and a position in the New York Statler, flagship property of the Statler chain, which had recently been acquired by Hilton in what was at the time the largest single real estate transaction in U.S. history. While working as food and beverage manager of the Buffalo Statler in upstate New York, he had been invited to give guest lectures at Cornell's Hotel School.

His brief was to bring some element of consistency to the company's food and beverage operations. Most needed a well-formulated business plan; stewarding was shockingly inadequate in others; the quality, quantity, ingredients, preparation methods, and presentation of certain basic dishes (an omelet . . . a hamburger) ranged all over the lot depending on the specific experience of the chef, the cooks, and/or the general manager. IHC's customers required a certain assurance that the basics would be familiar and of uniform acceptability. Many hotels were running unorganized old-fashioned "hotel dining rooms," featuring a stereotypical selection of items, more or less well prepared, listed on boring, poorly printed menus. Over a forty-month period

Balas visited every property and assisted general managers in upgrading their restaurants, bars, and banqueting operations. Some managers found him meddlesome; others welcomed the opportunity to share new ideas.

In San Juan major problems had plagued restaurant and banqueting operations since the hotel's opening. An investigation by Balas revealed widespread theft and waste. A number of the senior food and beverage people were dismissed on the spot. Surveying the chaos and facing a major need to serve a large banquet that day, Balas by chance met Harold Talalas (who ran the banqueting activities at a large restaurant and catering establishment in New Jersey) standing in the hotel lobby while on holiday in Puerto Rico. Balas: "Do you have a tuxedo?" Talalas: "Of course." Talalas was put in charge of the banquet, beginning a career which was to span some thirty years, on and off, with IHC.

In 1958, Trippe invited John B. Gates to leave his position as a senior executive with Russell Burdsall & Ward, the world's largest manufacturer of industrial fasteners (i.e., nuts and bolts) and join Pan Am as vice president – finance. Gates and Trippe were regular golf partners in Greenwich, Connecticut, and Bermuda where both had homes, and both were active as fund-raisers for their alma mater, Yale University. It could not have been a simple decision for Gates to take a cut in salary to switch to Pan Am. Trippe must have been at his most persuasive, as he explained the exciting growth which he foresaw for the international travel industry, and the very attractive stock options and executive bonus program in which Gates would participate as a Pan Am officer.

It soon became apparent that one of Trippe's chief wishes was that Gates reassume the chairmanship of the Yale Alumni Fund, a time-consuming activity on which he had had to cut back while at Russell Burdsall. And, oh yes, he could help Sam Pryor – a long-time Pan Am vice president in charge of governmental relations – with some important lobbying work in Washington. As Gates began to feel his way around the Chrysler Building executive suite, he discovered that there really was no such job in Pan Am as vice president – finance. John Woodbridge, the comptroller, had charge of accounting, tax, and audit activities; Robert Ferguson looked after cash management as treasurer; and dealings with banks, institutions, and Wall Street to fund Pan Am's capital needs were handled personally by Trippe. None of them seemed to be planning any change in function.

In mid-1959, Trippe assigned Gates to supervise Intercontinental and to assure its rapid growth. The commercial jet age had begun and the room shortage was getting serious. Trippe thought eighty or ninety hotels would be a good realistic target; and of course IHC should make token investments if necessary, and surely you, Gates, will find the financing without requiring Pan Am guarantees or making any commitments in Pan Am's name . . . a tall order indeed!

As IHC's new chairman, Gates quickly took charge. He changed the reporting arrangements of those involved primarily in development, design, construction and furnishing activities, to report to him. The IHC architectural, engineering, technical services and project purchasing staff were to be made part of the newly created Tourist Facilities Development Department of Pan Am. A general agreement was concluded with Bechtel giving that organization prime responsibility for project management and negotiating construction contracts; if IHC were to make investments all over the world, Gates wanted to be as certain as reasonably possible that the hotels would be built on time and within tightly controlled budgets. Work was begun on a detailed manual, containing a

Fidel Castro addresses his supporters in Cuba. The triumph of his revolution was one of a number of disruptions that affected Intercontinental's operations in 1959.

standardized hotel construction code of accounts; job descriptions for the various positions of those who would work in the program; approval procedures for each stage of development and construction; and a description of preopening planning and budgeting procedures.

Charles Trippe, fresh from Harvard, was engaged to work on development projects in the Pacific and Asia. Bob Smith, who had become convinced that hotels do not get built from behind a desk in New York, had persuaded Roger Lewis to let him move to Europe (but not that Pan Am should pay the moving cost) for a hands-on approach to promising potential projects which Lee Dayton had identified in Vienna and Geneva; Smith would now report to Gates. (Roger Lewis, whom many had seen as Trippe's probable successor, was to leave Pan Am in 1961 to become chief executive of General Dynamics Corporation.) Lee Dayton was to concentrate on the Middle East and south Asia. Full-time assistance was arranged from Pan Am's legal department and in short order new standard development, technical services and lease agreements were

drafted and professionally printed and bound. Peter Grimm was asked to resign – somehow he had not fitted into the image which Pan Am wanted for its hotel company – and was replaced with Dick Deichler. The eight member board of directors was replaced by a three man group: Gates, Deichler, and James McGuire, a Pan Am assistant comptroller who, as Woodbridge's representative, would make certain that the other two did not exceed their delegated authority under Pan Am's various rules and regulations. Board meetings would occasionally take place in a typewriter with resolutions and other documents circulated later for signature. The real control was in the form of two-to-three page summaries of the essentials of each proposed new hotel project, supported with financial schedules, which were sent from "JBG to JTT." They would be returned with an "OK" and Trippe's initials in the corner or, more often, with a series of penetrating queries and alternate suggestions handwritten in the margin. On the surface it appeared that the personal rapport between the two executives produced quick decision-making; in practice the marginal comments often required two or three more redrafts of the document – and from time to time lengthy conferences or telephone conversations, before final approval was obtained. The same procedure was followed for capital expenditure and payroll approvals above a certain rather modest dollar level.

Gates' first year was one of disruption on the hotel operating side. Castro's revolution had triumphed in Cuba, and the Dominican Republic was invaded by a group of rebel exiles. Tourists dropped both countries from their holiday planning. San Juan's operating problems meant that the hotel would barely cover its minimum rental commitment. Communist-inspired labor unrest in Venezuela marred the first year of civilian rule, which led many local and interna-

tional businessmen to adopt a wait and see attitude; consequently the Tamanaco experienced the novelty of empty rooms. A net loss of $154,000 was the result for IHC.

Each year, the Pan Am board of directors traditionally scheduled one of its monthly meetings outside of New York, to include a fact-finding visit to some other part of Pan Am's world. Most of the directors were chief executives of major corporations, bankers, private capitalists, or figures in international affairs, virtually all whom had access to locally prominent people in government and finance. In almost any country or city Pan Am's bringing them as a group was reason enough for doors to be opened for discussions at every level. And Trippe always ensured that IHC's willingness to take a role in hotel development was a topic of discussion with anyone who seemed, or ought to be, interested. A board visit to Australia, followed up by Pan Am's then executive vice president – Pacific/Alaska Division, Colonel Clarence Young, had produced an option on a centrally located hotel site in Melbourne, the former location of a farmers' market. Charles Trippe was moving his family to Melbourne on his first hotel development assignment; they were met on

Terence E. Hill, later Inter-Continental vice president marketing for Pacific/Asia, was the acting Pan Am manager for Melbourne in 1959.

arrival by Terry Hill, the acting Pan Am manager for Melbourne. Apparently not altogether certain as to the level of creature comfort available in the lands "down under," the Trippes carried many bundles of familiar home supplies, Kleenex, toiletries, etc., from the United States for setting up housekeeping. Charlie was able to meet leaders of the financial community and government and in relatively short order succeeded in organizing a company, Southern Cross Properties, Ltd. (SCP), to firm up the long-term land lease; undertake a hotel feasibility study; engage an architect, Welton Beckett Associates of the United States; locate sources of long-term debt, including a commitment from Ex-im for a U.S. dollar loan; identify institutional investors and an underwriter for a public share issue; and execute technical services agreements (TSAs) and lease agreements between SCP and IHC, the first of the new standard contracts to be signed.

Bechtel would undertake the bulk of the construction management responsibilities under the TSA. IHC would subscribe to one-third of SCP's share capital. The lease provided for a rent calculated at 75 percent of the GOP, and committed the landlord to fund annual additions to, and replacements of, furniture, fixtures and equipment in an amount equal to varying percentages of the original cost, the latter clause intended to ensure that the property could be maintained in good condition throughout the term of the lease. Because of the size and location of the hotel site, a large shopping center featuring an open plaza and handy access to the hotel's restaurants and bars was incorporated into the plan. As added security for the lenders and landowner, IHC's lease required that up to 100 percent of the GOP generated by the commercial center be made available to SCP if the rent from the hotel portion was insufficient to cover its financial costs in any year. The public share issue was successfully floated, an attractive construction contract was negotiated, and the 435-room hotel – the Southern Cross – would be in operation in less than three years from the date of Trippe's initial contacts.

Meanwhile in Europe, Bob Smith was being continually frustrated in his efforts to complete negotiations for Geneva and Vienna. Contacts with Dr. Kamitz, the Austrian finance minister, had induced a favorable government interest in seeing an IHC hotel in Vienna, and Kamitz had provided introductions to the leaders of the Austrian financial community. A site could be obtained through cooperation with the Eislaufverein, an ice skating club located between the Philharmonic Hall and the city park. IHC's commitment to renovate the club facilities (new offices, freezing system and piping for the outdoor rink) at a cost of about one million dollars, could be exchanged for 5,000 square meters of land directly facing the park. The next door neighbor's low-rise facility would ensure obstruction-free views from the hotel guest rooms, and the freezing plant could be designed to do double duty for air conditioning the hotel in the summer months. But despite a promising feasibility study and encouraging Bechtel construction cost estimates, the negotiations with the banks produced little result. Eighty percent of the industries in Austria and a substantial portion of the country's trade and commerce were controlled by these two banks, Laenderbank and Creditanstalt, each affiliated with one of the two dominant political parties. After months and months of meetings focused mostly on minutiae of the proposed TSA and lease contracts, there was no progress. At one particularly belligerent session, Smith, having been told that the IHC contracts were imperialistic, replied with a rather biting allusion to some of the worst excesses of the Hitler era. Whether neither bank wanted to be seen to be making compromises to IHC in front of

the other, or whether neither really wanted the project to go ahead, was never discovered, but Smith finally decided to walk away. Before leaving Vienna, he paid a courtesy call on Minister Kamitz, who was distressed at the news and summoned the two bank directors. He berated them for their failure after a year to reach agreement, was unimpressed with their pleas that they were really just trying to make the best possible deal for Austria, and gave them twenty-four hours to decide to negotiate in good faith, failing which the ministry would become IHC's sole partner and take up the equity for its own account. They yielded, and after another few weeks the deal was done. A Cooley fund credit was arranged for a portion of the debt with a savings bank providing the remainder, all under long-term loans. IHC would invest 25 percent of the equity, the banks 35 percent each, and the finance ministry 5 percent.

Horace Julliard was a Geneva real estate personality who in 1959 was planning to develop a large hilltop property overlooking the whole city of Geneva as a first-class multi-apartment complex. As an anchor for the project he envisioned a top-class hotel on which he was predisposed to work with Bob Smith and IHC. Through a series of introductions Smith was soon in contact with Philip de Weck, Geneva manager of the Union Bank of Switzerland; Joseph Kowalski, head of Promotex, a development company owned by Baron Edmond de Rothschild of Paris; Prince Sadruddin Aga Khan; Ernst Schmidheiny, chairman of Swissair and one of Switzerland's leading businessmen; and Maître Maurice Merkt, the chairman of Rolex. All were interested in seeing a new international hotel and conference facility built in Geneva. Countess Mona Bismarck, an American heiress, also became a backer. A feasibility study was undertaken, with Addor and Julliard as architects working with Dick Smith on hotel-related design elements. Horwath produced the market study and earnings projections while Bechtel prepared cost estimates. The feasibility report was passed by one of the bankers to the Swiss Hotelkeepers Association for review and comment. They in turn commissioned Jack Gauer, one of their members, to prepare an analysis – which turned out to be devastatingly negative. Smith prepared and distributed a careful rebuttal, but could not help but notice a certain reserve on the part of the investment group. De Weck invited Smith to Zurich to meet his bank's chairman, Dr. Schaeffer, who reaffirmed his continued interest in – though not necessarily support for – the IHC project. He had convened a meeting for his senior advisors to review the data with Smith; they reported that the other two banks which had been expected to join in underwriting the debt financing had withdrawn their support after reading Gauer's report. They would not recommend Union Bank's going it alone and no amount of discussion seemed to budge them from this position. At the last minute, Dr. Schaeffer arrived, was briefed, and stated slowly and succinctly his confidence in Pan Am/IHC, his support for the project, his belief that such a hotel was needed in Geneva, and his faith in the integrity of the feasibility study. During his monologue his nose began to bleed, and drip onto his collar and tie, but he remained cool and apparently under no strain. He apologized that he had not been able to attend the entire meeting and that he must leave for other appointments, asked Smith to continue his discussion, and expressed his belief that surely matters could be resolved. The room was silent; de Weck and Smith left, and in due course Union Bank financed the project.

As an adjunct to the main development activity, Smith also arranged for a consortium of the prestige watch manufacturers based in Geneva to lease jointly a large shop on the mezzanine lobby of the hotel to display and sell their products.

EASTWARD EXPANSION

I n 1960, the 170-room El Ponce Intercontinental opened in the middle of the tourist season on a landscaped hillside site overlooking the city. The hotel was owned by some of the same shareholders as the San Juan hotel, together with the Ferré family (Puerto Rico's largest cement producer), the Seralles family (Don Q Rum), Gloria Vanderbilt, and IHC. Ponce could be reached by car via a two-hour tortuous, winding highway over the mountains from San Juan, or by one of the four daily Caribair DC–3 aircraft twenty-minute flights, famed for their extreme turbulence. An architecturally unusual building designed by Bill Tabler, the hotel was unfortunately destined to be a money loser for most of its life. Optimism reigned at its opening, and for nearly a year it served some of the best food in the Caribbean, produced credible casino profits (until the local gambling community eventually discovered that the "house always wins") and seldom rented more than eighty rooms a night. General manager Leo Riordan had operated Calhoun's Weylin Hotel in the early 1950s and had been running a property in the Virgin Islands prior to being engaged for Ponce. As an ex-air force colonel, his reputation for attention to detail and often abrupt barking of instructions was well deserved. His office hours were unpredictable, but he showed up in the restaurant every night with his wife, Mildred (a former model), to oversee the operation and dine. Kane Rufe was executive assistant manager and Jim Potter was chief accountant, his first job with IHC. Osvaldo Herrera, a Chilean who had joined IHC from the Carrera, and had traveled throughout the chain for several years under Busquets' direction, installing and refining, and training staff in, food and beverage cost control systems, eventually settled down in Ponce as food and beverage manager.

The hotel won some awards in the United States for its handsome and expensively produced bilingual menus. Unfortunately, the New York agency which did the Spanish translations made some hair-raising errors: an English heading "From the Cold Buffet" read *"De la Bofetada Fria."* *Bofetada* surely appears as a word for "buffet" in the dictionary – but buffet in a Cervantes sense of "He was dealt a mighty buffet." Thus words meaning roughly "From a cold blow in the jaw" headed up the salad and cold fish section in the Spanish version. *"Del Horno Flamante"* was the translation of "From the Flaming Hearth." *Flamante* has nothing to do with fire: the hotel's grills were being described in Spanish as coming "From the brand new oven." Describing a stuffed baby chicken, the translator added the diminutive suffix *ino* (instead of *ito*) to the word *pollo* thereby offering the delicacy *pollino relleno* or stuffed jackass to Spanish readers. These menus became collectors' items.

Ponce was the first hotel for which the purchasing program was controlled by computer, a relatively rudimentary system, but unique for the time. From the earliest days "centralized purchasing" – and the savings presumably to be derived therefrom – had been promoted as a service to be provided under IHC's management. In practice, IHC purchasing had consisted of two or three

clerks in New York who transmitted purchase orders to Pan Am's purchasing department in the Long Island City office. Each order was handled on an ad hoc basis with no attempt made to negotiate volume pricing. Edward Dowling, a Notre Dame graduate who had joined Pan Am's purchasing department after discharge from the U.S. navy in 1946, was frequently asked to work on some IHC orders. He soon learned that these orders were spread among several people in Pan Am; seldom did the same person handle procurement of like items for two different hotels; the orders came in chronologically and were delegated to whoever had the time. Filing was chronological and not segregated for IHC within the Pan Am system. Answering questions from a hotel and reordering created many delays and much confusion. Dowling on his own initiative asked his supervisor to consider a separate section for IHC and by 1953 Dowling and a small group had been transferred to the hotel company. Pan Am continued to handle shipping. El Salvador was the first property for which IHC purchasing was responsible for procuring all of the furniture, operating equipment and operating supplies. Quantity furniture and equipment listings had been prepared by the interior design firm, and the kitchen and laundry planners. Levon Keenan borrowed a food and beverage inventory from a friend at the St. Regis Hotel which was modified for use in El Salvador. After the job was complete, Dowling used copies of the El Salvador purchase orders to create a computer-produced master list for future projects, using some key punch clerks whom he knew in Pan Am.

"The Intercontinentals", an early 1960s advertising campaign for IHC's properties in Latin America, featured match-books from all the hotels in the region.

One afternoon a representative of Liddell, an Irish manufacturer of linen, called on Dowling and asked how his firm might be of service to IHC. It was impossible to give him any accurate data on the magnitude of the company's consumption, or the types of products used. Dowling thereupon undertook a project of searching Pan Am's records to locate the past four years' IHC hotel purchase orders, from which product purchase records could be prepared. Thereafter IHC was in a position to negotiate and insist on volume pricing from suppliers. For three years, 1958–61, IHC made regular weekly container shipments of supplies and equipment to the hotels in the Caribbean. A full-time food buyer was added to the staff.

In 1960, Frankfurt, the financial center of West Germany, was already on its way to becoming one of Europe's most important transportation hubs. Pan Am operated a variety of flights from Frankfurt to America, and to other European cities, and a shuttle service to Berlin overflying Communist-controlled East Germany; daily east- and west-bound round-the-world-flights also called at Frankfurt. Pan Am's director for Germany, Thomas Flanagan, had firsthand knowledge of the short supply of first-class hotel accommodations in Frankfurt, and had arranged for Bob Smith to stop over in the city to meet some local officials. In a private Park Hotel salon Smith, Flanagan, and Eric Bleich, who had prepared the groundwork for the meeting, faced a high-powered group: Mayor Bockelmann; City Treasurer Klingler; Professor Gunzert, director of the Frankfurt City Bureau of Statistics, who had done a detailed study confirming Frankfurt's dire need of a large, top-class hotel; Georg Zinn, minister-president (governor) of the state of Hesse, in which Frankfurt is located; and their deputies and assistants. Bockelmann explained that the city needed a major hotel in which to host a world oil congress in June 1965, hoped that Pan Am/IHC could help in filling this need, and inquired how he and his associates could be of assistance. Smith took a bold approach, and proposed a 500-room property on a prime riverfront site to be provided by the city at a minimal rent, with thirty-year-term debt financing to be provided by mortgage and other banks, guaranteed, if necessary, by government, all subject to a satisfactory feasibility study. IHC would undertake to find equity investors. The German response was positive and immediate. However, the de Barry mansion site which Bob Smith had preferred had been promised to the Central Bank; the alternate and less attractive site, on the south bank of the Main River opposite the city hall, could be made available by the city even over the objection of a certain faction which did not want to see any high-rise construction on the Sachsenhausen side of the river. Nevertheless, on September 9 1960, while he was a guest on a shakedown cruise on the tanker *Esso Essen*, Bleich received a (collect) radio call from Professor Gunzert advising that the de Barry property was too small for the Bundesbank and that IHC could have it if it moved quickly. Bleich, who by this time was working full time on the project, sent out a call and within days IHC and Bechtel technical people arrived to begin site tests. Bleich's negotiations with the city produced a sixty-year lease on the 18,700-square-meter site with a rent based on an annual return of 4 percent on the 1939, pre-World-War-II property tax roll value, and an option to purchase the land after the hotel opened.

Bleich was at the time a forty-five-year-old Pan Am manager who was working as Flanagan's assistant. Born in Vienna, he was a student at the time of the Anschluss, Hitler's merger of Austria into Nazi Germany. Demonstrators thronged through the universities, harassing and upsetting routines. Bleich was from a Jewish family and could be a special target for the anti-Semitic wrath of the rioters, as well as for the SS who had already begun rounding up Jewish students. In order to take his final oral examination he reached the professors' chambers by climbing a ladder through a back window so as to avoid the troublemakers in the front of the building. He was awarded a doctorate in trade and economics. Consulting some U.S. telephone books, he found the addresses of several Americans who had the surname Bleich and wrote to them asking for an affidavit of support to immigrate to the United States. This was forthcoming and he booked ship's passage through the Netherlands and made a potentially dangerous train journey from Vienna which included being forced to disembark from the train at the German/Dutch border, and eluding the guards in order to reboard it as the engine began to pull away from the station. In the United States he was able to find support to bring his sisters out of Austria. He held a series of jobs, from cleaning to bookkeeping, before joining the U.S. army where, he had learned, it was possible to qualify for advanced technical training. After a series of tests he was accepted for a meteorological course at the University of Chicago, graduated as a weather forecaster and master sergeant, and was then sent for officer's training. He was eventually based in England while preparations were under way for the invasion of Europe. After war service and granting of U.S. citizenship, he joined American Airlines, and later its subsidiary American Overseas Airlines, to be posted in Europe – first Amsterdam, then Frankfurt – to handle weather and dispatch duties for transatlantic flights on their Shannon–London–Amsterdam–Berlin legs. He became a part of Pan Am when it acquired American Overseas in 1949, and provided weather forecasts during the Berlin airlift. Because of its inter-German Berlin service, Pan Am had a large number of aircrew based in Germany, and was anxious to secure some measure of German income tax relief for them, based on the special services which they performed in keeping Berlin accessible. Bleich, as a German speaker who understood taxation matters, was given the task and succeeded. His unyielding persistence combined with unfailing politeness

Dr. Eric H. Bleich (left) chats with Baron Rothschild, a shareholder in the Frankfurt and Geneva Intercontinental hotels.

and attention to proprieties led Pan Am to assign him other governmental liaison projects. After the initial Frankfurt hotel meetings, Bob Smith arranged for his transfer to the Pan Am development department.

With the land and debt committed, Smith quickly secured Countess Bismarck, Baron Rothschild, and Prince Sadruddin as equity partners. The remaining 25 percent of the equity was proving elusive to find. Dr. Hans G. Schroeder-Hohenwarth, then a mid-level bank officer working with the chairman of the Frankfurter Bank, had met Flanagan at a meeting of the American Chamber of Commerce in West Germany and the two had discussed the hotel project. As a high-class, small, private Frankfurt bank with prestigious clients, the Frankfurter Bank would be happy to see the hotel proceed; but it was not interested in an equity participation, being mindful of the accepted wisdom in banking circles that "hotels are only profitable after the third bankruptcy," when they can be picked up at a fraction of their cost. At a New York meeting of Schroeder-Hohenwarth's chairman, Dr. Hermann Jannsen, and Pan Am's Sam Pryor, Smith described the project in great detail and secured Jannsen's commitment to subscribe to 25 percent of the equity, DM10 million at the time. In taking the decision, Jannsen had exceeded the authority customarily granted by his partners and upon his return to Frankfurt they were disinclined to support him. After forceful prodding by Smith, the bank relented and undertook to sell lots of DM100,000 to various customers including HRH Prince Louis Ferdinand of Prussia, Hoechst Chemicalworks, the Frankfurt Fair Company, the Frankfurt Airport Authority and a Wiesbaden investor, Dr. Mueller Mark; the bank took some DM5 million for its own account. Dr. Schroeder-Hohenwarth joined the hotel company board and served as its chairman for more than two decades. He later became chairman of the bank.

At about the same time, Smith engineered the formation of a company to build three hotels in Ireland – Dublin (300 rooms), Limerick (100) and Cork (100) – with Aer Lingus, the Irish national airline, the Irish Tourist Board, private Irish investors and, once again, Countess Bismarck, Baron Rothschild, and Prince Sadruddin.

In April 1961 Indonesia's President Sukarno made a state visit to the United States to meet President John Kennedy, having chartered a Pan Am 707 jet to carry him and his entourage around the world – one of five such charters over the years. The purser on the flight was an American, Walter Spillum, who at the time was one of a special group of attendants assigned to VIP flights. He became a good friend of Sukarno and Pan Am eventually posted him to Jakarta as local manager, after the airline received permission for a single weekly jet service from and to Singapore (the tail end of an island-hopping trans-Pacific route: San Francisco–Honolulu–Wake–Guam–Manila–Saigon–Singapore). Sukarno had decided to use some of the funds which were being provided by Japan as war reparations to construct a major international hotel in Jakarta, and the 420-room, two-tower, high-rise building, designed by Abel Sorenson together with Japanese engineers, was rising when Spillum arrived. Over the course of several months, and another round-the-world Pan Am charter flight, Sukarno was made aware of Intercontinental, and his itinerary adjusted to enable him to visit some IHC properties; he was particularly taken with San Juan, because of the climatic similarities with Indonesia. It was arranged for Sukarno and Charlie Trippe to meet; shortly thereafter, at Sukarno's direction, a hybrid form of management agreement was hammered out by Trippe and representatives of the Indonesian Housing Development Bank, the entity which was to have responsibility for Hotel Indonesia upon completion. The agreement was heavily slanted toward the training responsibilities which IHC was expected to assume. The management fee was modest, and the salaries of the general manager and comptroller were to be for IHC's account. But specific commitments were spelled out in great detail regarding foreign exchange and tax concessions to be provided for a large contingent of training-oriented

OPPOSITE: Frankfurt-on-Main. The city was West Germany's financial center in 1960 but first-class hotel accommodation was in short supply and Robert Smith secured funds from high-profile investors to establish the Frankfurt Inter-Continental, which was opened in 1964.

During a round the world Pan Am charter, President Sukarno visited San Juan in order to inspect the El San Juan Intercontinental, prior to finally awarding the management contract for Hotel Indonesia, then under construction in Jakarta, to Intercontinental. J. P. Sutherland, general manager, greeted the Indonesian president.

President Sukarno and Walter Spillum, Pan Am director for Indonesia, practice on the gamelan in Merdeka Palace, Jakarta.

foreign hotel specialists who were to assume senior and middle management roles in the hotel, and the financing of overseas training programs for a group of promising young Indonesian graduates. A limited TSA provided primarily for graphic and interior design assistance, and on-site project management coordination during the preopening period.

At about the same time Charles Trippe executed agreements with the Burmese government for IHC to operate a hotel being constructed under a Soviet government aid grant at an attractive lakeside site away from the cluttered center of the old city of Rangoon. Complications, including an attempt by Hilton to sway certain bureaucrats away from the IHC commitment and genuine Russian repugnance at the thought of an American firm operating their gift, eventually killed the project just as IHC was arranging for the transfer of the hotel's prospective general manager.

Neal Prince was the chief designer at the interior design firm Walter Ballard Associates, in which capacity he had created and supervised the interiors for the Ponce hotel. Born in Texas and armed with degrees in architecture and architectural engineering from Houston's Rice University, Prince did military service with the U.S. army combat engineers in Italy. Returning to Texas, he became active in the Houston Little Theatre which produced a prizewinning play that he had authored. After a period as director of the Little Theatre, he went to the east coast and served for a season as director of a summer stock theater company in New Hampshire. A spell in New York with the Actors Studio brought him to the classical quandary of those bitten by the theater bug: a regular job supporting a regular diet or stick it out on the Rialto. Creature comfort won and through the Architectural League he secured a position with a firm which was noted for the design of hospitals; after several months of observation in New York's Bellevue Hospital, Prince became the firm's expert on the layout and planning of emergency rooms. In due course he decided against a lifetime in health care architecture, switched firms, and was assigned a project to design a motorway restaurant complex for Restaurant Associates, the New York area's most creative force in restaurant operations at the time. The job involved a complete package: architecture, engineering and interior. Prince took a genuine interest in the latter, and made a seminal career move to Ballard where, at Byron Calhoun's request, he did ad hoc work on a project to remodel the Hotel Jaragua in Ciudad Trujillo in the Dominican Republic, most of which work was never carried out, and a modest remodeling of the San Juan Hotel. Ballard had a contract for the interiors of the Phoenicia Intercontinental in Beirut and Prince was sent there to work on the interiors and also, because of his background, to represent architect Edward Stone in matters of interior layouts and finishes. All the furniture pieces were designed from scratch and were manufactured locally. In January 1961 Prince was hired to work full time as director of interior design in the Pan Am Development Department with the intention, at least in developing countries, that IHC would produce its hotels' interior designs "in house" and be reimbursed at cost under the TSAs. Prince shortly engaged Kenneth Smith, an interior designer from Ballard, and Charles Alvey, a specialist in graphics and industrial design.

In anticipation of the Phoenicia and European openings, Ed Dowling and Peter Balas were sent on a research trip to Europe and Asia to locate alternate sources of supply, particularly for kitchen equipment, china, glass, silver, and linen. This investigation turned up several small local manufacturers who were producing hotel-quality products at competitive prices, but who had never been involved in export sales. They were prepared to make products to IHC's specification, including original designs, in anticipation of a long-term relationship with a company which was obviously growing. WMF, a German stainless steel flat- and hollow-ware manufacturer; Beard, a Swiss silver-plate flat- and hollow-ware producer; Christofle, a quality French silver manufacturer who had never done high volume hotel plate; Bauscher from Germany and Schoenfeld from Austria, both chinaware producers; Schott-Zwiesel, a glass and crystal producer in Germany . . . all became major factory-direct suppliers to IHC.

The board of directors in Beirut had several members who in one or another of their other businesses represented various European manufacturers as agents in the Middle East. Each wanted to see his affiliate's products in the hotel. Accordingly, no orders could be placed without review and approval by the entire board. IHC was asked to obtain competitive samples and make recommendations; all the agency representatives were in an anteroom. Balas explained that price and prestige names were not necessarily as important as quality and durability, and thereupon banged plates from Limoges and Bauscher together; the Limoges cracked. The director whose personal interests favored Limoges repeated the exercise with the same result. The chairman intervened: "Bauscher it is." Forks and knives were bent, goblets chipped, silver platters flung to the floor, compromises proposed and discarded. By the end of the three-day meeting, all of IHC's proposals had been accepted at a total estimated cost well within budget.

1960 was another loss year for Intercontinental. The Cuban government "intervened" (a euphemism for expropriation) the Nacional Hotel, one of the last to be taken over, and presented a bill for the occupancy of general manager Bill Land's suite dated back to the fall of the prior government. IHC had to write off $850,000 on its Nacional investment. The IHC accounting office in Havana where Bill Busquets and his staff were based was abandoned, as were Warren Pine's and Busquets' homes and furnishings. Pine was strip-searched before his final departure; Busquets, who had been taking his files out of the country in small lots for several months, did manage to salvage the office calculator and Dictaphone. A shipment of linen destined for Cuba had been stopped in time at the New York docks, the manufacturer agreed to reinvoice at cost, and the Purchasing Department conducted a towel and bathrobe sale among IHC and Pan Am employees. Ponce had a shortfall in meeting its minimum rent. The political situation in the Dominican Republic worsened leading IHC to close the Jaragua, reduce the Embajador staff to 100, and release the casino operator from his minimum rent requirement. In Santiago, the owners of the Carrera were unwilling to make a firm commitment for much-needed modernization and refurbishing, and IHC opted to let the management contract expire. Plummeting worldwide oil prices sent Venezuela's economy into the doldrums and the Bolivar local currency, heretofore the region's most stable, was headed for its first devaluation in years. In Caracas, the Tamanaco had no profits, which led Deichler to question the expense item "employees' profit participation" in the accounts. This was his opportunity to learn that a benefit, once granted, cannot be taken away, even if there are no profits in which to participate. Only the Tequendama in Bogota was providing a steady income for IHC. Gates must have been wondering what he had gotten himself into; his favorite description for multiple disasters was "a barrel of eels – that's like a can of worms, but much worse."

Early in 1961 Busquets resigned to accept a promising position as financial controller for a major construction group in Chile, and was succeeded by Jim Potter as manager of hotel accounting.

At Gates' request Pan Am had added Max Hampton to its press and public relations staff to work full time (except when preempted by an airline disaster or other Pan Am emergency) ensuring adequate international press coverage for IHC. The "big story" for the next few years, of course, was to be a steady string of new hotel openings in every corner of the world. In the interim, getting travel writers to extol the glories of a Ponce or Curaçao holiday would tax his imagination and keep Max busy.

A partnership between Hilton and the Australian Chevron Hotel group had fallen apart just as a 200-room wing of a partially complete mega-hotel was to open in Sydney. Chevron's principal owner, a financier named Korman, had been overextended as the result of a recent takeover bid for a retail chain, and it appeared that there might be an opportunity to step into Hilton's position

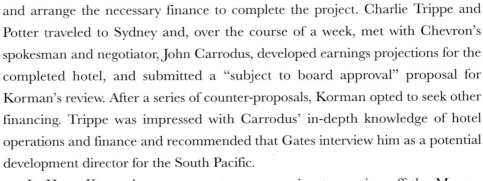

and arrange the necessary finance to complete the project. Charlie Trippe and Potter traveled to Sydney and, over the course of a week, met with Chevron's spokesman and negotiator, John Carrodus, developed earnings projections for the completed hotel, and submitted a "subject to board approval" proposal for Korman's review. After a series of counter-proposals, Korman opted to seek other financing. Trippe was impressed with Carrodus' in-depth knowledge of hotel operations and finance and recommended that Gates interview him as a potential development director for the South Pacific.

In Hong Kong, the government was preparing to auction off the Murray Parade ground, a super-central site immediately adjacent to the three pillars of the colony's financial power: the Bank of China, the Hong Kong and Shanghai Banking Corporation, and the Chartered Bank. Wheelock Marden, one of the established old guard British trading companies, Pan Am, and a Chinese entrepreneur had formed a joint venture to acquire the property. Wheelock would design and build, debt capital would be provided by Colonial Development Corp. (the British equivalent of Ex-im), and IHC would manage. The tender document

Hong Kong (opposite page) and (above) the heroine of a Cantonese opera. IHC negotiated a unique membership agreement for The Mandarin hotel on the waterfront.

set a construction completion date, which meant that only serious bidders with plans in hand and financing assured could hope for success. The principals of a Texas-based real estate partnership, Wyncor Development, happened to be in Hong Kong, read a newspaper notice of the event, went to the auction, bid up the price, and walked away with the prize . . . which eventually became the Hong Kong Hilton. Thereafter Trippe initiated discussions with Jardine, one of the premier tai-pan trading companies, which led to a membership agreement for the Mandarin hotel, a luxury property under construction on a prime site opposite the cross-harbor Star Ferry terminal.

One particularly unusual agreement was negotiated by Trippe during his years in the Pacific: a letter of intent with Seibu Railway Company of Japan, which provided for IHC to assist in arranging a long-term dollar loan to be used in the construction of a 600-room hotel and commercial center on land owned by Seibu near Shiba Park. A joint venture company of Seibu/IHC would be formed to furnish and manage the hotel under a lease, and a limited TSA would provide for IHC involvement in project design. The document set forth a procedure whereunder Seibu would have primary responsibility for day-to-day hotel operating activities in Japan, and IHC would market the property overseas, both under basic principles and policies to be agreed unanimously by the parties. Although the agreement represented a uniquely creative approach toward melding the

A monastery in Beirut. When the Phoenicia Intercontinental opened in the city in 1961 it was IHC's first venture outside Latin America.

interests and specific talents of two major organizations from different countries and cultures, the project, for whatever reason, did not come to fruition.

For the Ponce opening IHC had developed a planning and training procedure which was expanded in scope for the Phoenicia and was followed, with minor exceptions, in new hotels for nearly a decade. Since the company had no operations outside Spanish-speaking Latin America, staffing of key department-head positions for new hotels was going to have to be from new hires, mostly from Europe and the countries in which the hotels were located, and few if any of them would be familiar with IHC's management practices. Specifications for virtually everything used to furnish, equip and supply the hotel had to be determined, and goods ordered well before any staff had been designated for the hotel. Grimm had built a small staff to take responsibility for the preplanning and opening activities, coordinating with and assisting the new hotel's general manager to recruit and engage key staff, and assure the installation of IHC operating systems.

For the Phoenicia the team would include Peter Balas, to plan the food and beverage facilities, develop menus, recruit expatriate staff, and insure adequate restaurant service training; Levon Keenan, to develop and review the preopening budget with the general manager, and to organize training for front office, and the uniformed service and housekeeping departments; Jim Potter with two traveling accountants, Ben White and Bert Laacks, to set up and train staff for the accounting, cashiering, receiving, storeroom and cost control departments; Art Schermer, IHC director of maintenance engineering, working with the hotel chief engineer, to commission mechanical equipment, and establish routine maintenance systems; Tex Stovall, to organize the laundry, commission equipment and train laundry workers on equipment most of which had never before been used in Lebanon; Max Hampton to gather and shepherd overseas press, travel trade, and VIP guests for the inaugural events; Ed Dowling, to provide on site and overseas support to assure that all furnishings and operating supplies and equipment ordered by IHC were on site and in good condition; Neal Prince, Ken Smith, and Charles Alvey, to oversee the furniture installation and setting up of guest rooms and public spaces, and the production of printed graphics; and Jim Fox, as project manager, to be general coordinator of the team's efforts, interfacing with the general manager and construction project management, in this instance Bechtel. The extent of each person's involvement was related to the level of professionalism which was available among the locally recruited staff. In some cases this meant training from scratch; in other cases simply standing in the background to be of assistance. In Beirut, a highly qualified kitchen and restaurant supervisory staff had been recruited, but the front office reception, reservations, and guest billing systems were the first of their type in Lebanon.

General manager for this first Intercontinental venture outside Latin America was René Lambert, transferred from Caracas, and bringing the optimum in IHC experience as well as a sound base in the style and culture of France, the predominant European influence in Lebanon. He had succeeded in engaging Karl Walterspiel as executive assistant manager, a youngish professional who had literally spent his entire life in fine hotels – starting at his family's Vier Jahreszeiten Hotel in Munich, and including a tour as food and beverage manager at the Tamanaco in Caracas, and, just prior to Beirut, service as a manager at the newly opened Carlton Tower in London.

IHC purchasing undertook a massive procurement operation to supply the Phoenicia with a complete inventory of world-class food and beverages. Negotiations were conducted direct with European distilleries and vineyards, resulting in attractive pricing that was based to some extent on the perceived future business volumes to be generated by IHC's rapid growth, a card played loud and often by Dowling and his staff. Grant's whisky was to be shipped from Scotland at less than $1.00 a bottle. Frozen meats were shipped from the United States, and French beef and lamb were to be flown for special occasions from Paris. There were some

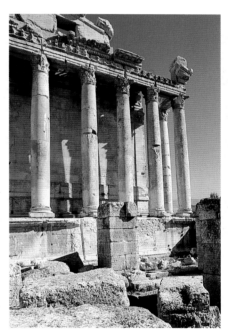

Baalbek, Lebanon. Celebrities were taken on a visit to the ruins during the Phoenicia Intercontinental's opening celebrations.

restrictions, of course, on the importation of products already plentiful, or being produced, in Lebanon, among them citrus fruits. Included in one shipment of several thousand cases was a single box of twenty-four bottles of Rose's Lime Juice, a product deemed essential by some for that staple of the East – the gimlet. There are no limes grown in Lebanon, but limes are citrus. What to do to spring this box – and the rest of the lot – from customs seizure? Solution: explain that the product was Rose Juice, of course! The two cases of American peanut butter included in that shipment sat uncalled for in the hotel's stores for many moons – and this product was subsequently removed from Dowling's computer list.

The Phoenicia Intercontinental opened and started accepting guests in late December 1961

Poolside scenes at the Phoenicia Intercontinental in Beirut. "Sous la Mer", the hotel's bar, featured underwater views into the swimming pool.

with most of its bedrooms, two restaurants, a rooftop lounge, and the lobby bar completed and in operation. Three days earlier the ceiling of the lobby at the head of the escalator from the street, directly opposite the reception desk, had begun to sag, and one after another of the suspended acoustical tiles had started to fall, leaving a gaping hole and, overhead, a view of the maze of pipes, conduits, and ducts that deliver power and water and air to the floors above. It seems that earlier in the week a workman had been sent to crawl into this space to make a repair; the wires which supported the grid for the suspended ceiling panels had impeded his travel, so he'd simply snipped a few!

Over the next weeks, the beauty parlor and barbershop, the street bar (featuring panoramic views through back bar windows into the depths of the swimming pool; it was named "Sous la Mer"), the ballroom, and the pool cabanas and snack bar became operational. Hampton had discovered a party of U.S. celebrities who were participating in a promotion for a new Mediterranean cruise ship route, and negotiated for them to visit the Phoenicia while in port. Joan Fontaine, Nancy Herrera, Hugh O'Brien, Zachary Scott, Gloria Swanson, and the *New Yorker*'s Charles Addams were aboard. They were treated to side visits to the ancient ruins at Baalbek and Byblos, and a flight to Jordan to visit Jerusalem, between receptions and luncheon at the Phoenicia.

For the gala opening which was scheduled a few weeks later, the Beirut board of directors wanted a major international entertainer – someone in the Frank Sinatra category. Budget realities produced Dorothy Dandridge instead, at the time a leading motion picture, nightclub and recording artist in America. Gates and Deichler came from New York; the president of Lebanon cut the ribbon; a high-powered *grande cuisine* luncheon was served to *le tout* Beirut; Le Paon Rouge nightclub opened with Miss Dandridge mostly drowned out by the merrymakers; and the hotel was well and truly opened.

While the Phoenicia was preparing to open, relationships with the owners of the San Juan hotel were deteriorating; Gates opted to accept an offer to buy out the lease and sold IHC's interests, recording a small gain on the transaction, but not enough to offset another year of overall corporate loss-making. Pete Sutherland, the San Juan manager, was tapped for Melbourne and sent to Australia to prepare for an August 1962 opening.

Moshe Mayer was an Israeli industrialist, property developer and builder who had constructed the Ducor Palace, a 100-room hotel on Mamba Point, a hilltop named for a deadly snake, in the city of Monrovia, capital of Liberia. He had other projects underway in the city, including an elaborate palace for President Tubman and a 100-room enlargement to the hotel. He had also concluded an attractive arrangement with the Ivory Coast government to develop a huge tract of lagoon-fronting land in Abidjan into an African "Riviera." The first step was a 200-room hotel on which construction had begun. Mayer had made equity investments in both this and the Ducor Palace and controlled the management. An introduction to Gates produced a genuine rapport between the two, out of which quickly came proposals for IHC also to invest in the two properties and take over the operation.

Pan Am had a long history in Liberia, having built the international airport at Roberts Field (an hour's drive from Monrovia) as part of the air route system from Brazil to Africa created for military support in World War II; was managing the airport under a technical services agreement; owned a small hotel at the airport; and operated all its African jet flights through Liberia, which was also a major crew layover stop. (The Liberia Company – an entity which had widespread natural resource development rights in the country – was owned by members of the Trippe family, among others.) Pan Am had hopes of adding Abidjan to its West African route system which also included Dakar, Accra, Lagos, and Leopoldville. The investment in Abidjan was to carry a governmentally guaranteed dividend; the Liberia investment carried full commercial risk. Fortunately, a program of insurance had been created by the U.S. government to encourage investment in developing countries, whereunder a U.S. company could purchase protection against expropriation, non-remittability of dividends, and other economic risks, at affordable rates. The insurance, administered by the U.S. Agency for International Development, was available in countries with which the United States had negotiated enabling treaties, and among these were both Liberia and the Ivory Coast. With this protection, the projects were "go" for IHC, and the Monrovia hotel became the Ducor Intercontinental, the company's first property in Africa, on April 1 1962.

John Gates had been in charge for two and a half years during which time he had set in place an extensive framework for rapid growth, but was becoming concerned about IHC's operating leadership. A major corporate hotel operator needed a major hotelier at its helm, and Gates had become convinced that Dick Deichler was not that man. The choice to succeed Deichler was Robert Huyot, hotelman par excellence. His résumé included a sixteen-year stint as general manager of New York's Carlyle Hotel – the ne plus ultra of residential *hôtellerie*, where he had created the elegant Café Carlyle and enjoyed the custom of John and Jacqueline Kennedy; three years as manager of the prestigious Waldorf Towers; the obligatory series of up-the-ladder junior management positions in such properties as the Crillon and du Louvre hotels in his native France; and most recently the responsibility, as vice president and general manager, for opening the new Loew's Summit Hotel in New York and, as vice president and general-manager-designate, the planning of the deluxe Regency Hotel which was shortly to open on Park Avenue. While building this major hotel industry career he had earned a bachelor of arts (*cum laude*) degree with a major in philosophy, and law (*cum laude*) degree from French schools; had taken courses in accounting, U.S. business law, labor relations, public speaking, and real estate appraisal at New York's Columbia University, as well as a two-year course at the New York School of Interior Design; and had studied oil painting at the Art Students League (and shown his paintings at Georg Jensen, Fifth Avenue), cabinet-making at the Museum of Modern Art, and landscape design at Hunter College. His hobbies included trap shooting, flying as a private pilot, and garden landscaping.

A view in Pakistan. After four years of negotiation construction on the Karachi Intercontinental started in 1962.

Lee Dayton had been laboring for four years to put together a viable hotel project in Karachi. Early on he had made the acquaintance of Yusuf Haroon, a Pakistani businessman who had also played an important role in local and national politics, following in the footsteps of his father who, in colonial times, had been a member of the Indian National Assembly and had been knighted by the British. The Haroons owned *Dawn*, Pakistan's leading English language newspaper, of which the nation's founder, Moh. Ali Jinnah, had once been editor. The United States and Pakistan were close allies, and Washington had already indicated a willingness to make Ex-im and Cooley funds available for a hotel project. Haroon was prepared to make a substantial investment and to find local equity partners, but the pursuit of necessary approvals at government level had been time-consuming and frustrating. In 1958, a military government headed by Field Marshal Moh. Ayub Khan had taken control of the country after several years of ineffective civilian governments, and had forced all politicians, among them Haroon, out of government service. Ayub Khan was reluctant for the government to do deals with these ex-politicians. Unlike several other countries, the authorities were not inclined to grant a concession for duty-free imports of equipment and furnishings for hotel construction. Dayton had persisted, and eventually the government agreed to support the hotels proposal by allowing Pakistan International Airlines, the national carrier, with whom Pan Am was currently involved in a technical assistance program, to purchase up to 30 percent of the hotel equity capital. In addition the government clearly expected further IHC proposals for hotels in Dacca (the provincial capital of East Pakistan and future co-site of the National Assembly), Lahore (the West Pakistan provincial capital), and Islamabad (the future site of the national administrative capital) near Rawalpindi. To overcome the problem of high import duties, the government would agree to accept debentures in lieu of payment of customs charges, interest on which could be capitalized for ten years through the issuance of additional debentures; repayment would commence only after Ex-im loans were fully amortized. The hotel would enjoy promoted industry status, carrying a short-term income tax holiday and an assurance that a portion of the hotel's foreign exchange earnings would be available to service dollar loans, to pay management fees, to remit a portion of expatriates' wages, and to import goods and services needed for the continued operation of the hotel at international standards. This package was a major achievement for Haroon and Dayton. By early 1962, Bechtel was ready to start construction on a 300-room Tabler-designed hotel in Karachi; architectural layouts, feasibility studies, and Ex-im loan applications were being prepared for Dacca, Lahore, and Rawalpindi (instead of Islamabad); and drafts of a prospectus for a public share offering were being reviewed. IHC would borrow rupee Cooley funds and subscribe to 25 percent of the shares.

In Yugoslavia, to punctuate its independence from Moscow's control, the government was negotiating to permit Pan Am to add Belgrade to its round the world route two days a week. Mark McKee, a wealthy businessman from Cleveland, Ohio, and member of Pan Am's board, was an inveterate traveler, frequently seen on Pan Am's planes with only a seaman's bag for luggage, who searched for interesting destinations in every part of the world. He had been an early discoverer, among Americans, of the Dalmatian coast resorts at Split and the medieval city of Dubrovnik. McKee introduced Gates to a Yugoslav travel agency with whom Gates and Bob Smith, with the occasional participation of the secret police, conducted exploratory negotiations aimed at IHC's involvement with hotels to be built in these two cities and the upgrading of the existing Hotel Esplanade, a 120-room turn-of-the-century relic of the Austro-Hungarian Empire in Zagreb. Smith describes his first Esplanade breakfast being served by a waiter with a three-day growth of beard, white jacket covered with food stains, black fingernails, and a hairstyle clearly created without the intervention of brush or comb. The menu offered neither fruit nor juice. While no agreement was ever reached for new construction on the coast, the city of Zagreb, the government of Croatia, the travel agency and IHC did conclude a technical services arrangement for a redesign of the Esplanade; Prince and Dick Smith quickly produced designs for reconfiguring some of the guest rooms and redecorating the hotel from top to bottom. But what to do about future operations? The well-entrenched socialist system in Yugoslavia could not stomach direct control of management by capitalist foreigners. Gates created a hybrid form of relationship to suit the circumstances – a "membership" contract whereunder IHC would provide short-term operations and accounting personnel to introduce international standards of service and controls; overseas reservations, communications, and promotion services; and access to IHC's operational staff for continuing training and other assistance. The hotel would be renamed Esplanade Intercontinental, and a structured program of site inspections would be developed to assure IHC that acceptable service levels were being maintained. In the event, the refurbishing of the hotel (which included new uniforms and graphics) proved a major staff morale booster, and under the leadership of general manager Branko Jakopovic the Esplanade was transformed into the leading and only international standard hostelry in the country.

The membership agreement format also proved to be the means for IHC to overcome hurdles in finally reaching agreements with the Oberoi interests in India to finance construction of a 350-room hotel in Delhi, a project on whose design IHC had been cooperating for some time. In this case, IHC agreed to accept preferred shares for its services under the TSA; to make a rupee investment from loans to be negotiated locally, hopefully from Cooley Funds; and to join Oberoi in an application to Ex-im for a dollar loan to cover the import of mechanical and other equipment not available in India. The continuing relationship for the completed hotel would be governed by a membership agreement which provided for the joint selection of a general manager, an individual who, it was understood, would be provided by IHC. This arrangement overcame opposition by those in government who were fearful of economic colonialism replacing the all-encompassing Western domination of the colonial era; and it enhanced a spirit of goodwill under which Pan Am would soon receive fifth freedom pick-up rights to carry passengers between Karachi and

Delhi twice a week on its round-the-world flights. Work could now commence on the Oberoi Intercontinental and a framework was established for possible further cooperation with Oberoi on new hotels for Bombay, Agra, and Calcutta sometime in the future.

During the period leading up to the opening of the Phoenicia in Beirut, Charles Alvey had designed a crest for the hotel as well as a logo combining "Phoenicia" with "Intercontinental" and was disturbed that it was impossible to create an obvious visual connection with the existing corporate three-section Mercator emblem, a signature piece which was somewhat dated to his and Prince's taste. Working on his own, Alvey developed a proposal for a new corporate crest, utilizing a single globe, with longitudinal arcs, and the words "Intercontinental Hotels" superimposed horizontally across the center. Alternately an individual hotel's crest could be inserted into the space in the center. It bore a clear relationship to the well-established Pan Am blue globe crest. Senior management approved and Prince's group began adapting the new graphics for use in corporate and individual hotel's advertising, internal promotion, and tableware.

In South America, Mario di Genova had succeeded René Lambert in Caracas where two years of losses had led the government-owned hotel and tourism organization, Conahotu, to convert its

Zagreb, Yugoslavia. Negotiations to upgrade the existing Hotel Esplanade in the city were successful and by 1964, when it eventually reopened as the Esplanade Intercontinental, it was the country's only "international" hostelry.

outstanding debt from the hotel into equity and emerge as the largest single shareholder. Leftist unions were flexing their muscles and were particularly antagonistic toward the Tamanaco because of a perceived, and unwarranted, notion of a prior close relationship between the hotel and the ousted Perez-Jimenez. With IHC's assistance di Genova assembled a key group of senior staff including Fred Hatt in the front of the house, Sergio Fieschi in food and beverage and Manuel Arriandiaga as controller. The Naiguita supper club was revitalized with such entertainers as Eartha Kitt and Sammy Davis, Jr. (for whom a private plane was sent to Jamaica, when other transportation failed). Pool passes were provided for fashion models, and slowly the hotel reemerged as the capital's social center; and returned to profitability.

Ernst Etter left the Tequendama in Bogota in response to an offer to join Harley Watson who had become vice president in charge of Sheraton International's newly established overseas development effort after leaving the San Juan Intercontinental. The two were based for the time being at the Park Sheraton on New York's west side.

Shortly after Huyot's arrival, Gates convened a meeting of all the Latin American general managers (plus George Lawrence, the Ducor incumbent) at the Embajador in the Dominican Republic, to introduce Huyot . . . and also himself since he had to date had almost no personal involvement with the region's hotels. The company's ambitious growth plans were explained in detail, the new logo and crest were discussed, and an attempt was made to reestablish a sense of continuity and stability, which had been shaken during the recent past history of four different presidents in less than five years. The managers were clearly impressed. They felt at ease now that a distinguished hotelman was once again in a leadership seat and they could not help but be charmed by Gates' charismatic personality, quick wit, and occasional eye-twinkling smile. Not a frequent public speaker, he had a pronounced stammer; he often joked that it gave him extra time to plan a riposte in debates or negotiations with adversaries. Huyot, commencing his speech to the group, assured them that he, like John Gates, would limit his comments to forty minutes. Gates jumped up and challenged the comparison: "But you d-d-don't stutter."

Huyot thereafter set off on a familiarization trip to learn about the hotel group which he was inheriting. He was not particularly impressed with what he saw. Hotels for the medium-priced business traveler did not appeal to him; nor did he believe that this was the long-term marketplace in which IHC could prosper. The Tequendama was busy and profitable, but to Huyot it lacked flair and international excitement. Only the Tamanaco struck him as being a model on which to build for the future. Returning to New York he pored over the architectural plans of all the hotels currently under construction and, concerned that the company was replicating its 1953 product in 1960s Europe, visited the construction sites to see what adjustments were still possible. He added air conditioning to two guest-room floors of the Frankfurt hotel and supported Prince's group in design changes to Geneva and Vienna, where the local architects were creating interiors which Huyot judged to be sterile, unwelcoming, and unresponsive to international travelers' needs and expectations. He spearheaded an immediate review, revision, and codification of IHC's architectural and design standards, and thereby began the evolution of IHC's basic product from three star commercial to four star luxury.

Turning to food and beverage operations, Huyot reinforced Balas' efforts to create "restaurants" instead of hotel dining rooms – facilities which could actively compete with individual dining places in the city while satisfying the needs of the hotel's overnight guests. Within the spaces provided in the hotels then under construction, they decided to introduce a Café Brasserie instead of a hotel coffee shop, and a themed restaurant with a menu of international selections instead of the stereotyped hotel dining room familiar in most European and colonial hotels. There were some disagreements with certain architect/designers who felt strongly that all the hotel's facilities had to be unified in a single design concept related if possible to the building's exterior in style, color, and finish. Thus the Frankfurt architects had determined to clad all of the interior walls of the ground floor with a buff polished dark wood veneer, while the outer "walls" were curtains of glass; the back of the reception desk and the inner wall surfaces of the bar, restaurant and brasserie would all look exactly the same, regardless of the function of each area or other design features such as carpets and furnishings.

Where there was a vista of note, the hotels included rooftop bars and nightclub limited-menu restaurants, although these facilities put extra demand on guest-room elevators and compromised guest-floor security to some extent, and the dancing facilities required expensive and carefully constructed sound attenuation features. All the restaurants should, if possible, be supported from a single centrally located kitchen; if the hotel size required restaurants to be on separate floors, the kitchen whose outlet would serve three meals daily should also be the source for guest-room service. The "up market" restaurant should reasonably strive to achieve recognition in the Michelin one star category.

August of 1962 would bring the opening of two major hotels within a three-week period: Hotel Indonesia in Jakarta and the Southern Cross in Melbourne. Bill Land, the last Nacional general manager, had been on site in Indonesia for nearly a year witnessing the completion of what was the most modern building yet built in the world's sixth most populous nation, a far-flung archipelago super-rich in natural resources and with some of the most densely (Java, Bali, Madura) and thinly (Kalimantan on Borneo) populated areas on earth. A Soviet aid mission had constructed a major sports stadia complex which was to host the Asian Games; Hotel Indonesia had to be ready for this international festival. The hotel had the first high-speed elevators in a publicly accessible building and the first escalator anywhere in Indonesia. Virtually the entire inventory of food and beverage had to be imported, as high-volume, quality agricultural products and an effective

distribution system were non-existent in the archipelago. The departure of the ship carrying thousands of cases of canned and frozen foods from New York was the excuse for an Intercontinental promotional bon voyage party at the dock. Unfortunately, the ship went aground in Chesapeake Bay, and the order had to be duplicated. When the goods eventually arrived, the boxes were transferred direct to trucks waiting on the dock and delivered by military escort to the hotel with gun-carrying guards atop each vehicle.

Typical of the hundreds of unique problems which had to be solved before the hotel could operate was the question of currency exchange rates as they applied to guest billings and menu pricing. Foreign currency transactions were covered by a mass of regulations which provided for a collection of different exchange rates for different purposes. A procedure had been in force which required foreign visitors to declare all the currencies which they brought into the country and, upon departure, prove that they had spent at least a certain amount per day – accounted for with official exchange receipts – during their stay. It was easily established that all foreign overnight guests at Hotel Indonesia would have to settle their accounts in foreign currency or with a foreign credit card and that room rates would be quoted in dollars. Since the bills had to be denominated and printed in rupiah – the local currency – there had to be some nominal exchange rate to convert to dollars or yen or sterling, etc. No one could take a decision, so with a week remaining before the opening, Walter Spillum called on his close relationship with the palace, and IHC representatives were summoned to an audience with President Sukarno. The problem was explained, and the president discussed it briefly with the ministers who had also been invited. The solution was simple, but one which only he could have taken: someone was to check periodically with "the market" (i.e., find out what the currency was being traded at on the street or in Singapore) and convert the dollar room prices at that exchange rate, a ratio which was to become known as the "bookkeeping rate" and would be adjusted from time to time by the hotel's controller. Menu prices would be set in rupiah at levels which would not discourage local custom, but were high enough for the foreign currency costs of producing and serving (expatriate salaries plus the cost of imported ingredients and beverages) to be adequately covered by those paying in foreign currency. This weighty business out of the way, Sukarno jokingly changed the subject to matters of levity: could he help in finding masseuses from Japan for the health club; how could IHC make sure that people didn't think the so-called Presidential Suite was a place where he would be doing private entertaining; could he please see some of the elevator attendants in their new uniforms one day soon to be sure that the Western cut and fit didn't detract from these girls' beauty.

The hotel had been designed, at Sukarno's direction, without air conditioning in guest rooms in the taller of the two towers. These rooms featured an outdoor corridor with rooms on one side only and had balconies with floor-to-ceiling sliding glass doors with screens; the room doors to the corridor were louvered and screened so that these bedrooms were quite airy, albeit humid, if there were a breeze. No amount of cajoling seemed to budge him – he cited the example of the open air, trade-wind-swept lobby and bar of the Caribe Hilton, which IHC had showed him during his familiarization tour to San Juan.

In July, Soviet deputy premier Anastas Mikoyan visited Indonesia to dedicate the Asian Games complex and was given a tour of the nearly completed hotel where he commented on the lack of guest-room cooling. Within days orders from above materialized, directing that window type air conditioning units be procured from a certain source in Japan, the terrace windows be altered to accommodate them, and the job be completed in three weeks.

As the hotel had been financed with Japanese war reparation funds, all of the imported equipment and supplies were sourced in Japan. The limited TSA provided for the locally built furniture in certain of the restaurants, public spaces, and a portion of the guest rooms to be designed by IHC; however, the message had not been passed to the local project group which had been working on the hotel prior to IHC's being engaged. Thus two sets of furniture were arriving simultaneously and territorial disputes broke out between the two installation teams. The practical compromise: Group I delivers its furniture, puts it in place, and departs from the hotel; Group II, with Prince and his IHC staff acting as hands-on foremen, replaces Group I furniture with Group II furniture on a nonstop, twenty-four hour, D-Day-minus-one timetable. (The Group I furniture later came in handy when furnishing staff housing.)

Bill Land had been told that French cooks were to be employed, and had engaged a complete brigade from Paris. All of them had worked together, but none had ever worked in a developing country, considered by some to be a "hardship" posting, where all of the equipment was Japanese and unfamiliar. With two days to go before the unofficial opening, the group presented a series of demands concerning housing, equipment, hours, wages, etc. Balas and Land faced them down and shipped them back to Europe. The Phoenicia lent four of its kitchen chefs, and the show went on. Joop Ave, a young official in the Indonesian foreign ministry who did double duty in protocol matters at the palace, played an invaluable role behind the scenes in matters of organization and in familiarizing IHC's executives with the realities of conducting business successfully in Indonesia.

The inaugural ceremonies were choreographed in minute detail as to the arrival of President Sukarno, the seating of guests, the speech making, the temperature (warm to hot in the banquet room), the entertainment program of traditional dance and music, and the unveiling of plaques and impressive original art. Bob Huyot represented IHC – in a white suit and brocade vest which some said smacked of Somerset Maugham. At the last minute someone, somewhere, had decided that the original 600-person guest list ought to be expanded, so after the "official" guests were in place another 1,500 stretched in a queue from the security checkpoint out into the city, all of them holding invitations. The local president-director beamed with pride as he explained that plans had been changed, and suggested that perhaps more food should be produced during the speeches.

Most of the IHC opening team thereafter departed for Melbourne. Many who were involved with the Southern Cross recall it as one of the very few instances where the building was virtually complete and furnished, with a high portion of "punch list" items already corrected, at the time of the opening. There had been a couple of minor flaps: one of the owning company's directors, a knighted gentleman of a certain age, had expressed some concern at IHC's selection of silver individual one- and two-portion coffee- and teapots. He and his wife felt certain that china was the only acceptable brewing vessel for a proper "cuppa." A last-minute crockery order avoided a possible tempest over a teapot. Early in the construction process, the concrete slab for the fourth floor collapsed. The contractor and project manager surveyed the damage, gave precise instructions, went off together for a long lunch and returned to find the site immaculate and the builders ready to pour the slab anew. Unusually for construction work in Australia in those days, the job was completed without labor slowdowns or stoppages, and ahead of schedule.

The Southern Cross was also the first Intercontinental to open in a location where virtually any local resident could afford, and be reasonably expected, to be a patron of one or more of the hotel's dining or drinking facilities. The hotel had four bars, each serving a different clientele with different price levels and different product offerings . . . something for everyone. The one common, and uncommon by world standard, feature was the 6 p.m. closing when all beverage sales abruptly ceased – water was pumped into the beer lines – everyone stood one pace back from the bar, and

the premises were vacated no later than 6.15. The quantity of beer and spirits consumed during "the swill," as those last thirty minutes were affectionately known, was prodigious indeed. On the first day, the entire accounts staff had to be stationed at the bar cash tills to make change while the bartenders strained to keep up with the demand for glasses of grog. And because of the unusual pricing (seven pence ha'penny for a glass of lager in one of the bars) some tills soon ran out of change . . . all afternoon the general cashier circulated through the hotel replenishing the stock of coppers in the various bars. On opening day 5,000 bar and wine glasses were put into use.

Pan Am moved its Melbourne administrative office into the hotel and had an attractive sales office in the shopping arcade. John Carrodus, now working on Pan Am/IHC hotel development activities, had been enlisted to introduce his wide circle of acquaintances from the worlds of Australian business, finance, racing, and entertainment to the Southern Cross. General manager Pete Sutherland had hired George Milne from the Menzies, Melbourne's busiest hotel at the time, as executive assistant manager; he also had a following of valued guests, many from sports and military circles.

OPPOSITE: Melbourne. Intercontinental opened its first Australian hotel – the Southern Cross – in 1962.

In his remarks at the inaugural luncheon, the prime minister Sir Robert Gordon Menzies, observed that travel and tourism was the sort of industry he liked – one which had no air-polluting smoke pouring out of the top of it.

The Southern Cross was the nation's first international standard hostelry – and effectively more than doubled the inventory of first-class rooms in a city where there was very limited demand on weekends, except for sporting events. Melbourne's airport could not yet accommodate intercontinental range jets. During the early days of 30 to 35 percent occupancies, the housekeepers turned on the guest-room lights in 75 percent of the rooms each evening for a couple of hours so that passersby would assume that the hotel was busy; well-known Melbourne personalities were paged in the lobby and cocktail lounges so that those already there would assume the pagee was somewhere about.

Australians were great travelers, however, and typically contacted travel agents or their banks' travel departments for their hotel and transport arrangements. Terry Hill, who had been lured (or more accurately, coerced) away from Pan Am to be the hotel's director of marketing, focused early on the travel agent network for special attention in launching the hotel, setting a pattern which IHC would later follow worldwide. Within a few years his Australian network was one of the larger business producers for IHC system-wide.

One of the Southern Cross's successful restaurants was its Club Grill. Decorated by Scollard Moss, a designer associated with the architectural firm Welton Becket Associates, in clubbish wood paneling and red leather, it featured a wine display bar and a rotisserie and charbroil grill where hearty cuts of beef, veal, lamb, and fowl could be cooked in full view of diners. Balas made a mental note to include this type of facility in designs for future hotels in locations where the basic raw materials would be plentiful.

Immediately upon his return to New York, Bob Huyot prepared a detailed summary of his observations in Jakarta and Melbourne, in many cases establishing new IHC standards of performance and hotel design, a pattern which he would repeat after each opening for years thereafter. He commented on telephone equipment and operators' answering routines; on portion sizes and wine selection; on menu design and staff appearance; on the garnishing of buffet platters – he was partial to parsley; on the flakiness of croissants and the crispness of laundered shirt collars. He traveled with a thermometer and measuring tape to check on water and air temperature, as well as chair, table, and desk heights. Dick Smith, Prince, Balas and others took note and made hasty adjustments to projects in progress.

By the end of 1962, despite reporting another loss – $245,000 this time – Gates could look back on three and a half years of dramatic change in the company's direction: three major new hotels opened, sixteen new projects designed, financed and under construction in eleven countries; a development group producing at least six or seven new deals each year; a strengthened operations organization under Huyot . . . all achieved almost within Trippe's guidelines of zero net cash outflow for Pan Am. It was Gates' belief that in its development role Pan Am/IHC was entitled to be reimbursed for its efforts in the same manner as any independent developer – with the exception that no profit should accrue to IHC at this stage; that would come later when the hotel was in operation. By including in a hotel's capital budget an amount roughly equivalent to the payroll and out-of-pocket costs incurred on the project by Pan Am/IHC development officers, Gates could theoretically operate this function on a break-even basis.

The TSAs provided for a service fee, a large portion of which went to Bechtel, and for reimbursement to Pan Am/IHC on a time plus 150 percent overhead basis for all work performed by the technical services, and operations, staff during the design and construction phases, with these amounts credited to the cost centers in which the individuals were included. Thus, if manpower were being efficiently managed, the by now thirty-five-man tourist facilities development department ought to be, and nearly was, self-sufficient.

To finance IHC's hotel investments in Ireland, Australia, Austria and Lebanon, Gates, Smith, Dayton, and Charlie Trippe had arranged local currency bank loans, with the shares – or the IHC lease – as collateral, and with back guarantees from Pan Am in Vienna and Melbourne. In Pakistan and India, Cooley loans provided the funds. Only in Germany and Switzerland where super-stable local currency all but eliminated any likelihood of devaluation – one of Trippe's overriding concerns – did IHC invest dollars, provided by Pan Am, of course, to purchase its equity. The plan was to repay these loans from future operating and owning company dividend earnings. As noted, IHC had taken out U.S. AID insurance for its African investments.

The introduction of jet aircraft had more than doubled Pan Am's profits to $15,000,000 in two years and by the end of 1962 plans were being made to move the company's head office into the world's largest commercial office block which stretched sixty stories skyward atop New York's Grand Central rail terminal. The building was crowned with a heliport for a commercial shuttle service to Idlewild International Airport, immediately beneath which the 33 foot high illuminated letters of Pan Am's logo and crest proclaimed the building's principal tenant and namesake to anyone approaching the city from the suburbs and to all who traveled on New York's Park Avenue.

OPPOSITE:

The Mayfair Restaurant in the Southern Cross, Melbourne. The hotel also had four bars; more than 5,000 glasses were used on opening day.

At the end of 1962, Mario di Genova was elected vice president Latin America, with a mandate to oversee operations in this region, while continuing as general manager at the Tamanaco.

TWA, Pan Am's principal competitor across the Atlantic, had been late in ordering jet aircraft, and had overextended itself by the time these new planes came into service. Controlled by the once flamboyant, later reclusive, Howard Hughes, and under attack by its bankers, TWA's management had sold some of its new 707s to Pan Am and, by late 1962, had reached an agreement for a merger with its rival to create a transatlantic U.S. air colossus. Suddenly Pan Am's year-end balance sheet had to be decluttered of any IHC entanglements other than a single figure under the investment heading. In the last weeks of December, Charlie Trippe contacted his friends in Australia and arranged termination of Pan Am's guarantee of IHC's borrowings by paying off half the loan with funds reborrowed locally from Pan Am's regional office. Working to the December 31 deadline, Eric Bleich convinced the Austrian bank instead to accept a guarantee which he negotiated from the Frankfurter Bank. In the event, the U.S. courts consumed so many months in adjudicating the relative rights of the bankers and Howard Hughes in the control of TWA that the economic conditions no longer supported the merger proposal, and it died.

A colored photograph of an IHC hotel, the Southern Cross – the first ever – appeared on the cover of the Pan Am annual report for 1962.

A WORLDWIDE CHAIN

IHC's remarkable level of growth activity had strengthened Gates' position in the Pan Am scheme of things. Robert Smith's success in Europe had been rewarded with a Pan Am vice presidency. Reassigning Charlie Trippe from his Asia/Pacific development function to a newly created position as director of finance, Gates was able to engineer the transfer of the accounting, control, financial reporting, and cash management functions from the Pan Am comptroller's department to IHC. There was one proviso: Lyle Warner, a veteran of Pan Am's Alaskan and trans-Pacific island airport building era, would become IHC comptroller.

Another area which Gates and Huyot believed ripe for enhancement was sales and marketing. Panamac, the airline's worldwide computerized reservation and communications system – the world's first – was to come on line in 1963, and IHC's booking system would be integrated therein so that every Pan Am sales point could become a contact for an IHC sale. Reservations agents would have to be trained and the Pan Am connection would have to be strengthened in support of IHC.

Gates was assured by Juan Trippe that one of several rising stars in the Pan Am sales organization could be made available to head IHC's expanded sales effort. Gates selected Henry (Hank) Beardsley, a Princeton graduate who had spent his postwar career in marketing and sales positions at American and American Overseas Airlines, where he was manager of the London, and later Scandinavian, offices. When AOA was taken over, he opted to join Pan Am and became director of sales for Europe, again based in London. After a tour as sales manager in Washington, he was appointed director of passenger sales for the United States, reporting to Willis Lipscomb, the airline's vice president in charge of traffic and sales. Hank was not anxious to leave the airline, and Lipscomb assured him that he could say no, which he did. At Juan Trippe's annual Christmas reception at his home – a much-prized invitation to which was the ultimate authentication of acceptance in Pan Am's senior ranks – Gates told Beardsley that he could not accept his decision. The next morning Hank was summoned by Trippe, who turned on the charm and made the offer which couldn't be refused: try it for a year, and if it doesn't work out, you come and see me and I'll find you another slot in Pan Am.

Beardsley's first challenge in IHC was to produce an awareness program at Pan Am USA. The airline's overseas managers and staff in IHC operating and target locations were well aware of IHC's activities; in many cases they had assisted in making the original local contacts, and in some cases served on the board of directors of IHC hotel owning companies. But the sales and station managers in the United States, at the time the country of residence of the majority of the airline's passengers, were only peripherally conscious, if at all, that Pan Am was in the hotel business in a big way and would soon be managing property assets worth about half the cost of Pan Am's

original jet fleet. At the point-of-sale customer contact level, each reservations agent would soon have computerized access to IHC's room availability and the possibility of making a room sale as an adjunct to an air ticket sale. Using Pan Am trainers, Beardsley organized a systemwide hotel indoctrination program for Panamac operators. Using his entrée to his former colleagues, the U.S. city sales managers, he traveled the country giving IHC presentations at sales meetings, management club gatherings, and city office briefings. His first hands-on experience in addressing the specific overseas sales support needs of IHC hotels would come with the meetings he would shortly have with hotel general managers and sales directors at openings in Ireland and Frankfurt.

At the end of May 1963 IHC was faced with the task of opening four hotels – in Frankfurt, Dublin, Cork, and Limerick – within a two-week period, straining corporate resources beyond their limits. Fortunately, Bill Busquets was available to return from Chile to take charge of the accounting systems installation in Frankfurt.

Dublin, Cork, and Limerick were opened over a four-day period; each involved a similar ceremony of bagpipe serenade, flag raising, ribbon cutting by the mayor, drinks party and inaugural

Farmland in County Cork, Ireland. The Cork Intercontinental was one of three hotels that were opened in Ireland in 1963.

luncheon with speeches. The three hotels had benefited from government per-room cash grants introduced to encourage tourism-related construction. The city of Dublin had made a special grant to partially underwrite the cost of a ballroom, accommodating 1,000 diners, with a specially constructed spring-based dance floor, the largest such venue in Eire and a much needed social facility for the city. It was inaugurated with a charity ball. In order to conform to very tight budgets, the three hotels' designs followed the motel style then popular in the United States: a central single-story block accommodating the lobby and reception, an all-purpose restaurant and central kitchen, pub bar, and administrative offices as well as technical and laundry facilities. The guest rooms in Limerick and Cork were in two-story, fifty-room wings connected to the central building by covered, glass-walled passageways through landscaped gardens. Also separate from the central block, the Dublin room block was a simple eight-story egg-crate type structure which incorporated an up-market restaurant on the rooftop. The interiors had been contentious; a design consultant nominated by the Irish Tourist interests had veto power and a strong preference for stark ultra-modern furnishings using natural materials (stone floors, nubby linen wall-coverings) in neutral gray and beige tones. The result could well have won a prize for up-to-date abstract distinction (if one were offered in Ireland), but from the guest viewpoint was cold, unwelcoming, and somewhat uncomfortable.

Leo Riordan, an Irish American, had been transferred from Ponce to be general manager and regional operations director for Ireland; the family Siamese cat had spent six months in quarantine in a kennel which Riordan had insisted be kept at no less than 72° Fahrenheit, a near impossibility in rainy Dublin where central heating was uncommon. Max Hampton assembled a group of U.S. and British writers and travel agents, who were taken to a wide range of tourist sites packaged around and between the hotel events.

In Limerick Mildred Riordan was seated next to the lady mayoress, garbed in ancient robes and chains of office, at the opening luncheon. The conversation went something like: "I'm sorry, but I must apologize for my ignorance. I've never spoken to a lady mayoress before. What do I call you?" Reply, with a genuine smile: "Frances will do."

In Frankfurt, on June 6 1963, with a host of government and financial community personalities looking on, the ribbon was cut to open West Germany's (and Europe's) largest hotel. Bechtel and IHC had met the commitment, given at the ground-breaking exactly two years earlier, to have the property open in time for the World Petroleum Congress due to begin in a few days. Curt Peyer, a German citizen who had been operating IHC's Embajador in the Dominican Republic for four years, was general manager. Bob Huyot gave his opening remarks in German, French, and English, recognizing the hotel's international clientele and its multinational group of shareholders.

The hotel's decorative furnishings included a collection of costume and scenic watercolors for a production of *Le Nozze de Figaro*, a set of costumed doll figures from *Don Carlo*, and handmade tapestries depicting characters in *The Red Shoes*, all by the German theatrical designer Hein Heckroth. A collection of fine antique Nymphenburg and Meissen china was displayed in showcases in function rooms of the same names. A set of original Picasso pottery platters decorated a shelf above the beer and drinks counter in the Brasserie. Black and white photo murals of old Frankfurt filled the spaces between bedroom doors on the guest corridors. Each suite featured a leather-covered Eames lounge chair. And Prince had gathered more than 1,000 pieces of original art by young German artists, which were displayed in the guest bedrooms. The building was wired for IHC's first mechanical room-status system, a series of lights and switches whereby housekeeping was notified of a checkout, and later the reception desk notified that the room had been cleaned and was ready to rent again, without the need for telephone calls or written messages transmitted by pneumatic tube or telautograph, as heretofore.

During the construction of the hotel an opportunity had arisen to construct an office building for IBM on the north portion of the site across Wilhelm Leuschner Strasse from the hotel tower, adjacent to a small shopping arcade and open plaza. Trippe was unwilling for IHC to make its proportionate equity investment in the office project; fortunately, Baron Rothschild stepped into IHC's shoes and completed the financing. The city gave a back guarantee for the bank loans and design was begun. Suddenly, without warning, the Bonn government decreed a nationwide moratorium, effective June 16 1962, on all office construction in order to curb an excessive boom then in progress in Germany, but threatening the

IBM building's construction schedule. Schroeder-Hohenwarth and Bleich, with city support, successfully presented a case that the city had granted its building permit on June 3; and that, in any event, the office building and hotel were an indivisible project and less than one-third of the north site was being used for office space, the remainder being devoted to shopping, the large underground carpark, a motor-fuel filling station and a separate computer service center.

Photographic murals of city landmarks featured in the corridors of the Frankfurt Intercontinental.

Two months later the Hotel Ivoire opened in Abidjan on the Ivory Coast. A number of last-minute technical failures included a yet-to-be-balanced air conditioning system which kept bedrooms in the frigid zone in order to adequately cool the extensive lobbies and banqueting room; several inadequate drip pans under the bedroom fan coil units with resulting steady dripping through the room foyer ceilings; and a split in one of the hot water pipes – just after the foreign press checked in – which shut down all water for several hours. The general manager organized an emergency warm water delivery service, utilizing garbage cans and freight trolleys, manned by room boys.

In preparation for the arrival of President Houphouët-Boigny, some 1,000 guests assembled in the carpark in front of the hotel. The entire diplomatic corps was in attendance, many in colorful national dress, the remainder in dinner suits with black tie. No one had told Huyot that black dinner jackets were the proper dress in the Cote d'Ivoire, and he had packed only a white one; fortunately, he was able to borrow Max Hampton's black tuxedo jacket. And then the lights – every single one in the hotel – went out. Everyone stayed in place; the housekeeper offered to fetch candles; the television cameramen fumed. The sirens wailed, announcing the president's approach . . . and as his car pulled into view, the power returned with a burst of blazing light.

Only half the stocks of tableware had arrived, not enough to serve the entire several course gala banquet, a sit-down affair. The courses were interspersed with dances and other traditional entertainment; while the dancers danced, the tables were cleared, the plates and silver quickly washed, and rushed back into use in time for another course. During the festivities, Moshe Mayer and Bob Huyot were decorated by the president.

IHC formed a joint venture to design a hotel with museum on the site of the Gare d'Orsay in Paris, working with the illustrious French architect Le Corbusier. After many months' work it became clear that the monumental concepts of Corbusier were not conducive to an efficient hotel design, and the project was dropped.

Britain's decolonization program reached Southeast Asia in 1963, where a newly created Federation of Malaysia, consisting of peninsular Malaya, the island city of Singapore, and the North Bornean states of Sarawak and Sabah, was scheduled to achieve independence on August 31. The Philippines, going back to an old agreement made by the sultan of Sulo granting jurisdiction over North Borneo to the British North Borneo Company, reasserted a claim for Sabah.

OPPOSITE: Singapore Harbor in the early 1960s. The opening date of the Hotel Singapura Intercontinental coincided with the Malaysian Federation's birthdate.

Indonesia, more belligerently, denounced the whole project as a "neo-colonialist plot to encircle Indonesia." Faced with this opposition, the British asked the United Nations to review and certify the plebiscites which had been conducted to ascertain whether the people in the territories supported union with Malaya, and, with the apparent agreement of Manila and Jakarta, postponed Malaysia's birthdate to September 16, a date which an astrologer had already selected as a propitious one for the opening of the 200-room Hotel Singapura Intercontinental.

The Malayan Chinese Association (MCA), a political party which had lost control of Singapore's limited local self-governing administration under colonial rule to Lee Kwan Yew's People's Action Party, had begun construction on a block of flats on Orchard Road near to the point where commercial activity yielded to the leafy residential areas of Tanglin and Stephens Roads. Although the MCA was still powerful in Malaya, serving in a coalition with the predominantly Malay ruling party, it had abandoned work on the apartment building. A group of local businessmen negotiated a very attractive long-term lease with MCA, and under a limited TSA negotiated by Charlie Trippe and David Salisbury (a Pan Am development officer who was working almost full time on IHC's Bangkok project) planned to complete the building as a modern hotel. Richard and Fred Eu, sons of a famous Singapore magnate Eu Tong Sen, and S. C. Huang (known as Bongsie), an Indonesian born in Bangka, where his father had been a foreman in the Dutch tin mining operation, and educated in Shanghai, formed a public company to carry out the project. Dick Eu was a managing director of the family bank, which was to provide some loan capital. Fred Eu and Huang together controlled the local Diners Club franchise; Fred was also an entertainment promoter and Huang, with a steady income from motorbus and other businesses owned in Jakarta, had acquired a small tourist-class hotel located a few hundred meters from the Singapura, which featured a well-known restaurant and nightclub, the Golden Venus. The public share issue for the hotel was oversubscribed, and the shares went up to six times their offering price within days of the flotation. Additional bank finance was negotiated with Citibank with IHC/Pan Am assistance. There was no up-to-date hotel in Singapore in 1963 and the total inventory of rooms charging first-class rates totaled less than 400.

Dick Squier was assigned as general manager and was able to assemble a group of department

heads almost all of whom were Singaporeans, or Europeans who had lived or worked in Southeast Asia. The hotel would contain a twenty-four-hour coffee shop, a cocktail lounge featuring a piano bar with a music-hall type singer/pianist, a retail pastry store, a pool club and outdoor satay stand, a bank and shopping arcade, and a showroom restaurant with non-stop dance and vocal music provided by a top-class Philippine band contracted through Fred Eu. The opening festivities were overshadowed, of course, by the jubilation of Malaysian independence; however, the finance minister, Dr. Goh Keng Swee, was available to officiate.

Sukarno's reaction to Malaysia was devastating and immediate; mobs in Jakarta stormed the Malaysian embassy without police or government restraint, and subsequently sacked and torched the British embassy (150 meters from Hotel Indonesia) and evicted embassy and other British Jakarta residents from their homes. Kane Rufe, who had become general manager of Hotel Indonesia, and Walter Spillum were in Singapore for the Singapura opening. When word of the events in Jakarta reached them, Walt contacted his boss, Bert Torrance, the Pan Am Singapore manager, and wheels were set in motion to secure authorization for sending the Pan Am 707 aircraft which was overnighting in Singapore into Indonesia to help evacuate the British families who were being delivered to the lobby of Hotel Indonesia by the mobs who had trashed their homes. Spillum and Rufe returned on the aircraft; the evacuees were accommodated at the new Singapura, which enjoyed two days of 100 percent occupancy.

These were to be the last full-house days for many months. On September 21, Indonesia suspended all trade with Malaysia, sent infiltration-minded troops to Indonesian Borneo, and unleashed "confrontation" against Malaysia punctuated with, mostly bungled, terrorist attacks in Malaya and Singapore. A sizable segment of hotel demand in Singapore had been from businessmen doing business in Indonesia, and Indonesians shopping and trading in Singapore. With travel between the two abruptly suspended, hotel demand sagged. Tourists became almost non-existent. The Commonwealth reacted by dispatching troops from Britain and Australia to defend the new nation, whose 15,000 men under arms could be no match for Sukarno's 400,000 military forces. The Indonesian front office cashiers who had been brought to Singapore to assist in training had to return ahead of schedule, and via Bangkok.

The bar and coffee shop were instant successes. At $5.00 per drink the Pebble Bar frequently took in as much as $4,500 on a weekend evening. During the early years Fred Eu was able to book artists who were in Asia doing performances for U.S. troops in Vietnam into Singapore for three or four days – one outdoor stadium performance, one television show, and two nights at the Singapura. Shirley Bassey, Lionel Hampton, Louis Armstrong, and Frank Sinatra, Jr. were among the more notable to appear at the hotel.

Shortly thereafter the Mandarin opened in Hong Kong. IHC had developed a major international promotional program for the property and within a couple of years Panamac was generating a sizable portion of the hotel's room bookings. It was a glamorous, deluxe property, and its general manager Tony Ross, a veteran of London and Bermuda hotels, had installed many innovative systems including a computerized front office that relied on punch-card generated input.

Within weeks the system had proven to be unwieldy, requiring more staff than a comparable mechanized guest billing system – an experience that was being duplicated in the New York Hilton which opened the same year. At Ross' request, IHC provided a team to study the accounting control installation and make detailed recommendations for integrating, or possibly eliminating, the computer.

Charlie Trippe was busy reorganizing the finance department and redesigning the monthly financial statement. A financial director was to be appointed to concentrate on hotel accounting, taxation, insurance, and IHC shareholding matters within each geographical area. Potter was initially assigned to Asia/Pacific. In the past IHC's accounts had not included the profits or losses of any subsidiaries except when remitted as dividends. In the new reporting each hotel's results were detailed to show the net income to IHC being derived from all sources under the applicable operations (or membership) agreement. Income derived from IHC's equity investments were presented in another section. The total sales of IHC included the in-hotel sales of leased hotels, but only the management fees of operated and member hotels. Charlie Trippe had long-term goals of emphasizing the growing size of the company's operations and making management continually aware as to the relative profitability of each property to IHC.

As part of Beardsley's task to enhance the IHC-Pan Am connection, he switched the Intercontinental advertising account to J. Walter Thompson, the agency which had been producing Pan Am's media program for many years. In the first discussions the question of the brand name arose. Many felt that the six-syllable Intercontinental when combined with a two- or three-syllable city name was too big a mouthful. People in Germany were already referring to the Frankfurt hotel as the "Interconti," dropping two syllables. U.S. press coverage of IHC's European openings had too often identified the chain as "International." Pan American had solved the problem with "Pan Am." What could IHC do? J. Walter Thompson was given the assignment. After several weeks of interviews, customer research, and discussions with IHC staff (Charlie Trippe suggested "Inntel"), the agency made its recommendation at a suitably impressive presentation, complete with demographic studies, statistical samplings, logos, sample crockery, matchbook covers, etc., etc. . . . a name which is friendly and welcoming – hold your breath – "Dolphin." The audience was uniformly underwhelmed, and the matter was dropped, until the next time.

Another problem faced by Beardsley and Charlie Trippe was how to allocate the costs of the expanded sales and booking system to the hotels. The contracts provided for IHC to be reimbursed for a proportionate share of corporate advertising, and a formula had been established based on number of rooms, and supported by an annual audit of costs certified by IHC's outside auditors. But while the contracts also appointed IHC as sales and booking agent, no fee system had been specified other than "on a cost basis consistent with other hotels in the group." After a great deal of study, it was determined that the results of IHC's worldwide sales and booking services would be best reflected by some measure of international travelers' usage of an IHC hotel. As part of regular "source of business" monitoring, hotels would make a calculation of total room nights sold, classified as between foreign, local, and aircrews. "Local" was usually defined as guests who are residents of the country in which the hotel is located. Aircrews would also be considered as "local." An annual estimate would be made of total "foreign" room nights at all IHC hotels and compared with IHC's budgeted system sales and booking costs to calculate a cost per foreign room night, which would be used in monthly invoices to the hotels based on the hotel's actual "foreign" room nights. The hotels which had a high proportion of guests who were regularly exposed to IHC international sales efforts would be paying a larger portion of the system cost than a hotel whose guests were largely residents of the local country who were principally exposed to the hotel's own local sales activities, and who usually booked directly with the hotel. No cost allocation system will satisfy everyone, and this one was no exception.

Huyot succeeded in luring Ernst Etter back to Intercontinental as general manager designate for the Vienna hotel, which was already six months behind schedule and would hopefully open in January 1964.

Pan Am reported 1963 earnings of $23,568,000; the economies accruing from all-jet transatlantic service had led to further reductions in tourist class fares to a low of $210.00, a drop of 47 percent since their introduction in 1952, despite an 18 percent rise in U.S. consumer prices over the same period. The airline announced its order for six supersonic Concordes for service to the United Kingdom and France, although these aircraft could not operate economically non-stop between New York and most of its other continental Europe destinations. A full page of the annual report was devoted to a listing of IHC's hotels and a picture of the Frankfurt property. No mention was made, however, of IHC's fifth successive annual loss – $345,000.

To manage the new Geneva Intercontinental, André Hamburger, a Swiss, was transferred from the Victoria Plaza in Montevideo, a hotel which had managed to cover its costs and minimum rent by converting several floors for rent and use as offices. Demand from Argentinean travelers was sporadic and the economy of Uruguay was lethargic at best.

Hamburger located a former Victoria Plaza colleague, Max Herr, by then managing the Avila Hotel in Caracas, and engaged him as executive assistant manager for Geneva. Huyot's executive secretary/administrative assistant Maryan Kiernan, fluent in French, was hired in the same capacity by Hamburger. The hotel opened on the last day of January 1964, with ceremonies presided over by the mayor, State Councillor André Ruffieux, Chairman Schmidheiny, and Bob Huyot, who repeated his trilingual speech format. This being Switzerland, nothing was allowed to go wrong; all the staff were professionals, though on the serving side virtually all were from Italy, Spain, and other European countries and were provided with housing by the hotel. Geneva was a relatively small city, with a population around 200,000. Its appeal as a tourist destination was limited, particularly when compared with Switzerland's more idyllic Alpine lake resorts. But as the former headquarters for the League of Nations whose services and properties had been transferred to the United Nations, and as a cosmopolitan city which the world consciously equated with peace negotiations and understanding among nations, Geneva drew a large number of diplomats and their hangers-on. As a banking center, though perhaps junior to Zurich, it boasted prestigious private banking houses which came to be the particular favorites of newly rich individuals and nations, many emerging from years of colonial domination. It was in these markets that the hotel would have to seek its clientele. The hotel's location bestowed a panorama of spectacular views and easy access to international organizations upon its guests, but at the price and inconvenience of a five- to ten-minute taxi ride to and from the city to conduct business. However, being away from the close-in city center, the hotel could offer a high level of security without significantly inconveniencing local businessmen and residents in their daily activities, an advantage which would prove invaluable in the days of international terrorist attacks which would begin in earnest a decade later. The list of important high-level international meetings which have taken place at the hotel, or with the participants staying at the hotel, is legion, and the frequent news coverage of these events has put Intercontinental on most of the world's television screens year after year. OPEC, the international oil cartel, became a frequent user of the hotel's conference venues and suites.

On a cold winter Sunday, Ernst Etter was visiting the Vienna hotel site – the opening day had been rescheduled, once again, for the first week of March – to collect telex messages, and noticed a young man strolling about looking at the building. Etter asked him if he knew that this was the Intercontinental Hotel. "Oh, yes – and I would like very much to meet the manager," came the reply. Etter: "Well, he's standing in front of you – would you like a tour?" From this chance meeting came an offer for John Edmaier to return to Austria from a position which he then held in a club in Nassau, Bahamas, as executive assistant manager. Etter was anxious to have a senior executive who knew the Austrian hotel scene and had had experience with North American management systems.

A Lippizaner horse at the Spanish Riding School, Vienna. The Intercontinental was the city's largest hotel and more than doubled the number of first-class rooms in the market.

Meanwhile in New York, Levon Keenan, searching through the company's files of prospective employees hoping to find a German-speaking candidate for the Vienna front office manager's position, came upon an out-of-date application from a thirty-year-old Viennese who had studied as a Fulbright scholar in the United States; later attended the Austrian Hotel School; married an American, and returned to the United States, where he had worked at the Broadmoor – a famous Rocky Mountain resort – and at the Clift (San Francisco) and Santa Barbara Biltmore in various management positions. Currently he was vice president and general manager of, and had opened, Washington's newest and best hotel, the Madison. Huyot had been impressed with the media and direct mail campaigns with which it had been promoted. Keenan was sent to Washington for an interview; obviously this was not a likely front office manager; and clearly this was someone whom Bob Huyot must meet personally, the sooner the better.

Hans Sternik explained to Huyot his professional goal of multi-unit management. Huyot explained IHC's growth opportunities, pointed out that such regional positions as existed were already filled, but that more would surely arise, offered him the Vienna resident manager's position, and assured him that he would succeed Ernst Etter, who would be transferred to another location before the end of the year. Sternik agreed and arrived in Vienna on January 9.

The hotel received a lukewarm reception among the Viennese public. Hoteliers from other properties were particularly unfriendly. The building and its interiors – particularly the facade, the lobby with a row of huge dirty gold columns, the blue and silver restaurant, and the ballroom with plastic-domed indirect lighting coves in the ceiling – were severely criticized as being in the worst American taste, despite the fact that nearly everything which was visible in the hotel (exception: some of the suites which Prince had partially redecorated at the last minute) was the work of architect Appel and interior architect Jacsh, both Austrians.

Max Hampton had arranged for a special article in *Esquire*, to feature photographs of a spectacular gourmet dinner in the hotel's Four Seasons restaurant. All the regular furniture was removed, to be replaced with chairs borrowed from one of the imperial palaces. Waiters were costumed as eighteenth-century footmen, one for each two of the thirty-six guests – a cross-section of leaders in government, business and the arts. The main course, flaming and lavishly garnitured, would be carried in on trestles: whole roast saddle and leg of lamb.

For this special event, the meat was to be flown direct from Paris. This French cut of meat, which includes the back ribs and both legs, is known as a "baron" of lamb (*agneau* in French). Etter and the chef were getting nervous that the shipment seemed to be lost, when one morning the front office daily report's "no-show" (guest booked, but didn't arrive) list included the name of one Baron D'Agneau. A phone call to reception revealed that a commercial telex had arrived the day before announcing the Baron's Air France flight number and the front office had sent a car and public relations staffer to the airport to greet this obviously important French nobleman, who was nowhere to be found. French culinary terminology had apparently not featured in the front office manager's schooling and experience. This time the four barons were collected from the cargo depot and sped by taxi to the Intercontinental kitchen. The airline on which the *Esquire* photographer returned to America lost his film box, the photographs were never developed and the article was scratched.

On May 27 the hotel was overbooked by 180 rooms. Attendees at a medical convention were due to check out, and an equally large group of postal officers was due to arrive. The front office, perhaps bribed, had also accepted a one-night booking for a group of football fans who were coming from Italy to attend an international match between Inter-Milan and Real Madrid. Several of the medical group decided not to check out as scheduled, and there were no rooms whatsoever for the followers of Milan. In desperation, space was found in a small hotel 60 kilometers from Vienna and a bus and tour leader were dispatched to meet the group at the airport and divert them to the alternate accommodations. No way! After seeing where they were being taken, the football fans revolted and demanded to be taken to the Intercontinental, where they were determined to camp out in the lobby if necessary. Meanwhile, to avert open warfare, the postal delegates were being checked in through a side door and smuggled to their rooms on the service elevators. That front office manager's tenure was mercifully short.

That first summer in Vienna was busy and promising; by late fall, however, the occupancy had fallen to 15 percent. King Saud, who had been recently maneuvered from office, arrived for an extended period of medical tests and treatments, accompanied by a retinue of dozens, and took over two and a half floors of the hotel, thus precluding the possible winter shutdown which management had been contemplating as a last resort.

The Jerusalem Intercontinental was built and owned by the government of Jordan as a first step toward tapping that nation's tourism potential. Designed by Bill Tabler, it featured a main building

with seven three-story glass-fronted arches overlooking the old city from atop the Mount of Olives. IHC had assisted in negotiating an Ex-im dollar loan and Bechtel supervised the construction. An international flap had been caused when Jordanian public works construction of a road leading to the hotel apparently unearthed a Jewish graveyard. Word was flashed to Washington and to the Pan Am Building that Intercontinental was the culprit in this desecration. Lee Dayton sped to Jordan, convinced the prime minister to intervene and an orderly reburial was effected.

George Milne had been transferred from the Southern Cross in Melbourne to be general manager. Balas arrived in Jerusalem to learn that the hotel's entire shipment of food and beverages was being held up in Aqaba where the customs department, having never before been faced with such a quantity of largely unfamiliar goods, was poring over the documentation with a very deliberate lack of haste. Balas requisitioned a car and a fistful of cash and set off on the 200-mile journey to the coast. After finally locating the senior supervisor in the customs section, Balas gave a speech about the food being for His Majesty's banquet, the absolute need for the shipment to be released

today, and dire predictions of who would be blamed by the higher-ups in the capital if action were not taken at once. It worked, trucks were rented, and a caravan took off across the bumpy desert roads back to Jerusalem, arriving at the hotel at the same time as the press crew whom Hampton was escorting on a Holy Land tour.

The opening buffet was an experience like none other that IHC had ever seen. Max Hampton was gathering notes for use in a book describing his adventures in "hotel opening land", later published under the title *Throw Away the Key*. His account of this memorable buffet: "I saw an elegantly groomed woman, white gloves to her elbow, lift from the table a tray holding an entire ham and carrying it over her head in triumph to her table. Bowls of salads, whole turkeys, complete trays of appetizers were similarly swept away . . . Staff were not serving. They were running up and down the long tables trying to rescue the food, not dish it out. One dedicated small waiter clung to a large tray of sliced meat. Across the table, his opponent, a large man, tugged fiercely. He won. The little waiter fell back against the wall when he lost his grip on the tray. He was almost in tears." At

The view from the Jerusalem Intercontinental. The hotel's opening buffet was put at risk when its entire consignment of food and drink was held up by the customs department at Aqaba.

the end of the meal, some guests folded their glassware, crockery, cutlery and remaining food in the tablecloth or their napkins and prepared to take the bundles with them.

A few weeks after the opening the hotel was the venue for a Palestine Liberation Organization (PLO) summit conference attended by several important Arab leaders.

As the Jerusalem hotel neared its opening date, Lee Dayton had completed negotiations with Jordanian officials for IHC to assume responsibility for operating the 110-room Al Urdon Hotel, then being completed, and partially opened, in Amman, Jordan's capital. Jean Pierre Stauffer was selected as manager, the hotel renamed Jordan Intercontinental and a technical assistance program begun to deal with alterations which would be required to assure compliance with IHC standards. Balas, Keenan, and Hampton motored from Jerusalem to visit the Amman property and to pay a courtesy call on one of the members of its board of directors. Balas, at his most effusive, made a point of praising the tea which was served by their host, complete with knowledgeable comments on its provenance, bouquet and flavor. Would the director think it rude if Balas were to inquire as to its source; perhaps this fine beverage could be introduced in Intercontinentals around the world. After checking with the server, the reply came in two precisely clipped syllables: "It's called LIP – TON." After a long silence, Balas: "Of course."

Gates concluded a Mandarin-type membership agreement for the 550-room luxury Okura Hotel, due to open later in the year in Tokyo, and a marketing program was developed under Beardsley's direction.

In April, Mario di Genova moved to the head office as vice president – operations, and was replaced as vice president – Latin American Division in the Tamanaco by Pete Sutherland. John Carrodus was transferred from the development department to be Southern Cross general manager. Ernst Etter was named vice president – Europe Division and transferred to Frankfurt, succeeding Curt Peyer who was assigned to Karachi to oversee the opening of the company's first hotel in Pakistan.

Lyle Warner had been transferred to Jakarta as comptroller for Indonesia and under his direction TSA and management contracts were finalized for the 330-room Hotel Bali Beach, under construction at Sanur Beach on the island of Bali. He also negotiated a $5,000,000 purchasing agreement whereunder IHC would procure the furnishings not only for the Bali hotel, but also for two smaller hotels to be operated by Tokyo's Okura Hotel group: the Samudera Beach Hotel in Pelabuan Ratu, West Java, and the Ambarrukmo Palace in the royal city of Jogjakarta, capital of Central Java. The Hotel Indonesia management contract was amended, prolonging its termination date to coincide with the Bali agreement. IHC had been lobbying for the Indonesians to build a low-rise building in Bali and had engaged the well-known Hawaiian architects Wimberly, Wisenand, Allison and Tong, a firm specializing in Pacific Island style designs, to produce a model for a spectacular Balinese-temple-inspired hotel structure. The model was placed in the Pan Am office window at Hotel Indonesia and caused much comment which eventually filtered back to Sukarno, who promptly sent for Spillum. The president explained that the Bali Hotel would be a high rise, it would look like the modern best of Miami or San Juan, and it would be a source of inspiration to the Balinese who would thereby understand that Indonesians could build a building equal to the best in the world . . . and would Spillum please destroy that Disneyland model or remove it from Indonesia, at once!

In Karachi, the Tabler-designed Karachi Intercontinental reminded many of a confection coated in spun sugar, clad as it was in sparkling white molded cement lattice work tiles; others were reminded of a giant harem screen. The bedrooms featured tiled floors covered with handmade woolen area rugs, and original watercolor artwork by a soon to be famous local artist. Following the example of the national airline, the hotel had engaged educated young men and women for all customer service positions. Female room maids were designated stewardesses and waiters were stewards, for the first time elevating these jobs to a position of respect not heretofore known in south Asia. For a while, one stewardess brought her maid from home to perform the room-cleaning tasks while the mistress sat in the corridor doing *petit point*.

Pakistan president Ayub Khan cut the opening ribbon and at his prior request made a comprehensive inspection visit to every part of the hotel, where he was introduced to each department head and a representative sampling of employees as well as the IHC opening team member responsible for training and planning in the respective area. He was shown several suites by Prince, who miraculously appeared (courtesy of the fire stairs) at the lift door as it delivered the president from floor to floor, eventually eliciting a "Haven't we met before?" from Ayub Khan.

The guests invited from overseas were taken on a rail and air tour of Pakistan which included a hair-raising side trip via Ariana (the 49 percent Pan Am owned national airline of Afghanistan) to Kabul and Khandahar.

Juan T. Trippe (right) was Pan Am chairman for more than forty years. Here he is seen in the Presidential Suite of the Hotel Tamanaco, with Wilbur Morrison, Pan Am's senior vice president – Latin America, just after receiving the prestigious Order of Francisco Miranda from Raul Leoni, president of Venezuela, in recognition of Pan Am's thirty-five years of service to his country.

Unknown to anyone in IHC, but apparently with the cooperation of Pan Am, a U.S. CIA agent had been hired for one of the hotel's middle management positions. He started missing work for an hour on one or two afternoons a week, and apparently visited the U.S. embassy more often than a passport extension or other usual formality would require. Shortly afterward an IHC official with a prior career in Washington was casually asked by one of his former colleagues about the Communist tendencies of one of the Karachi owning company's directors, a man who was the quintessential capitalist entrepreneur. The source of this misinformation may have been the IHC "expat"; he resigned abruptly and departed for points unknown.

J. Walter Thompson produced a new series of advertisements emphasizing the uniqueness of the various hotels and highlighting the IHC credo that each property should reflect its local environment. Intended for the consumer press, each vertical, one-column-wide advertisement featured a line drawing of some typical local feature of the hotel's country, a short descriptive blurb about the hotel, and a bold face heading: "The Great [Name of Country] Hotel in [Name of City] is an Intercontinental." Unfortunately, the selection of sketches was not always made, or checked, by someone who was fully familiar with the country being featured. The first: "The Great Pakistani Hotel in Karachi is an Intercontinental" showed a regally bedecked elephant carrying a maharaja, typical of India, but unknown in Pakistan. (It was soon replaced with a camel cart.) One of the Jordan advertisements for a short time depicted a shepherd with a shofar, hardly a familiar sight in Amman.

Flanked by a pair of Pathan doormen at the inauguration of the Karachi Intercontinental on May 10 1954 (left to right): Yusuf Haroon – managing director, Pakistan Services Ltd. (hotel owning company); Air Vice Marshal M. Nur Khan – chairman, Pakistan Services Ltd. and managing director, Pakistan International Airlines; Field Marshal Mohd. Ayub Khan, president of Pakistan; Curt Peyer – general manager, Karachi Intercontinental.

Many of Bob Huyot's innovative ideas were being incorporated into the planning of new IHC hotels. These included rooms in guest corridors for ice machines from which guests could serve themselves – his preference was for in-room refrigerator units, a choice which capital cost considerations made unfeasible; retractable drying lines in guest shower baths, for wet bathing suits or self-laundered clothes; business lounges – an idea several years ahead of its time; street entrances for restaurants; an enclosed privacy cupboard for toiletries in guest bathrooms; direct dial telephones, but ones without the ability to phone from one guest room to another – he had a particular concern about preserving a guest's privacy; privacy booths for guests using their safe deposit boxes – at first hardly used and often converted to luggage storage, but essential as the years went by; provision for coin-operated cold beverage dispensing machines on the guest floors, eventually rendered unnecessary with the introduction of minibars in the late 1970s; and shoe boxes, a compartment in the closet with a locked door from the corridor where a guest could safely place his or her shoes for polishing by hotel staff at night – this was short-lived as there were too many clicks and slams as doors were opened and shut up and down the corridors in the middle of the night.

Virtually every IHC hotel opened between 1962 and 1964 was having difficulty achieving consistently acceptable levels of occupancy. In most cases each had more than doubled the number of first-class rooms in the city which meant that success had to come, at least partially, through diverting customers from existing hotels until such time as the growth in international air travel produced a major increase in total demand. However, IHC's experience in Latin America, and the typical trend in the United States, had been that guests automatically sought out the newest hotel in town. Somehow this was not happening in Vienna, and Karachi, and Dublin, and even Melbourne. The business traveler whom IHC was hoping to attract was not predisposed to quickly desert the hotel which had looked after him in the past. In his mind, new was not necessarily better.

In Beirut, René Lambert and a prestigious committee of French and Lebanese social leaders organized a major international charity event during the summer of 1964, the thirtieth *"Bal des Petits Lits Blancs."* The first to be held outside France, it was a fund-raiser for French children's hospitals. A private 707 jet charter brought the guests from France. They were based at the Phoenicia and treated to a three-day program that included an evening at the well-known Casino du Liban with its international Lido-style stage presentations, and a luncheon at the mountainside home at Aley of Madame Désirée Kettaneh (who had imported a huge tent specially designed in Paris by Lancel). The ball itself took place in the grounds and among the fruit and olive orchards of a palace at Beit-Eddin, some 45 kilometers from Beirut, which had been constructed and embellished over a fifty-year period, 1790 to 1840, by the Emir Bechir II. Charles Helou, at the time president of the National Council for Tourism, had put these and other government facilities at the disposal of the ball's organizers. Khahil Sarkis, a leading antique dealer, lent carpets and oriental objets d'art to decorate the premises. Three two-tiered buffets some 30 meters in length were decorated and filled with a spectacular variety of cold foods and rotisserie-cooked meats and fowl. Thirty cooks presided over the buffet, eight of them having spent a week at the palace in the temporary kitchen facilities constructed for this event. Five mannequins circulated through the dining area exhibiting the latest couture of Jean Patou and the jewelry, valued at some 30,000,000 francs, of Boucheron, Cartier, Chaumet, Van Cleef and Arpels, and Mauboussin. Security guards in mufti hovered near the models throughout the evening. During the meal guests received a copy of the Paris *Figaro*, the first page of which was devoted entirely to the ball with photographs of the guests departing from Orly and arriving in Beirut. Hundreds of bottles of champagne were served and the dancing went on until 4 a.m., after which guests were taken to Baalbek, the site of ancient Roman ruins, where hot croissants were served at dawn. For those still ready for more, a typical "mezze" luncheon was served at Byblos en route back to Beirut.

In Zagreb the refurbished Esplanade opened its doors in November. The collection of travel writers recruited by Hampton from the United States and several European countries were given a VIP tour of the Yugoslavian countryside, Zagreb, and the Dalmatian coast and repaid the favor with a barrage of magazine and newspaper articles which played no small role in "opening up" Yugoslavia to international tourism.

With twenty-nine hotels and 8,550 rooms in operation, IHC had doubled its number of locations in the four years 1960–4. And after a six-year drought, the company turned a profit of $491,000, while Pan Am earned $37.1 million.

Intercontinental News, IHC's first company-wide employee newsletter, made its debut early in 1965. Its twelve pages, edited by Tom Gerst, Max Hampton's assistant, contained a message from Bob Huyot on some aspect of management, articles about new hotels, pictures of interesting hotel events and hotel VIP guests, quotes from press reports of IHC activities, a feature on one of the hotels and its general manager, a feature on some head office department, and a list of management appointments throughout the chain.

In May, Charles Trippe was elected vice president – finance and Fred Eydt, controller. By this time Bill Busquets had returned to Chile and Dieter Spaethe and José (Pepe) González were appointed financial directors for Europe and Latin America respectively.

"Spec" Roll retired at the end of July, after more than thirty years with Pan Am/IHC.

Intercontinental's second hotel in Germany almost didn't get built and, judged from its first several years' earnings, perhaps it should not have been. Pan Am's Sam Pryor had hosted a group of businessmen on a visit to the Hanover Fair and they had been uncomfortably accommodated in railway carriages. Returning to New York, he reported to Gates that Hanover was a city desperately in need of hotel facilities. Bob Smith and Bleich set out to find a site and were successful in gathering a group of Lower Saxony businessmen to form the nucleus of a hotel company. Professor Hans Deutsch had been introduced to IHC and the Frankfurter Bank by Baron Rothschild. Deutsch had made a fortune and become well known in West Germany as an attorney specializing in restitution cases which he handled on a contingency commission basis: lawsuits against the West German government on behalf of individuals whose assets had been seized by the Nazi regime. Deutsch had become a small shareholder in the Frankfurt Intercontinental and, anxious to participate in other, hopefully high profile, Intercontinental hotel projects, had committed to a major portion of the Hanover shares.

Profit and loss projections which Bob Smith believed necessary to ensure the feasibility of the project were passed to Huyot for review. He and Keenan were incredulous: room rates were being proposed which were at least as high as Frankfurt, and occupancies appeared to ignore the fact that except for ten days a year there was probably no need for more than 100 additional rooms in Hanover; the proposed hotel contained nearly 300. It is not unusual for real estate developers and operators to disagree about forecasts; the independent developer wants to get his project financed and put to bed, collect his fee, and be on about another development. The operator wants plenty of cushion. When, as was the case, developer and operator are the same entity, the argument degenerates into an interfactional spitting match: "You are responsible for killing this project!" "You won't be around to take the blame when the losses pile up!" The projections were revised and re-revised, certain reductions were made to the project capital cost (guest room air conditioning and an in-hotel laundry were deleted) and with less than unanimous approbation the project went ahead. In the midst of construction, Professor Deutsch was arrested on charges of perjured testimony (paintings which he claimed had been taken from a client by the Nazis were actually in the USSR) and was unable to meet the capital calls on his Hanover share purchase contract. IHC secured agreement to step into his place, and was eventually unsuccessfully sued by Deutsch over the transaction.

The restaurant and banqueting facilities of the hotel were attractive and very busy from the opening day; not so with the bedrooms. Substantial losses led IHC some years later to buy out most of the smaller shareholders, and the property remained in the red until worldwide inflation in the 1970s pushed room rates to a level sufficient to cover the property's inflation-proof debt service. Eventually a casino and *Bierstube* were added.

In India, the New Delhi Oberoi Intercontinental's official September 1965 opening had to be postponed because of hostilities which had broken out with Pakistan, largely over the Kashmir issue. Each side occupied towns in the other's territory and tank engagements – the fiercest since World War II – took place along the border not far from Lahore. Max Hampton and Bill Belcher, the IHC project manager, who had joined the company in 1962 in Indonesia where he had been working for Cal-Tex, were stranded in Delhi as all nighttime landings (Pan Am's round-the-world service came through at around 4 a.m.) were prohibited for security reasons. Hampton's press people's trips were canceled in time, except for one intrepid social editor from Washington, D.C., who turned up smartly dressed and beautifully coifed in the employees' cafeteria which was doing duty, unneeded as it happened, as an air raid shelter. General manager Bill Land, formerly of Havana and Jakarta, was calm and unperturbed.

India and Pakistan at the time shared honors for the most impenetrable bureaucracies in the world. A huge civil service hierarchy controlled all government action through thousands of regulations, all of which seemed to produce "no" for an answer, or a referral to another office. No one wanted to be the fellow who took the responsibility for saying "yes." Processing IHC's paperwork for remitting the first fee from India, the basic permission for which had been secured years earlier from the highest levels of government, and the related acceptance of income tax returns (you couldn't remit until you proved that provision had been made for the payment of the applicable taxes, a logical policy), stretched out over several years with personal visits by IHC executives and continuous follow-up by lawyers and public accountants in Delhi and Calcutta. Once the first remittance passed, however, subsequent approvals were usually forthcoming without incident.

In Indonesia political instability was building up to a major explosion. Kane Rufe had been sent to Jakarta to replace Land after having served in the Dominican Republic as a caretaker operations manager charged with keeping the Embajador hotel open at the lowest possible cost during the period of transition from the rule of Rafael Trujillo to whatever government might emerge to succeed him. Hotel Indonesia, under Rufe's leadership, had become self-sufficient in a city where ordinary infrastructural services were slowly decaying. The hotel had its own taxi fleet, its own staff housing and laundry service, its own staff medical services, its own auto-repair service, its own

OVERLEAF:

The Taj Mahal is about 100 miles from New Delhi where IHC's first hotel in India opened in 1965.

This 1965 advertisement in the *New Yorker* featured page boys from Hong Kong's Mandarin hotel and introduced the group's general managers.

transportation pool, its own stocks of reserve equipment – toilet bowls, chairs, light fix-tures, sinks, pumps – and spare parts, and oversaw a program of rice, sugar, and cook-ing oil distribution for the families of its 2,000-man staff. A piece of land in Sukabumi, some eighty miles south of Jakarta, had been ceded to the hotel for the development of a cattle ranch and vegetable farm. Beef cattle were imported from Lombok, and an expatriate staff consisting of a veterinarian, an agronomist, and a mechanic was recruited to administer the project under Lyle Warner's general supervision. The ranch was the frequent site of politically inspired skirmishes between pro- and anti-Communist groups among the employees and the nearby villagers.

In Jakarta, Rufe had managed to steer the hotel in a politically neutral vein, being certain that policies reflected the stated positions of President Sukarno and the cabi-net. There was a great deal of anti-West propaganda, loudly broadcast by leftist groups throughout the nation with the U.S. often decried as a "NECOLIM" (neo-colonial imperialist) power. Rufe successfully walked a tightrope; the four-page English language newspaper controlled by the foreign ministry once praised him for being a "real" believer in freedom and democracy, unlike the political leaders of the West.

A group of employee members of the hotel's PKI (Indonesian Communist Party) union – each political faction had a separate union and a group of adherents among

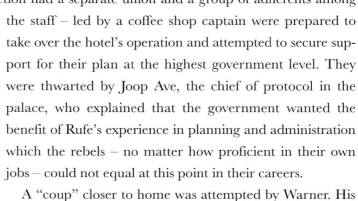

John Carrodus, vice president – South Pacific, entertaining one of the paramount chiefs of American Samoa, who was also one of the owning company directors of the Pago Pago Inter-Continental.

the staff – led by a coffee shop captain were prepared to take over the hotel's operation and attempted to secure sup-port for their plan at the highest government level. They were thwarted by Joop Ave, the chief of protocol in the palace, who explained that the government wanted the benefit of Rufe's experience in planning and administration which the rebels – no matter how proficient in their own jobs – could not equal at this point in their careers.

A "coup" closer to home was attempted by Warner. His business style – confrontational, bombastic – was the oppo-site of Rufe's. Warner interpreted Rufe's cautious diplo-macy as weakness and lack of management drive and he too approached Ave, seeking a sign of government approval for a push to replace Rufe with his own candidate. When this filtered back to New York – partially the result of a "poison pen" letter criticizing several of the expatriate employees – Charlie Trippe flew to Indonesia, con-ducted an investigation and, with Huyot's support, set up a working council of the IHC/Pan Am people to be directed by Rufe. Warner went on leave in connection with his wife's need for medical treatment, and Potter was sent to Jakarta to fill in and investigate further.

And then during the night of September 30 1965 a group of disgruntled pro-Communist and allegedly pro-Chinese military men and leftist civilians attempted to overthrow the government. Their real aim was to neutralize the army, the only serious obstacle to a Communist takeover of the nation (by murdering its senior leadership). The army resisted and the coup was crushed,

followed by a period of widespread destruction of the PKI organization and its sympathizers in the armed forces. The coffee shop captain disappeared on October 1 and never reappeared. Rumors circulated that the coup leaders had prepared lists of individuals to be eliminated or deported; Rufe was one of them.

American Samoa is a 76-square-mile collection of islands in the South Pacific, an unincorporated territory of the United States with a population of 25,000 about 1,300 of whom reside in the capital Pago Pago. In an attempt to develop a tourism industry the government organized a hotel company to be owned communally by the villages of the islands and financed through small business administration loans from the United States government. Pan Am operated three weekly flights from Honolulu to Sydney via Pago Pago and a weekly circle route Honolulu–Pago Pago–Tahiti and return. It was logical for IHC to be involved with the hotel. Designed by Wimberly in the architectural style of local dwellings, the multibuilding complex would contain American

A Samoan island view. The Pago Pago Inter-Continental opened in 1965 in American Samoa's capital.

Samoa's first full-service restaurant and bar open to the public. Decorated with shells, tapa cloth and lavish plantings, the hotel received its first guests in early December. Prior to the hotel's opening, beer had been sold in one or two local establishments but liquor had been limited to a naval base facility, the Goat Island Club. Recognizing that virtually every American Samoan was one way or another ultimately a shareholder of the hotel, the chiefs cooperated with the hotel to provide husky security personnel who would be universally respected. Initially 100 rooms, the property was later doubled in size. Unfortunately Pago Pago boasts one of the world's highest annual rainfalls, and never gained any real popularity on the tourist circuit. While at the airport preparing to depart for Tahiti, Gates received a telex from Charlie Trippe advising that Charlie had been asked to become Pan Am's treasurer.

Prince Rainier and Princess Grace of Monaco (center) in the Dublin Intercontinental where they were guests of honor and patrons at the *Grand Bal des Petits Lits Blancs*, escorted by René Lambert, general manager, and his wife Suzanne.

René Lambert had been transferred to Dublin and in 1965 was instrumental in bringing the *Bal des Petits Lits Blancs* to Ireland. It was staged at Powerscourt, a majestic stately home in County Wicklow, and Prince Rainier and Princess Grace of Monaco took the places of honor at the dinner, during which guests were entertained by the Paris Opera Ballet.

Leo Riordan moved to Amman, and Ernst Etter replaced Lambert in Beirut. IHC's 1965 profit jumped to $1.5 million, and Pan Am's to $52.1 million.

Early in 1966, the question of Intercontinental's name was to arise again. This time the prestigious firm of Lippincott and Margulies, creator of many internationally known brand names and corporate identities, was engaged. They were told to come up with a name which reflected the nature of the business, one which could be pronounced the same way in most languages, and one with ideally two, but no more than four, syllables. They used computers to grind out possible three-consonant, two-vowel combinations. The recommendations: Forum (a meeting place in Roman days), Intel (obviously a good name for a computer) and Meridian (which hadn't already been appropriated by Air France). The committee settled on Meridian and Gates took it to Juan Trippe. "I don't think I like it. Intercontinental really says it all, and by the way have you taken care of . . . " was the response.

Once again a solution was found in-house: why not split the word Intercontinental into two hyphenated words "Inter-Continental," with a capital "C"? This should end the press confusion with International. Charles Alvey had found that the longitudinal

Ernst Etter (right) replaced René Lambert at the Phoenicia Intercontinental in 1965. Here he welcomes Haile Selassie I of Ethiopia and Lebanese president Charles Helou to the hotel.

world crest was proving too small for incorporating some of the individual hotel crests; he designed a new crest with the name of the chain in a surrounding circle with laurel leaves. The "hyphen" when printed would be in the shape of a diamond which could be enlarged to include a letter "I" in a typeface similar to that in the new company name logo. To further emphasize the corporate brand name, new hotel names would have the city name follow Inter-Continental. This format was introduced in the spring of 1966 and, with minor modifications and short-term deviations from time to time, has served the company for thirty years.

In late 1965, Bob Smith and John Gates had interviewed Paul Sheeline, a Harvard Law School graduate, with the thought that he might join the development department or serve in an administrative position attached to Gates. After military service in North Africa and Europe during World War II, including undercover work with the French Resistance behind German lines, Sheeline had joined Sullivan & Cromwell, one of Wall Street's old-line law firms. In a few years he concluded that being in the law to take a Friday afternoon call from a client who was looking to a merger announcement on Monday, which meant twenty-hour weekend days of document preparation for the attorneys, was not for him; he'd rather be the guy who made the call. He spent eleven years with Lambert & Co., a financial partnership venture capital firm, and after leaving Lambert had been working as an advisor to U.S. AID on an investigation of business opportunities for potential U.S. investors in Morocco. Gates offered him the vice president – finance position and he joined Intercontinental on January 1 1966.

Huyot continued to be concerned that consistent operating systems be installed and maintained in the hotels. He was determined that a set of operating manuals be developed for each functional area of hotel activity; an accounting manual written by Busquets in the late 1950s and updated from time to time by Potter was the only such volume in existence. Balas and Steve Fedak, who had replaced Schermer in charge of maintenance engineering, were to give top priority to the preparation of food and beverage and maintenance manuals, respectively. Virginia Baker, a Cornell graduate, was engaged as director – housekeeping, joining IHC from several years at Realty Hotels in New York where she had been manager of the Barclay Hotel, and in charge of a several million dollar remodeling of the Biltmore Hotel. Juan Callobre, a Cuban who had worked at the Nacional, San Juan and Ponce hotels for IHC, and briefly at Realty, was named director – front office. Each went to work on departmental manuals, and would be scheduled to assist in training at openings and to make periodic visits to hotels throughout the system to assure that operating standards were being maintained.

One of Pan Am development's earliest priority locations had been Bangkok. The airline had played a role in selecting the site for the international airport, which doubled as an air-force base, and had worked with Thai Airways under a technical assistance program. The Pan Am round-the-world service stopped in Bangkok every day in both directions, and Thailand had one of the most liberal open skies policies regarding international air traffic. As early as 1958 IHC formed a company to construct a hotel in the capital, Bangkok Intercontinental Hotels Co., Ltd (BIHC). By 1960 a lease option had been negotiated between Pan Am and His Majesty's Private Property on a 26-acre site then part of the Srapatum Palace grounds (the residence of HRH the Princess Mother), for a period of thirty years at an attractive rent. But only one or two potential investors had been identified. Charlie Trippe, who had just taken over the IHC development role in Asia, was able to obtain an appointment with the Thai prime minister, Field Marshal Sarit Thanarat, and shared an audience with foreign ambassadors presenting their credentials. Marshal Sarit listened to Trippe's presentation, which was well larded with statistics concerning the economic effects of tourism, and reacted favorably, assigning his aide-de-camp and private secretary, Colonel (later General) Chalermchai Charuvastr, to be the contact for further negotiations. IHC was seeking an equity participation of 15 million baht (then $750,000). Chalermchai reckoned that the hotel, one way or another, would be paying at least this much in taxes in a three-year period – it looked like a good investment for the government. Tourism was in its infancy in Thailand, way down on the list of foreign exchange earners, but Sarit had a clear future vision and had created the Tourist Organization of Thailand with a modest budget to promote the nation's attractions to international travelers, with Chalermchai as the chief executive. Within fifteen years tourism would emerge as Thailand's leading foreign exchange generator. An Ex-im credit was negotiated; the business-oriented agreements limited the final draw-down of funds to the end of the construction phase of the project, and only upon an acceptable certification that all funds were available to complete on budget; and placed restrictions on future dividends so that the borrower would be required to maintain adequate cushion to cover future loan repayment obligations. The economic officers in the U.S. embassy were unhelpful – they thought hotel construction was not a basic economy building enterprise, and it was necessary to outflank them and deal direct with Washington.

Providing the necessary guarantees was a problem. In other countries the guarantor had had a mortgage or other claim on the property as collateral. In this case the land belonged to His Majesty the King, making such a lien unthinkable. Finally, after long and difficult negotiations by Chalermchai, Trippe, and later David Salisbury, three banks agreed to jointly and severally guarantee the Ex-im loans for a fee with no further security. At the time, share transfers in Thailand required a detailed registration procedure, and there was no easy market for quick transfers. To attract institutional investors to the project, Trippe proposed an issue of debentures to be underwritten by commercial banks, which the banks could hold in their own name or for their clients' accounts, with the bank able internally to effect transfers (without stamp duty or other formality). The National Lottery and the Crown Property (a quasi-governmental agency which owned and managed large tracts of publicly owned land, as distinct from HM Private Property) each subscribed to equity along with IHC, a local brewery (Singha Beer) and some private investors. Chalermchai was elected to the board, and shortly thereafter, by then a major general, was named chairman to preside over a group which included a representative of His Majesty, the heads of five leading banks, two government ministers, the heads of the lottery and Crown Property, and four representatives of Pan Am and IHC.

Joseph Salerno was the project architect. The firm with which he was then associated had designed the Pan Am terminal at New York's Idlewild airport. In order to emphasize the relationship of the hotel buildings with the large garden spaces, he created two low-rise wings of bedrooms surrounded by ponds, lawns and plantings, connected by outdoor walkways to a dramatic four-story high, elongated pyramid-shaped central building with an orange-tiled roof. An audience was granted by King Bhumibol for the model to be shown. General Chalermchai, Bob Smith, Charlie Trippe, a vice chairman of Ex-im, and Salerno made the presentation. His Majesty walked around the model and finally judged it to be either Indonesian, or possibly Japanese, in inspiration and suggested that the national library would be a good source for the understanding of local architecture. Salerno explained that he had not wanted to copy local designs since he thought of them as intrinsically royal or religious in nature, but that he would incorporate individual local motifs into the finished product. The main building and its roof remained controversial (at the time of the opening Prince Kukrit Pramoj, a leading politician and intellectual, said it reminded him of a crematorium), in a country where most people had probably been expecting an American company to create an ultra-modern high rise. It became a city landmark.

While the hotel was under construction it was clear that demand was growing rapidly; financing was arranged (Ex-im, IHC, debentures, and a new issue of preference shares underwritten by Siam Commercial Bank) and plans drawn up for a second phase 190-room eight-story tower, construction on which would begin shortly after the opening of the original 224-room property.

Siam Inter-Continental's inaugural date was set by the royal astrologers, and Her Royal Highness the Princess Mother honored the hotel with her presence. Unfortunately some of the essential furniture and equipment – telephone instruments among them – were on ships which had been delayed en route by a massive gridlock in the port of Saigon. Thus tent cards "Our telephones went to war" sat on most of the bedside tables for two weeks after the opening. One irate guest to a smiling unflappable lobby receptionist: "I must have a room with a phone; I have to call room service!" "Oh, never mind, sir, room service doesn't work either."

In Singapore, which had become independent of Malaysia in August 1965, a confrontation was brewing between far leftist elements and the more moderate labor unions who were pillars of gov-

The Siam Inter-Continental in Bangkok. Its garden is spectacular, with ponds, plantings and lawns surrounding two low-rise bedroom wings.

ernment support. The main hotel workers union was affiliated with the leftists, and the Singapura Inter-Continental was a symbol of international capitalism. For what were clearly political reasons, negotiations were doomed to failure on a new labor agreement, despite the fact that all salary and related economic issues in the proposed settlement had already been agreed through direct contacts with owning company board members. General manager George Milne, who had switched jobs with Squier in Jerusalem, was asked by the local authorities whether IHC was prepared to stick out a long strike and, if so, how the security services could be of help. On the day of the final showdown, three groups of riot control troops were positioned behind the hotel; Milne invited all employees who wished to remain in the hotel to do so – and the rest went on strike and started to set up picket lines at the hotel's front door. The troops, headed by a towering 6 foot 5 inch commander, immediately forced the group from the hotel property, arresting one or two who resisted, into two corners on the street where they could not hinder access to the building or the property through its driveways. Posters went up the next day showing dollar signs being extracted from workers' pockets by a cigar-smoking kangaroo (Milne), and being wafted away in a Pan Am plane to a munitions factory to be converted to bombs to be dropped on Vietnam. This was a pretty major internationalization of a local union dispute whose few unsettled issues included the disposition of lost and found guest property, and the pooling of tips. Obviously larger forces were at work. The hotel remained open and the coffee shop served three meals a day for resident guests; a key staff of department heads (and the head man in the boiler room, whose son was a union leader) were accommodated dormitory-style in the restaurant; and guests (including aircrews and tour groups) came and went for five weeks. During this period a major rally against the U.S. presence in Vietnam was organized by the leftist union group – it was rumored that the attendees would move from the stadium to the Singapura in a massive show of support for the strikers. But the police and security services cleverly avoided this post-rally event through traffic diversions which made it impossible for the group to reassemble. The strikers became frustrated; one afternoon a can of red paint was thrown against a tourist bus entering the hotel's driveway; the next day pictures of the paint-spattered vehicle appeared in Bangkok and Hong Kong newspapers. This was enough; the government shut down the pickets' tents and the forty-two-day strike was over.

OPPOSITE:

Bangkok's Grand Palace.

Milne made valuable arrangements at the Singapore airport to do catering for Cathay Pacific and establish a daily contact around 8 p.m. to advise the number of unbooked rooms in the hotel; the local airline handling agent then sent an equivalent number of layover passengers to the Singapura. For at least three years thereafter the hotel's occupancy seldom fell below 97 percent.

During the last year of construction of the Hotel Bali Beach, funds for local salaries of the hotel trainees and the on-site construction workers were advanced from Hotel Indonesia. No bank in Bali had sufficient currency to handle these payrolls, necessitating bi-weekly hand-carrying of boxes of rupiah by plane from Jakarta to Bali; a month's payroll filled two empty twenty-four-bottle beer cases. A freestanding freezer in which shipments of frozen foods could be stored prior to periodic shipment over land, and by ferry boat, to Bali had been ordered by the hotel for installation on the docks at Surabaja. The ship carrying the freezer docked in Jakarta en route to Surabaja; the captain was unsure how to set up this piece of equipment, so it was arranged for the hotel chief engineer to travel on the ship to Surabaja. Ben White, the IHC controller for Indonesia (who had succeeded Warner), also traveled on board carrying one of the monthly cash shipments.

Both carelessly ignored the fact that from the point of view of Indonesian port officials they were arriving from overseas, not Jakarta – and that one was carrying a very large quantity of Indonesian currency. White was put under guard in a port office; he and the guards played chess for five hours, while the Bali controller managed to contact senior officials who could order his release. The hotel's freezer trucks, which were on the same ship, were unloaded and delivered to the customs gates without wheels. These "lost" wheels had to be "found" and purchased, in order to move the trucks on to Bali.

The Hotel Bali Beach had hoped for an opening on June 6 – "6–6–66" – Sukarno's birthday. The disruption of all activity in Indonesia following the aborted September 30 1965 coup delayed completion until November. At the last minute, the hotel's landscaping crew had traveled around Bali with trucks and appropriate certificates that were exchanged for attractive mature trees or shrubs wherever they might be found, thanking villages for contributions.

The Pan Am board of directors was making a tour of Southeast Asia and scheduled itself to participate in the Bali events. The international airport was still under construction, which meant that all attendees had to travel from Jakarta via the national carrier, which at this time had a very limited fleet of operable aircraft, or by whatever alternate means could be arranged.

In the wake of the coup an interim government was in place led by a presidium headed by General Suharto and including Adam Malik (foreign minister) and the sultan of Jogjakarta, Hamengku Buwono IX, a patriotic leader who in the past had been in charge of tourism activities. The relative ranks of the various senior invitees were not always clear. Making a seating list was well-nigh impossible. Joop Ave had been assigned to be master of ceremonies for the opening. He surveyed the gathering throng of guests and quickly requested a desk, three page boys and a table location chart. As each guest arrived, Ave made an appropriate greeting, assigned a table number and sent the guest, with a page boy, to his place. Ave knew every Indonesian guest (someone from IHC stood near to identify those few foreigners he hadn't met), and could balance the seating around the room so that no one's sense of rank, honor or prestige would be offended . . . a brilliant tour de force.

Traveling back to Jakarta the last group of about 100, mostly overseas, guests was to be transported in a military Hercules troop/cargo aircraft. Ave took one look at the airplane and the group and quickly arranged for the hotel to deliver a full bar and hors d'oeuvres to the airport. He gathered the guests and advised that they would be flying in a U.S. built aircraft, that while the bucket seating might not be up to Pan Am or Air France comfort levels it would be a safe journey; if any problem, take it up with Uncle Sam. Ave took over at the bar, while Kane Rufe and Siegfried Beil, the Hotel Indonesia resident manager, played waiters for this airborne drinks party on its two-hour journey above Java. No one on board would ever forget or regret that adventure.

Just prior to a dinner at Hotel Indonesia for the Pan Am board, the hotel suffered a brown-out: there was sufficient power for lighting but not for air conditioning or elevators. To keep things moving, Ave urged Foreign Minister Adam Malik to enter the stuffy banquet room and very demonstrably remove his jacket. The others followed suit, and everyone relaxed. The power returned during coffee. Malik bade farewell to the group with the words: "You will always remember that we Indonesians received you warmly."

A few days later, the Inter-Continental Dacca would open and many of the IHC brass traveled direct to Dacca after a stopover in Bangkok. Bob Huyot met the Siam Inter-Continental owning company board who were a bit nervous that their hotel's first four months' operation had not produced high occupancies and yet IHC had convinced them to go ahead with an enlargement. Huyot, thinking he was consoling them, explained in a businesslike manner that hotels in the United States generally didn't make money until after the third year. He was apparently unaware that IHC's forecasts for Bangkok showed profits in year two. In the event, through IHC adjustments in rental payments, BIHC recorded modest profits from the start, and was eventually able to pay sizable cash and stock dividends.

The Dacca hotel contained 300 rooms because Karachi had 300 rooms. It was a political necessity for the main city of East Pakistan to have a facility equal to that in the West. There was little economic justification for more than 200 rooms and the hotel was under financial pressure from day one. Since the two hotels were owned by the same company, profits from the one could to some extent subvent losses from the other.

Dacca general manager was Max Herr, who had been promoted from Geneva to the Reforma in Mexico City, and en route had married Maryan Kiernan, with a reception at Mayfair Farms, the well-known dining and catering establishment to which Harold Talalas had returned after his on-the-spot banqueting debut at the San Juan Intercontinental. Fred Peelen was executive assistant manager, transferring from Ponce where he had been hired by Balas to be in charge of the food and beverage operation. The Dacca hotel was an architecturally eye-catching structure, designed by Tabler with arches shading each guest-room window and colonnaded terraces and extensive gardens. During the non-monsoon months, the beds of flowers and shrubs were dazzling.

Nearly two years after the opening, Peelen was abruptly told to leave the country; Maryan Herr, who was out of the country, was asked not to return. It seems that they had regularly visited the home of one of the attachés from the U.S. consulate to play bridge. This official, introduced to Peelen by Levon Keenan, who had met the couple in Beirut, had a habit of appearing at the Dacca airport twice a week when the PIA 707, the only non-Communist airline then serving China, transited en route to and from Beijing. Pakistan security could not take any action against the attaché and his intense curiosity about those boarding and disembarking the China flight. But it seemed to them strange that the same evening every week the hotel car deposited what they thought were two Americans (Peelen was Dutch) at this official's residence. An unfortunate error, but not an improbable incident in a career with Inter-Continental in those days.

In 1966 Pan Am scored another first by announcing an order for twenty-five Boeing 747 "Jumbo" jet aircraft at a total cost, including spare parts, of $600,000,000. Each aircraft would carry nearly three times as many passengers as, and at lower cost per seat mile than, the 707 aircraft currently in use. The order would double Pan Am's total jet lift capacity. Within a year a total of ninety-five of the planes had been ordered by Pan Am and fourteen other U.S. and foreign-flag airlines; Pan Am's would go into operation first – by 1969 if production proceeded on schedule.

Problems had developed with the IHC standard lease and management agreements. Charges by IHC for services foreseen in the agreements but not specifically identified or quantified raised continual questions from hotel owning companies, and sometimes from exchange control authorities. Allocation methods inevitably produced arguments as to fairness. The replacement provision for furniture and fixtures was expressed as a percentage of original capital cost rather than

related to inflated replacement cost levels. And there was no specific provision for other capital expenditures. To deal with these shortcomings, Gates modified the agreements to include an "all exclusive" charge to reimburse IHC for system services – which were to be described in the contract – of a fixed percentage of gross revenue; this would preclude arguments about billings for specific service items, and allocation methods. A provision for capital expenditures including replacements of furnishings, also expressed as a percentage of gross revenue, would be included among the deductions for calculating GOP on which the rent or IHC management fees would be based. The first of the new form lease agreements was negotiated by Gates with the Ayala organization in Manila during a three-day visit in November.

Pan Am served Accra, Ghana, once or twice a week on its "milk run" flights down the coast of West Africa. State Department and Pan Am personnel had been in discussions with the ministers in the post-Nkrumah government concerning the Ambassador and Continental Hotels in Accra. A major African trade and agricultural fair was to be staged in Ghana in early 1967 and the government wanted the two hotels under international management with a full-scale training plan in operation prior to the fair's commencement. Bob Smith flew overnight to Accra with copies of the new form lease in his bag. On the next morning at a meeting with a group of Ghanian officials the contracts were reviewed, negotiated and agreed to in a few hours. Smith asked who would give the final authorization for the government. The chief of the military triumvirate running the country at the time was the reply. Leave the documents with us and we'll get them approved. Smith preferred to take the documents to the leader himself, that very afternoon. The problem: no one, including the leader's office, knew where he could be found. The negotiators initialed each page of the agreed documents and left them with Smith who, with the local Pan Am director, set off for the U.S. embassy to find help in locating the leader. No one had any idea, but according to the first secretary the ambassador was hosting a reception at his residence that evening and

perhaps the leader might show up. Smith went, explained his mission to the ambassador, and waited for an hour or so. The leader arrived with his entourage, was greeted by the ambassador, and ushered into a private room with Smith, who explained the situation and produced the initialed documents. The leader borrowed Smith's pen, signed, accepted Smith's thanks and departed. Smith was on that night's flight back to New York, and the next morning delivered the two signed long-term leases and commitments for rehabilitation of each hotel to Gates less than forty-eight hours after leaving the office.

IHC assumed operation of the hotels in 1967. Leo de Franco was assigned to install training systems. He had managed the Varadero Oasis in Cuba and the Carrera in Santiago, had been selected to manage the Rangoon property before the project collapsed; and had then spent five years in Indonesia developing and directing training programs for Hotel Indonesia and for Hotel Bali Beach, where he had been scheduled to be general manager. Within a year it was clear that the Ghanian government, for all its good intentions, did not have sufficient resources to carry out its obligations. Sheeline flew to Accra and negotiated an IHC withdrawal before the end of 1969.

Pan Am's 1966 annual report announced a record $83.7 million profit (including an $11.8 million capital gain on the sale of its 50 percent interest in Panagra). IHC earned $1.045 million. John Gates was elected to the Pan Am board of directors.

MANAGEMENT CHANGES

Early in 1967 an expanded senior management group was announced. Sheeline, di Genova and Beardsley became senior vice presidents. Carrodus and Rufe were named vice presidents for the South Pacific and Far East, respectively. Balas became vice president – food and beverage.

Huyot was concerned that most of the new general managers who were being hired, or promoted into their positions, had either not been exposed to a modern business education or not worked in hotels where the latest management methods were practiced. From his own experience, he knew that typical European hotel-trade education, and the related apprentice system, taught people how to do a wide range of specific jobs in hotels and restaurants with a high level of proficiency; what they did not teach were such matters as budgeting, the understanding of financial reports, marketing, personnel motivation, maintenance engineering and business management philosophy. Huyot envisioned a highly structured program of workshops for general managers and their assistants to instill certain uniform elements of management style. The cost was beyond IHC's means at the time, but as a start Huyot contracted with Cornell University's School of Hotel Administration to begin a series of three- or four-day seminars for groups of managers in Europe, Asia and Latin America. One or two general managers with particular promise were to be selected each year as IHC scholars and sent to appropriate advanced management short courses at Columbia, Harvard, Stanford, and Houston universities. Kane Rufe was one of the first, attending Harvard between his departure from Jakarta and taking up his vice president position in Bangkok.

Balas had introduced a program of annual food and beverage achievement awards, one for each geographical region, to recognize a hotel where results reflected a high level of improvement in quality and profitability from the prior year.

In the course of a Pan Am board trip to Southeast Asia, contacts had been made at the highest levels in Vietnam and Cambodia which indicated an interest in Pan Am/IHC proposals for hotel development and airline technical assistance. A complete hotel survey team was quickly assembled and feasibility studies prepared for hotels in Saigon, atop the central railroad terminal in conjunction with an office block for Air Vietnam, Phnom Penh on the banks of the Mekong near the royal palace, and Siem Reap, opposite and with a full view of the main entrance to the temples at Angkor. An unidentified Chinese rice trader in Singapore was reportedly prepared to purchase large quantities of Cambodia's rice harvest and pay in a combination of foreign exchange and Cambodian ryals, using a portion of the proceeds to invest in the hotels. (Such a purchase would deprive the Viet Cong of a major food supply source, a prospect which would be much appreciated by the powers-that-be in Saigon.)

The Victoria Falls, Zambia. The Musi-o-Tunya Inter-Continental, Livingstone is close to this extraordinary sight.

The studies were presented to the Vietnamese and Cambodian governments, but there was no further response from either – except that several months later Cambodia and Air France announced a hotel development on the same Phnom Penh site with an illustration which looked remarkably similar to the one in IHC's feasibility study.

Pan Am was betting on a huge growth in international travel following the introduction of jumbo jets. Economies of size would drive fares to a level where affordable travel for the masses in most industrialized countries would soon be a reality. This meant that in most destinations, particularly those on established tourist routes in Europe, hotel accommodation would be totally inadequate. Juan Trippe, who never thought small, took the initiative and arranged for contacts with his counterparts at the major European airlines. His message: We and you are going to have a vast increase in capacity by 1970–1; there is a genuine lack of hotel accommodation in your country to accommodate the increased number of passengers we and you will be carrying to Europe; local developers and investors cannot be relied upon to do the job in time to satisfy our and your passengers' needs; we and you have to take the lead; we have experience in this sort of thing and have an expanding hotel operating company in place which can provide the technical know-how to rapidly develop a group of hotels in your country; if necessary we shall invest on a dollar for dollar basis equal to yourself in the equity for these projects, which will be managed by Inter-Continental. Trippe assumed that these national carriers would also have good local banking contacts to provide debt capital.

BOAC, Lufthansa, and UTA (the private French Airline then serving Africa, Southeast Asia and the South Pacific) responded positively, leading to master development agreements with IHC calling for the airlines and IHC to work exclusively with each other within the respective countries (in UTA's case the French overseas departments of Polynesia and New Caledonia). Two to three thousand rooms in the United Kingdom and West Germany were the original goals.

Since IHC was already doing business in West Germany, it would sell 50 percent of its existing equity in Frankfurt, Hanover and Düsseldorf (the latter committed, but not yet under construction) hotels to Lufthansa. The airlines would have a preferred allotment of rooms to sell to their customers at periods of prescheduled high occupancy such as trade fairs and international congresses. Lufthansa's agreement provided that at least one of the hotels developed under the agreement would be managed by a West German hotel operator. Because the airlines would be supporting the hotels with their sales organizations, IHC would agree to a lower reimbursable system cost than was provided in its standard contracts.

Balas, working with several of the hotels' chefs and travel and food writer Myra Waldo, spearheaded the publication of the *Inter-Continental Gourmet Cookbook*, authored by Waldo and containing local specialty recipes from Inter-Continentals around the world as well as travel notes about each featured destination. Waldo selected those recipes which used ingredients generally available worldwide, giving the buyer the opportunity to experience a wide range of world cuisines at home. This was a genuine novelty in 1967.

Institutions Magazine, a leading U.S. hotel and restaurant trade publication, gave its annual hotel design award to the Siam Inter-Continental; the Intercontinental Genève had won the award a year earlier. Both hotels' interiors were created by IHC's interior design department.

IHC's employees became eligible to participate in Pan Am's Supplementary Variable Annuity Plan, a contributory adjunct to the basic pension scheme.

For two years Eric Bleich had spent many days and weeks following up leads for possible IHC participation in the development of projects in the eastern European socialist countries. With the Zagreb Esplanade package as an example, he met one government functionary after another in Hungary and Czechoslovakia, trying to interest them in an IHC association. In Budapest he was granted an appointment, kept waiting in an anteroom for nearly a day, and finally told that the purpose of the meeting was to assure him that there was no possibility of cooperation. He became the proverbial salesman who is ushered out of the front door, only to reappear at the side or rear door. It was exhausting and frustrating, but he was tireless. He became friendly with many of the "no"-sayers and spent evenings with them discussing philosophy and the works of Mozart, Dvorak and Bartok. Few others would have persisted as he did, but eventually he met, one by one, certain forward-thinking individuals in both countries with whom he was able to work out a form of cooperation to bring Western technical and design

experience to hotel projects for Budapest and later Prague; to provide for training programs at IHC hotels in Austria and western Europe; and to incorporate the new hotels into IHC's worldwide reservations and communications system. A foreign capitalist company could not have day-to-day operating control over the hotels, of course, but regular informal consultation meetings with IHC European operations executives formed a workable basis for quality assurance. IHC would collect a fee directly related to occupancy levels in each property. Over the next few years Bleich would sign up similar arrangements for Inter-Continental in Bucharest, Belgrade, and Warsaw. During the same period Pan Am was able to open routes to many of the same cities, operated with 727 aircraft on shuttle services from Frankfurt, and later as co-terminals for transatlantic services through Munich or Vienna.

In June 1967, Israel made a preemptive military strike against its hostile neighbors who had been building up troop strength at the borders. The resulting six-day war halted air travel through the Middle East and cast a pall over travel to Europe. Sandor Stangl, who was executive assistant manager in Jerusalem, had been ordered to turn over possession of the hotel to the Jordanian army commander, whereupon he drove by car to Amman from which he and the Jordan Inter-Continental expatriates were evacuated by military aircraft to Teheran. As the United States was

Budapest. The Duna Inter-Continental opened there in 1969. IHC's presence in Hungary was the result of Eric Bleich's persistence and diplomacy.

presumed to be allied with Israel, there was a real concern that the Amman hotel, known to be operated by a U.S. company, might be attacked by angry demonstrators. Israel occupied all of Jordan west of the Jordan River including the Inter-Continental Jerusalem.

Most foreign residents of the area had assumed that some sort of war was coming, and expatriate wives and dependants, together with their personal effects, had left Jordan well before the actual outbreak of hostilities. Three months later Stangl was sent back to Jerusalem, now under Israeli occupation, as general manager, with Steve Fedak and Peter Hothorn, on loan from the Frankfurt food and beverage department, to take charge of reopening the hotel. Dayton had ascertained that the Jordanian government, the hotel's nominal owner, preferred to see the hotel in operation, with IHC management. Any IHC agreement with the Israeli occupational

authorities would have to protect the Ex-im bank's interests in the unamortized portion of the original construction loan, and assure the former staff continuing employment.

Arriving at the hotel, the team was overcome by an overwhelming stench. It seems that whenever the storeroom door was fully open, it concealed the entrance to the deep freezer which earlier looters had therefore overlooked. With no electricity the huge stocks of once frozen goods were rotting and putrid. The only safe solution was to refreeze everything before hauling away the contents for disposal. Eventually IHC returned to Amman.

A new form lease was signed with the Equadorian government social security system covering a 235-room hotel and casino in Quito which had been opened a few years earlier and been managed by a small U.S. operating company. This was IHC's first new acquisition in Latin America in seven years.

Three days separated the September 1967 openings of the Lahore and Rawalpindi Inter-Continentals in Pakistan. Both were designed by Tabler and financed with the same unique package of international and domestic public and private funding as was developed for Karachi and Dacca. President Ayub Khan in his opening remarks reinforced continued government support for tourism development. PIA provided air transport for an unusually large press and travel trade contingent from Germany, Hong Kong, Japan, the United Kingdom, the United States, Denmark, Sweden, Lebanon, Italy, and France, who visited the Shalimar gardens, the Lahore fort, the immense Badshahi mosque, the summer resort of Murree, the Khyber pass, the Bokhara palace carpet factory, archaeological sites at Taxila, the new capital at Islamabad and the frontier town of Peshawar, where the new Khyber Inter-Continental was in its early construction phase. Several IHC executives traveled with Lee Dayton to Kabul to survey conditions and visit the site of the Inter-Continental Kabul, construction on which had been begun by Taylor Woodrow under a British export promotion credit, and for which Dayton was negotiating an IHC lease.

Pan Am earned $65.687 million in its fortieth year; IHC completed its twenty-first year with a profit of $1 million.

Early in 1968 Huyot placed day-to-day operating responsibility for the group in the hands of Mario di Genova for Europe, Africa and the Middle East; and newly elected senior vice president Pete Sutherland, transferred to the head office from Caracas, for Pacific, Asia and Latin America. Manuel Arriandiaga replaced Sutherland as vice president operations – Latin America. Carlos Rodriguez became treasurer.

After his return from Europe Bob Smith had taken responsibility for all development activities, except for those projects in which Gates himself played the lead role, and supervised a staff of six or seven development officers active around the world. During the six years from 1962 to 1968 this staff had negotiated agreements and arranged the financing for more than thirty Inter-Continentals. Smith had taken the lead role in negotiations in Managua, Nicaragua, where he had friends from his airline days and in newly independent Zambia, where a lease was concluded

OPPOSITE: The Inter-Continental in Managua, Nicaragua, opened in 1969 with architecture reminiscent of ancient Mayan pyramids.

for a 200-room hotel in Lusaka, the capital, and a 100-room property near Livingstone overlooking Victoria Falls. IHC would invest in all three properties, with AID guarantees.

IHC had been working for several years to develop a hotel in Kinshasa, the capital of Zaire. Agreements in principle had been reached with the government and IHC attempted to find support in Washington. The initial reaction was that AID funds were supposed to encourage capitalist ventures and that IHC should find some non-government shareholders. Since there was no private capital available for hotel building in Zaire, the project lay dormant.

Several months later, IHC received an inquiry from the office which previously had turned down the project as to how it was proceeding, and whether they might be of assistance, making it clear that time was of the essence. Reynolds Burgund, an IHC French-speaking development director, was sent at once to Zaire, completed contract and financing negotiations in record time, with the full support of the U.S. government, and returned to New York with a neat package ready to proceed. A few days later it was announced that a senior U.S. official was making a tour of certain African countries, among them Zaire. No doubt he would mention the IHC Kinshasa project in his public appearances.

In West Germany a corporation was created to provide structure for the IHC–Lufthansa (DLH) association. This entity, with chairmanship rotating between IHC and DLH, would review proposals brought by either party for joint development in West Germany, approve the selection of general managers for the German hotels, review the hotels' rate structures, and plan for growth opportunities. Lufthansa representatives, principally Dr. Guenter Berendt, a financial executive involved with all of Lufthansa's commercial, non-airline activities, worked with Eric Bleich on a comprehensive program of development.

A hotel administration company had been established in Hamburg by a group of local hoteliers with the purpose of developing a hotel in the city. Its activities actually had largely consisted of frustrating progress by any other entity interested in starting one, and accordingly this Hotels Verwaltungs Gesellschaft (hotel administration company) had acquired a nickname in Hamburg financial and property circles, *"Hotels Verhinderung Gesellschaft"* (hotel hindering company). Bleich had obtained agreement in principle for the city to back guarantee loans for an IHC hotel and proposed that Verwaltungs join with IHC in locating a suitable site. Gates, in Geneva at the time, enthusiastically supported the idea and made a special trip to Hamburg to meet the partners. Eventually a lakefront site was secured, Baron Rothschild joined with IHC, DLH, and the hoteliers as equity partners, and construction began.

DLH maintained its head office in Cologne and accordingly was anxious for a hotel to be built in that city. The only really ideal site, along the Rhine near the famous Gothic cathedral, was "not available for a hotel" according to the city (not many years later a hotel did open on this property) and a secondary location had to be accepted. No outside investors could be found, so IHC and DLH each financed 50 percent of the equity.

DLH was instrumental in introducing Dr. Horst Capelle, manager of the Düsseldorf-based Arenberg family enterprises, to IHC; his group took a 25 percent share, as did the Springer publishing interests – solicited by Bleich – in the Düsseldorf hotel which IHC had begun for its own account in 1966.

In Venezuela, the government was interested in privatizing some of the business assets which it had acquired over the years, reaching an agreement to sell its majority interest in the Tamanaco to IHC; a study was undertaken to further develop the site, which could easily accommodate a banqueting/conference center, additional bedrooms, and expanded recreational facilities. Elsewhere in South America, the Victoria Plaza lease expired in the absence of IHC's interest in a renewal.

In New Zealand, the Inter-Continental Auckland, owned by a publicly listed company and underwritten by IHC and a group of established New Zealand trading and manufacturing firms, opened in March 1968. Located on a hilltop adjacent to the university and commanding a spectacular harbor view, it was a strenuous, albeit short, climb up (or down) 40 degree pitched streets from/to the business center, a walk not suitable for the less than fully fit tourist. As a capital cost control measure, the guest rooms were not air conditioned although, strangely enough, the chillers for the public space had ample capacity for the entire structure. The financing package was loaded with debt and New Zealand was only just beginning to welcome international jet service (a DC–7 that operated twice a week between Auckland and Fiji up until only a short time before the hotel's opening was Pan Am's last piston-engine plane in international service). Here was a hotel ahead of its time in terms of demand, but behind its time in guest comfort and convenience. Despite an excellent catering and bars trade, the property was in serious financial difficulty from the outset, and eventually government support was required to stave off bankruptcy.

New Zealand's strict control on imports forced IHC to develop local suppliers for many essential furnishing items. If an essential product was absolutely unavailable, the treasury would issue an import license, but only after a withering examination. In one case – an order for two heavy-duty ice-makers – it was suggested that IHC bring in a sample, let a local equipment manufacturer take it apart and duplicate its design, and then ship the sample back. Aside from patent laws, this was a commercially ludicrous notion, and eventually the authorities relented. One local manufacturer of television cabinets refitted his factory to produce the hotel's bedroom case-goods

New Zealand. The Inter-Continental Auckland opened in 1968, but international jet services were only just beginning to reach the country and the hotel faced financial difficulties from the start.

(headboards, tables, desks, chairs, dressers). The excellent quality and attractive prices brought him future IHC orders for export outside New Zealand.

In Zambia, President Kaunda officiated at the openings of his country's hotels. The Lusaka property soon became the temporary residence of every important visitor to the country, and has hosted several international meetings of heads of state, the most remarkable, perhaps, a Commonwealth conference at which Elizabeth II presided. At the Musi-o-Tunya Inter-Continental (translation: the "cloud that thunders," a traditional African description of the Victoria Falls) man is always face to face with nature. Monkeys delighted in visiting guest rooms; a heavy, lumbering beast once immobilized itself when both front legs wound up in the swimming pool – the same principle as "ha-ha" ditches in English gardens. A tragedy occurred soon after the opening when a hippopotamus collided with a vehicle carrying the hotel's controller and housekeeper and crushed the gasoline tank, which burst into flames.

Pan Am introduced an employee stock purchase plan which, to satisfy U.S. regulations, was required to be offered also to all employees of every controlled subsidiary. The plan provided, among other details, for payroll deductions on which interim interest would be credited at a nominal rate of 2 or 3 percent from the date of the deduction until the date of the stock acquisition. Explaining this program to the employees of IHC's Thai subsidiary produced hoots of disbelieving laughter. The question of stock ownership aside, it was inconceivable that anyone would want to give his money to Pan Am, when any bank in Bangkok would pay 8 or 9 percent interest any day.

An introduction by the Morgan Bank to the Dutch owner of the Hotel Continental in Paris gave IHC the opportunity to acquire an impressive, though run-down, hotel building in the very heart of the city. Paul Sheeline, whose activities had been largely centered on finding solutions to the continuing cash flow problems in IHC's Vienna and Geneva properties, took charge of negotiations, which dragged on for months, finally reaching agreement at a purchase price of $8,000,000. Government loans at 1, 2 and 3 percent interest rates were available for financing rehabilitation and improvement expenditures for historic hotel buildings and Sheeline, fluent in French, negotiated a financial plan maximizing the use of these loans. Gates took the proposal to Trippe for approval. It would be IHC's largest single investment to date, and the first 100 percent owned property outside Latin America. Trippe was certain that at least $2 million more should be forthcoming in low-interest French government loans: "Tell Sheeline to go to General de Gaulle and tell him that Pan Am's order for twenty-eight more Fan Jet Falcons will not go ahead unless IHC gets the $2 million." (Pan Am at the time was the U.S. sales agent for these private jet aircraft built in France by Dassault, and maintained servicing facilities for the planes at stations around the world through its business jets division.)

Sheeline managed to secure an appointment with de Gaulle's *chef de cabinet* and, questioning his own nerve, did as Trippe had directed. Ask and ye shall receive, as they say; the additional credits were granted. Trippe announced his own retirement at the Pan Am annual meeting not long thereafter, keeping this decision a secret, even from his secretary, until the announcement day. Harold Gray succeeded him as chairman.

The closing on the Paris acquisition took place in the Netherlands while, in the city of Paris, student riots were shaking the nation and making one wonder whether this was really the place to have made such a large commitment. After careful negotiations, the hotel's long-term tenants, among them Janet Flanner who, under the byline Genet, wrote the "Letter From Paris" column in the *New Yorker*, vacated the premises, and the property was closed for rebuilding. Fred Peelen, recently departed from East Pakistan, was sent to Paris to be the IHC operations person at the takeover and to coordinate with Bechtel and others on the remodeling program.

Late in December the upside down Tahara'a Inter-Continental opened in Tahiti – "upside down" because the lobby and restaurants were on the top floor, with the guest rooms and bougainvillea-draped lanais on the floors below, clinging to the side of a cliff overlooking a black sand beach. It was originally to have been part of a joint airline program with UTA, but the French carrier had pulled out in midstream (to open another hotel on a lagoon close to the airport), leaving developer Joe Long and IHC to make up the shortfall. Long, a very successful businessman who had built a fortune from supermarket-style drugstores in California, also owned the Hotel Bora Bora which was an hour or so's journey by plane and motor launch from Tahiti. French Polynesia presented a great challenge in adapting to local cultures. One morning each week five flights – Pan Am, Qantas, Air New Zealand and two UTA – arrived within a few hours of each other. On other days two was the maximum and on one day there was none. But after the second week, no uniformed service staff appeared for work on the peak day. Explanation: that's the day when there's so much luggage to move and so many people crowded in the entrance lobby, it's better not to work.

Pan Am closed the year with earnings of $49.2 million and IHC at $1.636 million, both results negatively affected by civil unrest in Europe during much of the year.

Henry Ogden Barbour (Professor Barbour, as he was most frequently known) joined IHC as vice president – manpower development. Barbour, a Cornell graduate, had had a successful career in club management and was a regularly visiting adjunct professor at the Michigan State University Hotel School. He was a well-known culinarian and lectured frequently on wines and wine appreciation.

After an extensive tour of the system he began to develop a proactive training program for IHC, with concentration on management methods – particularly participative management and management by objective – and career growth. Huyot was anxious that as soon as possible all IHC general manager positions be filled by candidates from within the company, and that in the midterm this practice should apply to corporate positions as well. There should be two-way personnel motion as between hotel operations and head or regional office staff.

Hans Sternik was elected vice president – Middle East and Eastern Europe, and continued as general manager of the Phoenicia where he had succeeded Ernst Etter, who moved to Paris to take charge of the remodeled Inter-Continental Paris upon its reopening.

Düsseldorf, at the head of a grassy plaza leading to the Rhine, Managua, a pyramid-like structure reminiscent of a Mayan temple, and Kabul, a modern high-rise on a hilltop looking over the city, opened in 1969 adding 700 rooms to the group.

In the Philippines, shortly after the end of World War II, the Zobel-Ayala interests had begun a visionary long-term land development project for a large tract of land in Makati, a suburb of Manila, owned by the family. The Zobel-Ayalas had come from Spain in colonial times and were important leaders in a

OVERLEAF: The restored Inter-Continental Paris opened in 1969. It is popular for banquets, fashion shows and other events. The final negotiations for the property took place during the student riots of 1968.

variety of businesses in the Philippines including insurance, banking, and agriculture. The plan called for a complete new community of residential villages at differing economic levels; a complex of office towers; light manufacturing; retail and commercial centers; health and recreational facilities; parks, museums, and theaters; sports clubs; hotels; condominium apartment blocks; and an up-to-date, well-maintained infrastructure that would support and connect the various elements.

By 1966, Ayala was ready to start its first hotel project, a 400-room property designed by Leandro Locsin, a local architect, working with Bechtel which had been engaged by Ayala for project management and control. IHC had had non-conclusive preliminary discussions with Ayala many years earlier when Makati was still a gleam in a visionary eye. Bechtel brought the two together again and the property was being built to IHC's standards. A last-minute hitch developed when IHC attorneys pointed out that the lease signed two years earlier might prove to be unworkable in a few years time when a U.S.–Philippine treaty granting U.S. corporations pari passu rights with Philippine corporations would expire. An existing law made it illegal for foreign persons to engage in certain trades, among them the retail sale of food, and IHC as hotel tenant would surely be selling food. Potter was sent to Manila to find a solution. Hilton already operated a hotel in Manila under a management agreement, in which circumstances it acted as an agent for the owner, which was the legal seller of the food. This route was not available to IHC since not all of the shareholders of Mermac, the Ayala hotel landlord company, were Filippinos. The solution was for a new Ayala company, owned by Philippine nationals, to lease the hotel from Mermac, and hire IHC as manager under an operating and management agreement. The details were negotiated over a two-week period and new documents executed in good time.

The first lady of the Philippines, Imelda Marcos, cuts the opening ribbon at the Inter-Continental Manila. Looking on are Mrs. John Gates, Robert Huyot – president of Inter-Continental, John Gates – Inter-Continental chairman, and Ferdinand Marcos – president of the Republic of the Philippines.

President Ferdinand Marcos and first lady Imelda were the chief guests at the hotel inaugural, the social event of the year. The hotel was an instant success and was to be a consistent money earner, even in times of national crisis.

Early in Bob Smith's IHC career, he had thought of the World Bank as a likely source for capital. At a speech in the Waldorf-Astoria Martin Rosen, the executive vice president of International Finance Corporation (an agency of the World Bank formed to work with private enterprise in developing countries), explained IFC's policies to a large group of executives. He ended up with a list of investments IFC would not finance; "hotels or tourist projects around the world" was high on the list. After a visit to Kenya in the mid-1960s, and with the knowledge that Pan Am was planning a service to Nairobi, Smith felt that IFC might make an exception for Kenya. Here was a country whose chief, and perhaps only, easily developable export product was tourism. There was no other industry which could do so much for the economy in a relatively short period of time at a manageable level of capital investment.

Smith made his argument to Rosen, and won him over. But to

A Samburu woman in traditional dress.

IHC's Nairobi hotel opened in 1969.

change his board of directors' bias would be difficult, and the initial application for equity and loan participation in a Nairobi hotel project was turned down. By extending the scope of IHC's involvement to include investments in game park lodges, IFC participation was finally secured.

The Nairobi hotel opened on May 29 1969 with President Jomo Kenyatta cutting the ribbon. Fred Peelen was general manager.

Bob Huyot was combining his official duties with a honeymoon, which would also take him to Budapest for the opening of the Duna Inter-Continental. He had apparently forgotten his thermometer, and carelessly attempted to use the bidet in his suite without testing the water first. When he turned the valve steam shot forth, the result of a faulty plumbing connection, and he was taken forthwith to the local hospital for examination and treatment.

President Kenyatta of Kenya signs the golden book of the Inter-Continental Nairobi on the opening day as Robert Huyot, president of Inter-Continental, and Fred G. Peelen, the hotel's general manager, look on.

Gates, for all his charm on social occasions and unassailable business integrity, was not always the easiest man to work for or with. He and Bob Smith for some reason were never comfortable with each other. Gates set high standards for himself and did not feel it necessary to expect any less from his associates. Charlie Trippe, for one, could be extremely frustrated at Gates' handwritten notes in the margins of drafts prepared by Charlie, pointing out possible fallacies in his reasoning, or maybe just correcting a spelling error.

Gates always operated on a "need to know" basis, holding things close to his chest insofar as possible. In the spring of 1969 he asked Sheeline to let him know how much space IHC and Pan Am development occupied in the Pan Am building. "For what purpose?" "Just get me the numbers." Based on these figures Gates was negotiating an attractively priced lease in a new suburban office block near the rail station in Greenwich, Connecticut.

The move of IHC's head office was duly announced and IHC's architecture department given the building plans to lay out the new offices. The figures for IHC's Pan Am building space had been just that: the square feet devoted exclusively to IHC. They did not include corridors, passenger and freight elevator lobbies, reception areas, washrooms, copy machine locations, mailrooms, office and cleaning supply storerooms, or telephone switching rooms, all of which IHC shared with Pan Am departments on the various floors in which IHC had space. The newly leased space would be far less than needed. By this time the rest of the Greenwich building was fully rented, and the move was canceled a few months later.

The simmering anger of the partner banks in Vienna finally reached a boil early in 1969 as another winter's losses piled up. They believed that IHC, which had foregone any operator's share of profit and made loans as necessary, was not treating their concern with adequate seriousness. Finally one bank threatened to bankrupt the hotel owning company, an act easily committed under Austrian company law and one which would have called up government loan guarantees, and a potential political scandal. This time IHC offered to settle the matter with a buyout of their interests, at a price (about 45 percent of par) which was probably near to the carrying value on the

banks' books. After six months of protracted and uncomfortable negotiations, handled mostly by Dieter Spaethe, the deal was done. The finance ministry declined to sell its shares; it had a more positive long-term outlook. The following year the hotel turned the corner and earned a profit of $1,000,000!

During the Sternik years in Vienna, groundwork had been undertaken with the government to enhance the attractiveness of the city as a destination. A key element was to utilize the imperial palace – the Hofburg – as a congress center. An association of the city's hoteliers, with IHC as leading partner, was formed to negotiate with the government to take over the management and promotion of the palace's meeting and banqueting facilities for the benefit of all potential users. Shortly after Edmaier's promotion to general manager, these plans were brought to fruition, with the Inter-Continental Vienna as exclusive catering subcontractor to the hotelier association.

Lee Dayton retired in June of 1969. During his last years, he had concluded lease agreements and put together financing for hotels under construction in Istanbul, Teheran, and Colombo, and a franchise agreement with the Taj Mahal Hotel in Bombay. Levon Keenan resigned from the company shortly thereafter to join a tourist development organization in Hawaii.

The Inter-Continental Nairobi. This photograph was used in the hotel's brochure and in one of IHC's African Division advertisements.

In the third quarter of 1969 Pan Am suspended quarterly dividends after twenty-eight consecutive years of payouts to shareholders. The airline reported a $25.9 million dollar loss; IHC improved its profit to $2.33 million.

In 1968, Gates had directed Bob Smith to get personally involved in expanding IHC's base in South America, with Warren Pine to assist him. In less than eighteen months Smith, who preferred, and was better at, hands-on work in the field to paperwork in an office, firmed up deals for 1,500 rooms in five hotels: Cali and Medellin in Colombia, Valencia and Ciudad Guyana in Venezuela, and Rio de Janeiro in Brazil. The Reforma in Mexico City was sold.

YEARS OF GROWTH

In 1970 Najeeb Halaby succeeded Harold Gray as Pan Am chairman and chief executive officer. IHC hired Chisholm Maher as controller, Stanley Dziuban as vice president – technical services, and promoted Sergio Fieschi vice president – food and beverage, replacing Balas who was transferred to London as general manager designate of the Portman.

The Inter-Continental Medellin was opened by Colombian president Carlos Lleras Restrepo on May 3 1970, on an Andean hillside location above the city in a lush garden setting and temperate climate noted for the cultivation of orchids. The hotel was owned by a group of leading Colombian financial and property companies. Pan Am had made a peso investment for its own account.

At the joint urging of DLH and IHC, and with the jumbo jet era in mind, the Frankfurt owning company agreed to build a 300-guest-room tower on the north portion of the site near the IBM building, replacing a small shopping arcade. A tunnel would connect the two buildings. In order to induce the shareholders to accept a near doubling of the hotel's size, it was agreed that IHC, as tenant, would subordinate its share of the GOP to such extent as might be necessary to service the debt on the new wing and to assure a continued dividend, with this stand-aside recoverable from future earnings. As a result, for several years in the 1970s IHC would have limited earnings from the Frankfurt property; the additional amounts contributed under the stand-aside were eventually recovered in the 1980s and, of course, the value of the property was greatly increased by the addition.

Recognizing that the company was scheduled to add at least twenty hotels in a two-year period, and concerned as to the most efficient means for managing this level of growth for well into the future, Gates and Sheeline engaged Booz Allen & Hamilton, an internationally known management consulting firm, to study IHC's growth plan and recommend an organization structure that would be efficient, best utilize the company's existing talent, and delegate authority and responsibility wherever practicable, while maintaining fiscal control and product integrity.

Their recommendation: decentralize as much as possible the day-to-day management of the hotel business while continuing fiscal control, new business development and policy-making at the center. Division chief executives (DCEs) were to be named, responsible for a geographically contiguous group of hotels and operating from a central location within the area, ideally in an IHC hotel; the optimum number of hotels in a single division would be twenty to thirty. Each DCE would have staff, the number and type to be determined by the specific scope of responsibility, but generally each would have directors for sales and marketing, food and beverage, finance, personnel, and operations analysis. Within the framework of approved annual

Journalists' Day is celebrated every year at the Inter-Continental Medellin. A major event is "La Macarenita", a bullfight staged in the hotel's own ring in which local journalists take on young cows and cheer each other's style and bravery.

budgets, each DCE would have profit responsibility for the hotels in his division. A senior vice president – services, based in the head office, would coordinate support services for the entire IHC group where individual division needs would not justify full-time staffing – in such areas as housekeeping, front office, etc; and maintain and communicate procedures, manuals, and standards applicable throughout the chain. The head office food and beverage function would be primarily project design related. The DCE offices would interrelate with the development staff through the establishment of priorities, participation in new hotel survey and feasibility teams, preparation of new project earnings projections, and final sign-off on project fact-sheets which contained a detailed listing of all of the facilities and services to be built into a proposed hotel. The DCE and his staff would take responsibility, based on their in-depth knowledge of local conditions in the area, for the definition of a new hotel and for the earnings which it would produce. The development and technical services people would build it as directed, and turn it over for operation. In theory this put a tremendous amount of authority into the field together with a need for the division staff to become totally knowledgeable about the travel and hotel business in their areas. The appointed DCEs, with elected designations as senior vice presidents, were: Mario di Genova – Europe and Africa, based in Paris; Pete Sutherland – Latin America and Caribbean, based in Miami; Hans Sternik – Middle East and Central Asia, based in Beirut; and Kane Rufe – Far East and Pacific, based in Bangkok. John Carrodus was to be senior vice president – services, and Paul Sheeline became executive vice president – finance.

The operational management group in 1969 before effecting the first phase of Inter-Continental's decentralized organization structure. Seated: John Gates – chairman; Robert Huyot – president (right). Standing (left to right): Henry Beardsley – senior vice president, marketing; James Fox – director, technical services; Fred Eydt – controller; R. Kane Rufe – vice president, Far East; John Carrodus – vice president, South Pacific; Hans G. Sternik – vice president, Mid East; Peter Balas – vice president, food and beverage; Leo Riordan – regional director operations, Pakistan; Ernst Etter – vice president, Europe; Manuel Arriandiaga – vice president, Latin America; Henry Barbour – vice president manpower development; J.P. Sutherland – senior vice president operations, Latin America, Pacific, Asia; André Mas – regional director operations, Africa; Mario di Genova – senior vice president operations, Europe, Mid East, Africa.

In Germany, an opportunity arose to acquire the Vier Jahreszeiten (Four Seasons) Hotel in Munich. IHC and Lufthansa each took 25 percent of the equity and agreed that this property would be managed by the German Kempinski group, which owned the Atlantic in Hamburg and the Bristol Kempinski, which had become an IHC franchised member hotel in 1969, in Berlin. The Vier Jahreszeiten owned an adjacent parcel of land on which an addition would be constructed, and the original hotel would be completely remodeled and restored, with state-of-the-art technical systems, and a rooftop swimming pool.

The introduction of the 747 proved premature in terms of customer demand, and the cost of putting it into service exceeded expectations. Pan Am's 1970 loss increased to $45.5 million; IHC's profit came to $3 million.

In the first week of January 1971, John Gates relinquished his position as IHC chief executive and was transferred full time to Pan Am as senior vice president – corporate development. Robert

Huyot was named IHC chairman and Paul Sheeline president and chief executive officer. Gates had been at the IHC helm for eleven and a half years. Under his direction, and frequently with his indefatigable personal involvement, the organization had grown from a money-losing regional fifteen-hotel chain operating in eleven nations to a worldwide group of fifty properties in forty-one countries, with twenty-seven additional projects under construction in eleven lands. He was a man who had kept his distance and mostly kept communications to a minimum. Within the organization, many were in awe of him, some felt uncomfortable with him, and others could never figure out where they stood with him. All respected him.

Pan Am placed its senior vice president – finance, Richard Knight, senior vice president – marketing, James Leet, and Bob Smith on the IHC board, along with Sheeline, Huyot and Gates.

1971 was a major year for hotel openings: Kinshasa in Zaire, Cali in Colombia, Valencia and Ciudad Guyana in Venezuela; the Okura Amsterdam, a franchised hotel, in the Netherlands; Bucharest, a franchised property in Romania; Cologne in Germany; Helsinki in Finland; the Portman, IHC's first hotel in cooperation with BOAC, in London; and in Iran, hotels in Teheran, Shiraz and Persepolis, the latter two franchise properties opened in connection with the shah's gala 2,000-year imperial anniversary celebration.

The Cali property, opened by Colombian president Pastrana Borrero, was a project owned by local financial groups in which IHC had a small participation. Located in an Andean valley, the hotel became the center of the community and was enlarged twice, adding specialty restaurants and entertainment facilities. With the Venezuelan expansion, IHC would be represented in most of the nation's principal business centers. IHC's first United Kingdom property was a conversion of a twin tower originally planned as residential apartments (part of the site Bob Smith had tried to acquire more then ten years earlier). BOAC and IHC shared the equity in a 60:40 ratio. Initially the property was not fully identified with IHC; its official name was The Portman – a Pegasus/Inter-Continental Hotel, Pegasus being a brand which BOAC was planning to use worldwide. IHC's partner in Helsinki was Finnair, and the hotel had been partially financed from West Germany by the Frankfurter Bank. The Teheran partners included Prince Sadruddin Aga Khan and IHC at 25 percent each, with the Iran Development Bank and Department of Tourism owning the remainder.

The company introduced a structured program to assure uniform minimum standards of personal service throughout the group. Known internally as "the year of the satisfied guest" and supported with hotel-training materials and posters, the program offered prizes and rewards to the hotels in each division, based on their achievement and improvement in customer satisfaction as measured by three unannounced visits by incognito inspectors to each hotel over the period of the program. Each inspector completed an eighty-page questionnaire covering all aspects of guest service. In addition a consumer advertising campaign featured side-by-side photographs showing some element of personal service being performed the wrong way, and the Inter-Continental (right) way, with appropriate verbiage about the company's commitment to detail.

A DM11,000,000 line of credit was negotiated with the BHF Bank (formerly Frankfurter Bank) to finance IHC's equity investments in the DHL/IHC jointly promoted hotel projects. BOAC, suffering with other international carriers from the glut of 747 seats on the market, decided to curtail its hotel investment activities potentially terminating a development which had been begun with

IHC for a top-class London hotel on an unparalleled location at Hyde Park Corner. The McAlpine organization, which had recently built the Inn on the Park across Hamilton Place from the IHC site and was the owner of the Dorchester Hotel three blocks away on Park Lane, stepped into BOAC's position enabling the project to proceed. McAlpine and IHC would each own 50 percent; IHC would own the furnishings and lease the property.

During the BOAC partnership IHC had had difficulty in securing design approvals from the various authorities which controlled building permissions in this part of London, among them Her Majesty's Privy Council, representing Queen Elizabeth as owner of the hotel site which was being made available under a long-term land lease. Sir Frederick Gibberd, a specialist in town planning and formal gardens, had been appointed to the design commission for the British Airport Authorities and, working with BOAC, became aware of the hotel project. He was engaged to do a new design, it was submitted, and this time approvals were forthcoming. This meant the envelope of Gibberd's building design was inviolate and IHC's architects struggled to fit the programmed 500 rooms into the spaces. One result was that there were more than 200 different room sizes and layouts in the building. The completed hotel, like Paris, would contain some fifty very small single occupancy rooms, not unusual in older traditional European hotels but difficult to rent to the modern international business traveler. As part of the final financing, IHC as tenant would guarantee an annual minimum rent, the company's first such commitment since Ponce and San Juan.

The Brotherhood of Teamsters, the workers union which represented Pan Am's clerical and sales employees in the New York area, was in the midst of a negotiation with Pan Am and was attempting to organize comparable workers in IHC some of whom were sitting side by side with Pan Am employees in the development, technical services and reservations departments. When the negotiation came down to the line, Pan Am concurred with a Teamster enrollment of IHC's office staff. In time IHC would have to negotiate a separate contract covering most of the employees in the purchasing, sales, marketing and accounting departments, as well as secretarial staff.

Robert Strachan joined Inter-Continental as senior vice president – finance. He had been introduced to Sheeline by fellow University Club member Bob Smith. Strachan had been a partner in the Wall Street investment firm, Paine Webber, and had experience in international finance.

Pan Am's financial position precluded its future funding of IHC's capital growth needs. However, IHC's balance sheet and cash flow could support additional debt. With the assistance of Banque Privée (Baron Rothschild) and Lehman Brothers, Pan Am's principal investment bankers, an off-shore fifteen-year, $20,000,000 debenture issue, paying interest at 7 percent, convertible to Pan Am shares at $18.00, was underwritten. These funds, and its own earnings, would be IHC's only foreseeable financial growth engine for the years ahead. The terms of the offering placed certain balance sheet restrictions and financial discipline on the company in order to assure lenders of a preference position as to the company's assets vis-à-vis the shareholder. As a result, IHC's financial statement would have to be published for the debenture holders each year.

In October Bob Smith and John Gates resigned from the IHC board and announced their retirements from Pan Am, ending a combined twenty-eight years of service to, and association with, IHC.

The Halaby administration had concluded that Pan Am needed a new look, both in management style and in public product image. Elliot Noyes, a leading industrial designer – best known for

the IBM corporate identity with which he had been involved – was brought to Pan Am as a consultant along with equally famous graphic designers. The new look must be sleek and modern and reflect the latest design trends, and IHC did not escape their attention. The Paris hotel was a particular target of their discomfort: the Rôtisserie was "Disneyland." A modern typeface known as Helvetica, popular for directional signs in airports, replaced Pan Am's traditional logo. IHC was directed to reconstitute its logo and crest in a similar typeface; the laurel leaves were replaced by six circular "balls," three on each side. IHC's in-house and contract designers were indoctrinated as to the new consultants' design theories and preferences. Suggestions were made as to acceptable new interior designers to be engaged for new IHC properties, among them Terence Conran, who was hired to create the interiors for hotels in Ocho Rios and Kingston, Jamaica. Pan Am's VIP Frequent Traveler Clipper Clubs were redesigned (out with the clipper ship nautical look; in with seas of white uniform-height, rounded-edged molded plastic, blue-cushioned seats). Work was begun on repainting the aircraft in the new livery. Only the Pan Am latitudinal global crest remained.

IHC's twenty-fifth year's earnings for the year rose by 10 percent to $3.340 million. Pan Am's loss widened by a similar percentage to $48.4 million.

Sir Hugh Barton, retired head of the Hong Kong Jardines Group, who had been instrumental in building the Mandarin, had put together a group of European banking companies and five airlines including BOAC, BEA, and DLH, with a goal to finance and build large moderate-rate hotels in major European air-hub cities, this in response to the introduction of jumbo jets and the need to house travelers in the economy compartment who would not be interested in accommodation at IHC or Hilton price levels. The group's brand name would be Penta. For at least three years Huyot had believed that this market was ripe for IHC as well, but with a different brand name, and obviously different standards. DLH brought a Munich Penta project to the IHC/DLH partnership and IHC agreed to invest in and manage the property as part of its yet to be named "economy" class division. An employee contest was held to select a name; the winner, Bill Wilkinson, an operations analyst reporting to John Carrodus, put forth "Forum" – a name which, unbeknownst to him, had been considered and forgotten in one of the name searches of the early 1960s. (Penta concurrently built hotels in London and Paris in partnership with, and under the management of, Grand Metropolitan, a rapidly growing British hotel, restaurant, dairy, brewing, and spirits conglomerate.)

Potter, who had left IHC in 1969 to join a charter airline company, returned as vice president – food and beverage, reporting to Carrodus.

Sheeline, in his six years with IHC, had developed a reputation for fairness, scrupulous business integrity and fiscal conservatism. He was always available to his associates and was one of the few in the IHC executive suite who was comfortable with, and sought out, opposing viewpoints on controversial issues. From the first he did not hide his real lack of knowledge of the workings of hotels, but he made it his goal to learn, which means to listen and inquire. For a period Gates had given him supervision over the technical services group and he had developed a sympathy for their problems as well as a conviction as to their role as service providers in the big-picture goal of assuring profitable hotel operations. He was keenly anxious that interdepartmental communication be open and frequent, with as little memo writing as practicable. He convened a daily "morning meeting" of the senior executives shortly after the office opened, for open discussion of the current and immediate activities and problems facing each of them. Since busy travel schedules kept one or more officers away from New York on any given day, a deputy would attend in their stead. When Sheeline was away, he designated an individual to chair the meeting. Lasting anywhere from five to fifty minutes it was a signature feature of his management style.

Twice a year the DCEs would converge on New York – and later at overseas locations – for an intensive week-long review of company-wide policies, problems and strategies. This was the opportunity for the field – the side of the business which was responsible for income generation – to interact with the policy makers. Changes in company direction, priorities, organizational structure and personnel policy evolved primarily from these conferences. Sheeline bent over backward to consult with all affected factions before taking policy decisions. He didn't want surprises; others should be spared them as well.

Early in 1972, Halaby resigned as Pan Am chairman to be replaced by William Seawell, a retired air force general, who had been running the Rolls-Royce engineering business in the United States. The "new" IHC logo and crest were discarded almost before they had had a chance to appear.

The Civil Aeronautics Board (CAB), the U.S. air regulatory body, had decided to review the U.S. air route structure for the Central and South Pacific. Pan Am, long the dominant carrier, wished to strengthen its long-haul routes with a local service program interconnecting island groups from the Marianas to Polynesia to Melanesia with hubs in Guam, Honolulu and American Samoa. Pan Am's case would be helped by a concurrent IHC commitment to hotel development in the area. For the first time, IHC was being permitted, even urged, to find projects in the United States, in Hawaii, where a full-time development officer was engaged.

The Okura membership agreement expired in 1972 and to maintain a position in Tokyo IHC negotiated a new franchise

with the Keio Plaza – Japan's and Asia's tallest hotel building, erected in the entertainment, shopping, and passenger rail exchange center of Shinjuku, at some distance from the traditional city center. Except for the forty-seven-story hotel, no nearby building was taller than 60 meters. IHC's compensation was to be based on foreign room nights generated at the hotel; Pan Am moved its aircrews, more than 125 rooms a night, into the hotel. The hotel developers took a gamble and won; the Tokyo city administration made Shinjuku its headquarters and skyscraping office towers, and finally other hotels, followed suit.

The Keio Plaza Inter-Continental, Tokyo, was forty-seven stories high and, in 1972, the tallest hotel building in Japan and Asia.

Hamburg and Helsinki opened within a few days of each other, and the Taj Mahal in Bombay completed construction of its new Inter-Continental tower wing and restoration of its historic older section, reopening as a franchised member of IHC. The Lee Gardens, a Hong Kong hotel in a market niche below the Mandarin, became a new franchised operation and was later branded as Forum. The Okoume Palace Inter-Continental opened in Libreville, Gabon, the first of what was supposed to be a group of "Hotafric" properties under a cooperation with UTA, the Franco-African consortium airline.

In June 1972 Huyot reached retirement age. He had made an indelible impact on IHC in matters of enhanced and defined product and service standards and analytical operational analysis. The hotel operating side of IHC was staffed with talented people at every level gaining experience worldwide, whose careers were being nurtured by the company. IHC was a known and respected product not only in the developing third world of its early years, but now poised to emerge as a leader in Europe where Hilton, the principal worldwide competitor, was already well established.

With Huyot's retirement, Sheeline felt the need of a professional hotelier in New York to supervise day-to-day worldwide operations of the chain. In September, after conducting an outside talent search, he concurred with the executive search consultant's recommendation, and named Hans Sternik executive vice president and chief operating officer of Inter-Continental.

Edward Trippe, younger brother of Charlie, had joined the development department in 1969. After completing studies at Yale, Oxford, and Harvard, he had spent two years with the airline, most of that time in Saigon, as a contracts officer. Hong Kong was an IHC high priority destination and, with the Mandarin by then fully established in its market, it was unlikely that the owners would renew the membership agreement when it expired. Jerry O'Donnell, who had been Pan Am's vice president – sales for the Pacific for many years, and was currently the head of the Hong Kong Tourist Promotion Board, introduced Trippe to Trammel Crow. Crow was a leading Dallas-based property developer who had just paid a record HK$25,000,000 for a site close to the

To promote travel to Hungary, the Duna Inter-Continental Budapest organized culinary and cultural festivals in several Inter-Continentals in the early 1970s. The first was in Hamburg, where Fritz and Agnes Haerlin, owners of the Vier Jahreszeiten and investors in the Inter-Continental, celebrated their thirtieth wedding anniversary accompanied by the Duna's strolling musicians. Rudy Muenster, general manager of the Inter-Continental franchised Bristol Kempinski in Berlin (left) and Fred G. Peelen, Inter-Continental general manager (standing), join the celebration.

waterfront on the Kowloon side of the harbor, on which he would build a large retail center podium with a hotel above. Agreement was reached on a TSA and operating contract; Hutchinsons, an old-line British trading and property company, would take 50 percent of the equity with IHC and Crow at 25 percent each; Citibank would provide the debt. Elliot Noyes visited the site and found the design pedestrian; he could not come to grips with its retail intensive aspects. The project died, however, with Crow's request for an up-front $1 million development fee from IHC, an amount which, at the time, Sheeline felt IHC could not justify, particularly since it was apparently not contingent on the project's going ahead. Within weeks, Sheraton stepped into IHC's place.

Determining annual bonuses for general managers had been an entirely subjective exercise, with a lack of consistency between the operating divisions. Barbour was conducting a "management by objectives" seminar program throughout the group and as a logical extension he developed a structured incentive compensation plan which would clearly define the possible scope of awards (0–30 percent of annual salary), require the establishment of annual goals (financial, quality, personnel, or whatever was most pertinent to a given property's needs) quantifiable wherever possible, permit the DCE some discretion (for example: reward a valiant effort in the face of unpredictable economic woes, or alternately reduce an award if outside influences, not under management's control, were the real cause of extraordinarily increased profits), and set dates for bonus payments. The plan was approved for implementation in 1972.

An offer from the Jury's Hotel group to acquire both the leases and owning company shares of the Irish hotels was accepted by IHC and ended the company's operations in that country, while recording a modest gain on the transaction.

In Hanover, at the first DCE semi-annual conference held away from the head office, Ernst Etter was honored at a retirement dinner attended by all of IHC's officers. After his IHC retirement he worked for a short time as manager of the Meridien in Paris, eventually retiring to Luzern.

IHC operating results, particularly in Europe, were behind plan for 1972 and salary levels for IHC officers were frozen. IHC's profit fell to $3 million while Pan Am was losing $29 million.

Late in 1972 Mario di Genova resigned and was succeeded as DCE in January 1973 by Peter Balas, who at this time was general manager of the Inter-Continental Paris, having switched positions with George Markides (formerly in Curaçao, and opening general manager in Manila) now at the Portman. Balas' division would consist of Europe and the Middle East. Central Asia was added to the Far East/Pacific Division.

DLH was showing signs of discontent with certain aspects of the IHC relationship. Hanover was continuing to produce losses and in DLH's judgment Bechtel's performance as IHC's designated project manager at the two Munich properties had been below par. IHC repurchased the DLH shares in Hanover, and arranged for strengthening project supervision on all the German properties. Additional capital calls were required to cover operating losses in Cologne and Munich.

United Airlines, owner of the Westin Hotel chain, was in a loss position similar to that of Pan Am. Spurred by conversations at airline chairman level, Westin and IHC entered into exploratory discussions to determine whether there might be some opportunity for an association between the two groups. Westin was strong in the United States, particularly in the middle west and west coast, and Central America, and had notions of expansion to Europe and Asia. IHC was unrepresented in nearly all of Westin's locations. A tentative program was sketched out whereby Westin's San Francisco and Los Angeles (or New York) hotels and the Paris and Frankfurt Inter-Continentals would be somehow marketed together, with each side taking bookings for the other. If there were positive results, then the relationship could be expanded.

Inter-Continental Colombo and Munich Penta opened in 1973. The former was a project financed by government and private interests, the first modern high-rise hotel in Sri Lanka. The latter was IHC's first significant entry into the Forum market, albeit with another company's trade name. Prime Minister Sirimavo Bandaranaike cut the Colombo ribbon. The Penta's capital and operating costs had been kept at reasonable levels by siting the hotel in a lower-land-cost, secondary neighborhood (which was nevertheless only two stops on Europe's most modern underground rail system from the heart of the city) and limiting the property's dining and other public facilities and guest services to the minimum required by guests paying a room rate 30–40 percent lower than that of a typical IHC hotel. Room service, for example, was limited to a complimentary

OVERLEAF: A window-cleaner at the top of San Francisco's Hotel Mark Hopkins in 1939 when the cocktail lounge with its panoramic view first opened. IHC negotiated an agreement to manage the hotel and it was renamed the Mark Hopkins Inter-Continental in 1973.

Continental breakfast box hung on the doorknob, and the contents of an automated in-room refrigerator, bar, and coffee heater which produced a record of consumption at the front office cashier; the system, provided by "Bell Captain," also included a room-status control mechanism.

A negotiation with a Honolulu developer culminated in a management contract for IHC to assume operation of the well-known Hotel Mark Hopkins, atop Nob Hill in San Francisco. The property was very much in need of a facelift and had been operated unsuccessfully by Regent. The developer's group was prepared to undertake a major rehabilitation, which eventually required partial funding from Inter-Continental. John Carrodus was transferred from the head office to be vice president and general manager of IHC's first hotel in the United States. The addition of this property ended the discussions with Westin.

In October 1973 another Arab–Israeli conflict brought war to the Middle East. It was a month before a truce was negotiated but a major result was the slowing in the flow, and consequent jump in price, of oil from the Middle East. The oil embargo lingered for several months; the cost of jet fuel for aircraft skyrocketed and international travel slumped in the fourth quarter on many routes. Pan Am's annual loss narrowed to $18.4 million; IHC's profit rose to $4.3 million.

Alex Furrer, a Swiss hotelier who had been in charge of the Inter-Continentals in Pakistan and had worked in Africa for much of his career, was elected senior vice president – operations and became DCE for Africa. Hans Sternik was named president of IHC.

To fill a void in Hong Kong, Ed Trippe negotiated a hybrid type of management services agreement for the Furama Hotel. A new 570-room, centrally located skyscraper with several dining facilities and bars as well as a rooftop revolving restaurant, the hotel was doing poorly and had an image as a downmarket tourist property. The personnel, purchasing, and accounting functions remained under the direct control of the owning company. IHC was responsible for other aspects of the operation, and would be compensated at a predetermined percentage of gross revenues. Despite a very modest room product, the hotel was competing head to head with the well established Hong Kong Hilton within two years.

Indonesia was to host the annual conference of the Pacific Area Travel Association (PATA) in the spring of 1974. To accommodate this event and its workshop, Hotel Indonesia and Hotel Bali Beach were to be enlarged under IHC TSAs. A new Jakarta hotel, to be built from the skeleton of a project known as Hotel Banteng which had been begun and abandoned in the early 1960s, was urgently required for PATA. Inter-Continental and other hotel groups had tried and failed in the late 1960s to put together a viable financing plan for the hotel. After interesting Cicofrance, a French construction company with major French government backing (which had just completed a large power generation project in Indonesia), and the IFC, IHC was successful in bringing these participants and the Indonesian government together to form a company to proceed with the project – now to be a 675-room hotel with the largest meeting and banqueting facilities in Indonesia, set in a lush 23-acre garden with pool, squash, and tennis facilities. IFC had insisted that IHC's management fees be subordinated to debt service. As the opening date drew near, it was clear that most of the furnishings would be arriving by sea and air at the last moment. With twenty-nine ships in the harbor containing IHC goods, permission was received to set up a branch customs station in the hotel's carpark, permitting all goods to be brought from port or air base direct to the site. The hotel was to be called Borobudur Inter-Continental, named for the eighth-century Buddhist monument in central Java.

Lance Brokenshire had been hired by Bechtel as project accountant for construction of the Melbourne Southern Cross, and he had moved to the controller's position with the opening of the hotel. Carrodus had appointed him resident manager; for six months he was acting general manager in Auckland, returning to Melbourne as general manager when Carrodus moved to New York. One of his many crises as general manager during the final days before the Borobudur opening was caused by the arrival of 10,000 frozen chickens, ten tons in all. Half had originally been ordered for Hotel Indonesia, which had changed its mind while the shipment was on the sea. The chickens, together with several cases of #10 cans of frozen orange juice, were being offloaded, box by box, from trucks into the hotel freezer by a human hand-to-hand "bucket brigade," when the Cicofrance engineer happened to ask what was going on. He was aghast to hear that some 17 tons of food was about to be placed on a concrete slab never intended for such weight, and an emergency construction gang overnight began building steel and concrete support columns and beams.

All the IHC general managers attending the PATA conference were put to work. Graham Jeffrey from Manila manned the front desk along with David Thorn, then the IHC director – front office. President Suharto officially opened five new hotel facilities simultaneously from the palace and then went on to visit each of them personally.

During an early inspection it was discovered that the contractor had ignored IHC's standards and used plywood for corridor ceilings, failed to extend fire walls between rooms from slab to slab, and disregarded other safety precautions. The contractor who built the boiler flue had run out of fireproof cement, and used ordinary mortar between bricks. One night Brokenshire, in bed with a fever, was awakened with a report that bricks had broken through the wall of the third-floor kitchen. Apparently bricks had started falling from high in the building and had piled up in the flue from the below-ground floor up to the fourth. The engineer on duty had quickly shut off the boiler. There was no hot water; laundry was sent to Hotel Indonesia. While a temporary flue was built up the outside wall of the building, guests were advised that the hotel was "experiencing a temporary problem and may not have hot water for several days. Please bear with us . . . We hope to restore full service soon." Construction workers remained in the hotel doing corrective work on these various problems for many months. In its first year the property achieved a 77 percent occupancy. Over the years it has been one of the most profitable in the group.

The hotel was to include a Japanese restaurant. Potter had negotiated with the Keio Plaza for them to plan the restaurant, provide training and assign key personnel to open and supervise the operation of "Keio Restaurant," for which services a franchise fee would be paid.

When Hans Sternik arrived for the inauguration he was impressed at the complete line of top-quality internal promotional pieces already in place throughout the building. Ray Hall, their Australian creator, had been assigned the task by Terry Hill, now division vice president – marketing. Sternik soon arranged for Hall to create a manual, complete with artwork photostats and instructions, for sign and poster board construction, which would be distributed throughout the chain, thereby upgrading, and establishing a uniform look for, internal selling graphics in IHC hotels.

Pan Am and Gulf Oil had formed a joint venture to develop a chain of motel-type properties in Europe, to rival the successful Esso Motor Hotels operation. A prototype was developed, and construction was ready to begin on a 160-room property on the outskirts of Wiesbaden, near Frankfurt; a site option in Aberdeen, Scotland, was also in hand. Gulf decided to drop the program and

Pan Am offered to sell the company (named Arcadia) to IHC, promising to reimburse IHC if the assets were a total loss. Aberdeen was scratched; Wiesbaden was completed and opened as a Forum Hotel in 1974. To be viable, it had to be operated as a family-run type of establishment.

Two 500-room resorts opened in the western hemisphere – in Rio de Janeiro, Brazil, and Montego Bay, Jamaica. Economic conditions in the latter country were in serious decline following the election of a leftist, populist government which seemed to find greater affinity with Castro's Cuba than with Jamaica's traditional trading and cultural partners. The Rose Hall Inter-Continental Hotel and Golf Club was the first of what were to have been three major IHC hotels in Jamaica: a resort property in Ocho Rios and a city business travelers hotel in the capital, Kingston, were

scheduled to open in 1975. Tourism was collapsing, Pan Am had discontinued service, and the outlook was grim. In Rio, the hotel was in a developing area of the city facing the Gavea Beach, with extensive recreational facilities – including a golf course – on the hotel premises or nearby. It took more than a year to begin building up acceptable occupancies. In both hotels, the general managers were replaced shortly after opening.

In Lebanon, the small Emir du Liban palace at Beit-Eddin, which had been the scene of the *"Bal des Petits Lits Blancs"* in 1964, became an operating dependency of the Phoenicia.

In eastern Europe, the Inter-Continental Prague and the Forum Warsaw opened their doors.

Skanska Cement, a Swedish firm based in Malmo, had built the Warsaw Forum Hotel and was working on the Victoria Inter-Continental in the same city. They had developed a good working relationship in

the socialist-bloc countries to which they brought and taught the latest construction skills and techniques, with large crews of overseas workers. Having worked with Dick Smith on the Warsaw hotel under the IHC TSA, they were anxious to avail themselves of the company's architectural design talent for three projects in the USSR. A unique TSA was concluded, the first for hotels with which there might not be any official Inter-Continental connection.

As support for Pan Am's Pacific Island local service route case which was proceeding before the Civil Aviation Board, IHC had contracted with Trammel Crow to work on a series of native-style 150- to 200-room resorts which he would finance, own, and operate under an IHC franchise in locations in Fiji, the New Hebrides, New Caledonia, Western Samoa, the Cook Islands, the Solomon Islands, and Tonga. To be identified as Inter-Continental Island Inns, they would pay a nominal fixed base franchise fee to IHC plus a percentage of sales at an escalating scale of rates based on achieved occupancy. The first property in Port Vila, New Hebrides, opened in 1975.

Joseph Smyth had joined IHC in 1972 from TWA, as vice president – marketing development. A Harvard Business School graduate, he had worked on airline accounts with major advertising

agencies. During his first years he had analyzed IHC's existing and potential customer base and concluded that the company should target its marketing effort on the frequent international business traveler. This meant identifying these individuals, communicating with them, and influencing them to choose IHC as their preferred hotel group. Using Pan Am's Clipper Club, and access to American Express mailing lists (through the cooperative promotion program which Amex offered to companies accepting its credit cards), IHC began to compile a data base of people who could be documented as spending more than, say, twenty nights a year in international hotels. Cooperation with other airlines identified additional potential clients. A few years earlier, as a sort of VIP recognition device, IHC had created its Six Continents Club. Smyth turned the club into a structured vehicle for frequent traveler recognition. With no computer-based data available from the hotels, it was not an easy job. He set rigorous targets and began a company-wide awareness of the importance of this market segment. With limited budgets for consumer advertising, Smyth selected a medium which all but guaranteed that IHC's message would get to the target market: airline in-flight magazines. Some years later exclusive contracts were made through In Flight, the airline servicing company, for IHC two-minute video segments to be shown in the World-on-Parade trailer which preceded each film on most of the world's airlines' international flights.

At the Dubai Inter-Continental, the coffee shop comes to you.

**Inter·Continental Hotels.
A World of Difference.**

At the Dubai Inter·Continental, a cup of coffee becomes more than a cup of coffee. It's an ancient Arab tradition served with warmth, ceremony and style. In addition to the exceptional facilities you'll find at all Inter·Continental Hotels — more than 70 around the world — each of our hotels offers something unique and distinctly its own. At the Inter·Continental London, you can watch the Household Cavalry parade right past your bedroom window. Inter·Continental gives you a world of difference. To the experienced traveller, it makes all the difference in the world.

❶ INTER·CONTINENTAL HOTELS
When you've seen one, you haven't seen them all.

Eleanor Leslie, a Goucher alumna, had worked as an IHC telephone reservations agent in the late 1950s in Long Island City.

For several years IHC advertising featured individual employees from every part of the world, reflecting the company's international scope and differing local traditions applied to some aspect of exceptional service.

She had been brought into the marketing group and, under Beardsley's direction, had eventually taken responsibility for design and approval of marketing promotional pieces (brochures, fact books, etc.) and coordination with J. Walter Thompson. Amplifying the message of the uniqueness of each Inter-Continental Hotel, as well as the relationship of each to its local environment, the signature line "When you've seen one you haven't seen them all" was developed and used as a basis for a full-color consumer advertising campaign that used photography specifically typical of the geographical region being featured in the advertisement. Over the years this line metamorphosed to "A world of difference," with pictures of hotels and hotel employees at work, and other variations on the same theme.

Through cooperation with Pan Am and Lufthansa, Smyth arranged in-flight passenger surveys to ascertain customer travel and hotel preferences. Everyone was happily surprised to learn that IHC was held in high regard among those who were familiar with the product, many of whom indicated their intention to use the chain in the future; the general recognition level among all travelers was, sadly, below that of Hilton, the principal competitor.

In June 1974 Hank Beardsley reached retirement age, and Joe Smyth succeeded him as senior vice president – marketing.

For many Inter-Continental hotels, incentive travel operations had become a major source of business. Vienna, Budapest, Geneva, Helsinki, Tahiti, and Auckland, among others, had succeeded in preparing tourist packages which attracted back-to-back 160 to 180 person charter groups for three to four months each year.

When Pakistan's first direct nationwide elections were conducted in 1971, supporters of Mujib-Ur-Rahman, the Bengali leader of East Pakistan, won a majority. Many leaders of West Pakistan, and the army, would not accept him as national leader. Protests in the East wing led to suppression and a war in which India involved itself against the Pakistan military, resulting in the break-up of Pakistan and the creation of a separate nation, Bangladesh, by 1972. IHC's investment in and operation of the Dacca hotel were revalidated shortly after independence. Yusuf Haroon was one West Pakistan leader who had supported the result of the election and he became unwelcome in the Pakistan of Zulfikar Ali Bhutto. He took up residence in New York and, as a continuing friend of IHC, was asked by Sheeline whether he would like to join the company to work in hotel development. As vice president – development he was head of the department by 1974.

Pan Am advised that the current energy crisis – jet fuel prices had doubled over 1973 – precluded any further investments or advances from them to IHC. Since IHC's known commitments would use all of the company's available funds, credit lines, and anticipated short-term cash flow, no investment in new hotels could be considered for the foreseeable future. Haroon and his development officers would have to find hotel owners who wanted IHC's services but not its cash. Consideration would be given to disposing of such assets as IHC's equity in the hotels in Caracas, Teheran, and Paris, and the Portman in London, subject to negotiating long-term management agreements on each property.

Pan Am's 1974 loss leaped to $81.8 million. IHC reported a profit of $2.3 million, for the first time including adjustments for equity accounting: the company's share of the profits or losses of subsidiaries in which it owned between 20 percent and 50 percent of the equity would be combined with its other income and expenses in calculating net profit. Since all of IHC's West German investments were greater than the 20 percent threshold, and most of the hotels there were still recording losses, this change in accounting treatment would have a negative effect on net profit. IHC's accounting had always been very conservative, in any case, providing reserves for any income which was not being promptly and regularly remitted – a frequent occurrence in some developing countries.

During 1974 and 1975, thirteen hotels would open including Ocho Rios in the Caribbean; the Victoria Inter-Continental Warsaw and Inter-Continental Zagreb in eastern Europe; and the franchised Khyber Inter-Continental in Peshawar, Pakistan.

Yusuf Haroon had made agreements for IHC to lease two deluxe hotels being constructed in

Riyadh and Mecca by the government of Saudi Arabia. Both featured extraordinary, if not particularly efficient, architectural designs (in one there was no direct connection between the kitchen and dining room, except across the lobby, a feature which was corrected under IHC's TSA), that had been created in response to an international design competition. Trevor Dannatt (United Kingdom) and Rolf Gutbrod (West Germany) were the winners for Mecca and Riyadh respectively. Both properties incorporated extensive conference facilities.

General manager in Riyadh was Raymond Khalifé. Shortly after the opening of the Phoenicia, Lambert had hired him and put him in a specifically designed training apprenticeship in the hotel.

In the course of the program he was assistant food and beverage manager, assistant front office manager, and then front office manager. In 1968 Siegfried Beil was passing through Beirut interviewing possible candidates for executive assistant manager in Bali and selected him. Two years later Khalifé moved to Jakarta as resident manager to general manager Leo Riordan who had been transferred from Pakistan. (On the second day after Riordan's arrival in Jakarta he is reported to have asked his most senior assistant how many employees there were in the hotel. "You have 1,858, sir." "Wrong! You have 1,857; I have one: you.") After eighteen months Khalifé was transferred back to Beirut as manager, and given responsibility for settling certain labor problems in the hotel.

Raymond Khalifé, above, area president – Middle East and Africa, and right, in 1963 as a management trainee at the Phoenicia Intercontinental Beirut.

The Riyadh hotel was packed from its opening day; it was the only top quality hotel in the city. Anyone wishing to do business in the kingdom had to negotiate in the capital. *Fortune* magazine described it as the most difficult place in the world in which to get a room. Many important international deals were sealed in the hotel's lobby.

OPPOSITE: The Riyadh Inter-Continental, Saudi Arabia, opened in 1975.

A training school was established to interest Saudi graduates in the hotel trade as a profession and a Cornell professor and several department heads went to the universities looking for candidates. Of the eighty original trainees, twenty graduated and two eventually became general managers of IHC-managed facilities in Saudi Arabia.

In Abidjan, Mayer's plan for an African Riviera was falling into place. The Hotel Ivoire had been twice enlarged to 750 rooms and a state-of-the-art congress center had been opened. A theater, ice-skating rink, shopping center, bowling alley, and expanded recreation facilities made the hotel complex a mini-city. A few kilometers up the lagoon the Forum Golf Hotel, a resort-oriented property, was to open in 1975. Plans were in place for a major golf facility.

In Istanbul a hotel which had taken more than six years to build finally opened in what was to prove a difficult location facing Taksim Square. General manager Rudy Richter introduced a practice of sending specially decorated cakes to embassies on the occasion of their national days. The pastry chef had an (apparently out-of-date) chart showing the flags of the United Nations member nations. They were surprised when the Chinese embassy returned its cake – until someone realized that the Nationalists' flag (from Taiwan) had been incorporated into the decoration.

The Saipan Beach Inter-Continental Island Inn had its genesis in a Pan Am competition with Continental Airlines for a route connecting Saipan and Tokyo. Ed Trippe had formed an owning

company involving Keio Plaza, Japan Travel Bureau (one of Japan's largest travel and tour operators), IHC and local Saipan citizens who contributed the site, but it was impossible to secure debt on acceptable terms. Pan Am finally agreed to guarantee the debt or, alternately, provide the funds itself and with a very tight capital budget, the project went ahead. The route was awarded to Pan Am but the award was overturned and the case reopened; Continental (which had built an attractive first-class hotel of its own next door to IHC) was ultimately the winner. John O'Shea transferred from the Tahara'a in Tahiti to be its general manager.

The Inter-Continental Maui was the first hotel to be opened in the Wailea development on the Hawaiian island's south shore. It was also the first Inter-Continental to open with a computerized guest reservations and receivables system. One important strategic goal was to develop a personnel program which would create a working environment that would make employees feel union representation to be unnecessary. Under a plan called the "Strawberry" program, everyone who worked for the hotel was to be invited to check in and spend a night utilizing all of its services so that he or she could understand the typical guest experience and appreciate how his or her job contributed to that experience.

The Inter-Continental London at Hyde Park Corner was a very special hotel. IHC had what appeared to be a stiff minimum rent to be covered. The hotel's capital cost was among the highest of any in which IHC had an equity investment at risk. At Sheeline's personal urging, general managers in IHC locations with significant outbound travel to the United Kingdom were to send letters to their hotels' best customers introducing them to the London Inter-Continental and its general manager, Graham Jeffrey. Jeffrey had joined IHC from the River Club, a top-quality social club in an apartment block overlooking New York's East River, which was especially known for its outstanding catering department. His first posting with IHC was in Rawalpindi. This was followed by Pago Pago, and later Manila where he was in charge when the hotel's "Where Else?" disco was opened and became the leading young adult entertainment spot in the city. He had also been involved in a bizarre incident involving the mayor of Makati who considered an attempt by the hotel to collect his overdue restaurant account to be an affront to his honor, and attempted twice to have Jeffrey jailed on some trumped-up technical violation by the hotel. He almost succeeded in preventing the Jeffreys' timely departure for London, but relented at the last minute. Jeffrey had attended Columbia University as an IHC scholar.

The London hotel is built on a site formerly occupied by two residences, one of which had been the private home, in the early 1930s, of the Duke of York, later to become George VI when his older brother abdicated. In the late 1960s squatters had occupied one of the houses which had been been severely damaged during the bombing in World War II and was derelict. To protect themselves, they had destroyed the entrance steps; if anyone wanted – and was granted – admittance a door was thrown down over the gap like a drawbridge and then pulled back in again denying entry to the unwanted. These residents had to be removed before construction could start. On the appointed day a police commissioner and two assistants stood before the building and addressed its occupants with a bullhorn, asking them to let him and his men come in to discuss a peaceful relocation. It seems that three police did not look particularly threatening to the squatters. However, unbeknownst to them, everyone out in the street who was seemingly going about his business was a policeman in disguise. Delivery trucks apparently delivering food and grog to a club up the street were crammed with riot police. Dustmen, window washers, post men, delivery boys . . .

all wore police uniforms under their unexceptional work clothes. When the drawbridge went down, the police went into action and stormed the house; it was all over in minutes.

The opening day ceremonies were presided over by Sir Gerald Glover, solicitor for McAlpine, and chairman of the owning company. Guest of honor was the Duke of Wellington, the hotel's neighbor at Apsley House across Park Lane, who had also participated in laying the cornerstone of, and topping off, the hotel. He commented that it "would be handy for breakfast."

Through a carefully laid plan of public relations, organized by Mary Gunther (who had developed excellent connections in London society from her years at Harrods and Liberty department stores), the hotel was early on able to host a wide variety of benefits and charity parties which served to bring London's leaders into the property. A superior banqueting product and a fine restaurant positioned the Inter-Continental in the forefront of London's hotels almost from the beginning. Sheeline need not have worried about the minimum rent; earning it was never a problem.

A porter welcomes guests at the Inter-Continental London. Opened in 1975, the hotel is on the site of a building that was once the home of the Duke of York, later George VI of England.

Abdul Rahim Galadari, a prosperous Persian Gulf trader resident in Dubai and a long-time Haroon associate (he had grown up in Karachi in a house rented to his family by the Haroons), had decided to build a new hotel, the first really modern one, in Dubai on a choice site across from the Creek, the sheikdom's traditional port. He had been put in contact with IHC, concluded a TSA and management contract and was ready to open the hotel in 1975. It had already been increased in size to 330 rooms during construction when it became clear that demand was sufficient to support a greater number of rooms than in the original plan. Patrick Board, a Britisher who had worked for IHC in Dublin (banquet sales manager), Amman (food and beverage manager), Pakistan (executive assistant manager, Rawalpindi), Paris (executive assistant manager in charge of food and beverage), Accra (general manager), New York (assistant to senior vice president di Genova), Paris (assistant to division chief executive di Genova), Pakistan (general manager – Lahore) and Kinshasa (general manager), was its general manager. The hotel was an instant success and amortized its debt in record time. It was not until 1978 that the hotel would need a sales department. It is probably the variety, quality, and up-to-dateness of its food and beverage outlets that have enabled the Dubai Inter-Continental to maintain its competitive position, despite the opening of other, in some respects more luxurious, international properties in the sheikdom.

Hans G. Sternik, president Inter-Continental Hotels Corporation, Graham Jeffrey, general manager, and Max Blouet, managing director, welcome the Duke and Duchess of Wellington to the opening of the Inter-Continental, London, on September 23 1975.

When it was new, and the only luxury hotel in the city, it was somewhat elite and intimidating to many local residents. One young man, very casually dressed, was walking along the Creek and thought he might have a look and a cool drink inside. The splendidly dressed doorman, after looking him up and down, politely but very firmly turned him away. The doorman has no doubt retired; the young United Arab Emirates national, Ahmed Ramdan, undertook a career in the hotel trade and would become the hotel's general manager in 1991.

The luxurious Inter-Continental London was chosen for United Press International's 16th Annual Conference of Editors and Publishers. Among the prominent speakers were the Rt. Hon. Mrs. Margaret Thatcher, leader of the Conservative Party, and Paul C. Sheeline, chairman of the board of Inter-Continental Hotels Corporation.

In Venezuela, in the wake of rumors of possible official moves to exclude foreign shareholdings in some of the country's industries, IHC took advantage of an opportunity to sell its majority position in the Tamanaco to a Venezuelan banking group, while continuing to manage the property. The funds from the sale would, hopefully, be available for growth.

During 1975 Jim Hynes was named vice president – personnel and manpower development (Barbour had left to become chief executive of the Culinary Institute of America, the premier training academy for chefs in North America); Peter Hothorn, vice president – food and beverage;

Victor Newman, vice president – technical services; and David Haeger, vice president – finance administration.

In 1974 Pan Am had applied to the U.S. government for a subsidy to offset the fuel cost increases which it was sustaining around the world, and was rebuffed. Shortly thereafter exploratory negotiations were opened with the government of Iran to provide some sort of financial support to Pan Am. By mid-1975 an agreement was reached whereunder Iran would lend $245 million to Pan Am which would be used to repurchase outstanding notes from insurance companies at deep discounts, thereby substantially reducing long-term debt on Pan Am's balance sheet. Additionally, Iran would purchase 55 percent of IHC's shares for $55 million, would receive purchase warrants on six million Pan Am shares at $2.50 per share, and would receive a seat on Pan Am's board. The deal was announced to the public, and Pan Am waited. For whatever reason, the shah never gave his approval and the matter was dropped.

Other attempts were made to negotiate the sale of all or part of IHC, in order to provide cash to Pan Am, but none got beyond the planning stage.

The Tahiti hotel's operation had not achieved an adequate return; Joe Long wanted to sell his interest to IHC, or alternately acquire the company's minority share; the latter choice was selected and IHC withdrew. The Ponce hotel, after a short period of profitability occasioned solely from housing some sixty workers from a major nearby construction job for nearly two years, was back deep in the red. Negotiations with the owners and the mortgage holder resulted in an agreement to close the hotel with IHC providing a full-time engineer/caretaker on the site to safeguard the property.

The Inter-Continental Dubai in the United Arab Emirates was opened in 1975 and has gone from strength to strength. Here general manager Ahmed Ramdan celebrates with his team after being voted best hotel in the Middle East in 1994 by *Executive Travel* magazine.

Results by mid-year 1975 were well behind forecast; an across the board review of operating costs had led to a $500,000 reduction in corporate overhead, much of it through canceling or postponing programs already budgeted in personnel resources and marketing, together with a few middle management head-count reductions. Provisions for management bonuses were reversed.

During the year the company's first five-year plan was completed, an exercise developed principally "from the bottom up," the reasoning being that an IHC business plan must of necessity start with the business plans of the individual hotels, which account for the bulk of company revenues. Near the end of 1975 Pan Am directed that IHC pay a dividend of $5,000,000, the first ever received by its parent.

Two tragedies befell Inter-Continental in the closing days of 1975. Hans Teufl, general manager of the Phoenicia, was in the building with a group of employees when a shell fired from the St. George Hotel across the street set fire to the Phoenicia auditorium where mattresses from the bedrooms had been stored for safety, causing a massive cloud of smoke. Teufl did not escape. Bob Kulka, a former manager of the Phoenicia and currently manager in Paris, was traveling with his wife to the Middle East for a holiday on an MEA flight which crashed in Dharan, killing all aboard.

Pan Am lost $46 million in 1975; IHC's profit was $2.6 million.

NEW MARKETS

Having made its mark as a pioneer in the Middle East in 1961 with the opening of the Phoenicia Inter-Continental Beirut, Inter-Continental rapidly expanded its position in the region throughout the 1970s.

During the mid-1970s IHC attempted to diversify into various related businesses. Contracts were negotiated to take over, and improve, airline catering and restaurant operations in Zambia and Zaire. Ed Krygsman, who had managed Marriott's extensive catering operations at New York's J. F. Kennedy International Airport, was engaged to oversee this effort. Bids were made on catering contracts for construction sites, universities and hospitals in the Middle East. Studies were made for constructing hydroponic farms in the Gulf States and Jamaica. A joint venture was formed to construct and operate a supermarket in the United Arab Emirates. Bids were made in conjunction with Pan Am to operate feeding facilities in Pacific testing stations, Oman, and nuclear submarine bases. These various discussions generated a great deal of activity but, in the long run, produced only frustration and little to show for the effort.

IHC made a concerted effort in 1975 and 1976 to divest itself of unproductive and/or money-losing businesses. It negotiated withdrawals in Auckland and Salvador. The lease in Curaçao was terminated. Negotiations were undertaken to dispose of the Embajador (Santo Domingo) and the El Prado (Barranquilla) and successfully concluded in 1977.

Through intensive efforts with its bankers Pan Am effected a debenture exchange which resulted in a credit to earnings of $103 million. Its revolving credit agreement was renewed, but this time with the shares of IHC pledged as additional collateral, putting certain restrictions on IHC's cash management.

West Germany, with several new hotels, continued to be a cash drain for Inter-Continental with no sign of a turnaround before 1979.

In 1974 Jack Fink, an Australian businessman who had made a great deal of money in carpet manufacturing, had started buying Southern Cross Properties (the Melbourne-owning company) shares on the open market and eventually controlled the largest single block. He was certain that the Southern Cross shopping center would be more profitable under his management than as part of the hotel lease. He convinced IHC to sell its Southern Cross shares and to modify the lease to exclude the commercial space. By 1976 he was pressuring to buy the lease altogether; an agreement was reached and IHC sold, ending its Australian operation after almost fifteen years.

The program of incognito inspections created for "The Year of the Satisfied Guest" had been modified and continued on a two-visit-a-year basis. The idea was for each hotel to have a comprehensive summary of one guest's total experience, which could be used as a management tool to reward excellent performance and identify areas where service standards might be weak. Occasionally an employee or a hotel executive would become personally offended by some aspects of the report; some French hotel workers likened the program to a spy scheme. In 1976 IHC's public relations department contracted with a freelance writer to serve as one of the "quality control" inspectors. An article describing her adventures was published as the lead article in the Sunday *New York Times* travel section and later syndicated in other newspapers . . . which produced more than 400 letters from readers offering an amazing variety of reasons why they should be selected as inspectors. Every letter was answered; genuine frequent travelers among them were made Six Continents Club members; four were actually engaged as inspectors.

At the end of 1976 IHC's investment and advances in Montego Bay had risen to $6,500,000, and the company was committed to three hotel leases in Jamaica under which all operating losses were for the lessee's account. If IHC were forced to keep the hotels in operation, and if the Montego Bay hotel were to be bankrupted, more than a full year of the company's total profits could be wiped out.

Pan Am's 1976 business loss was $8.4 million which, when combined with the debenture exchange credit, resulted in a reported $94.6 million net profit. IHC's profit rose to $6 million.

A hotel and congress palace was being constructed in Taif, the Saudi royal summer capital, to host a conference of Islamic heads of state. IHC offered to service the conference and brought 250 Inter-Continental employees from all over the world to staff the event. An executive assistant manager was assigned to each head of state. The royal protocol department was extremely satisfied and asked IHC to make an offer to operate a royal guest palace in Riyadh. Eventually the company was to be involved in fourteen hotels and palaces in the kingdom.

During construction of enlargements to Riyadh, and in connection with IHC's regular invoicing, payments were made by Saudi authorities against eventual review and approval of documents. During the interim period the company was required to provide bank guarantees

The Massarah Inter-Continental opened in 1977 in the royal Saudi summer capital, Taif.

OVERLEAF: The Inter-Continental Maui in Hawaii opened in 1976 as part of IHC's strategy to expand into resorts throughout the Pacific.

The Inter-Continental Muscat, IHC's first hotel in Oman, opened in 1977.

for the value of the invoices. At one point these guarantees totaled several millions of dollars, a significant exposure.

The first Inter-Continental in Muscat opened in 1977 and several franchised properties joined the group: Le Vendôme, out of the war zone in Beirut; the Ritz Carlton, an old-established hotel in Montreal; the Montfleury in Cannes; and two hotels in the Philippines owned or controlled by Ayala – in Davao, and in Calatagan, Batangas, a new resort being developed south of Manila.

A racetrack was being planned for Teheran by Stanley Ho, a well-known casino operator in Macao. Inter-Continental contracted to furnish and operate the food and beverage facilities in the clubhouse and grandstand. The kitchens were designed to handle a high volume of catering. The IHC hotel was operating to capacity and could not take on additional catering, even though there was substantial demand. The racetrack kitchen would enable the company to provide feeding services for factories (factory owners were required by law to have these for their workers), to operate mobile snackbars to park and sell meals near construction sites, and to substantially increase social catering to receptions, etc. The facility opened shortly before the overthrow of the shah. One problem during the racetrack's short life: there were not enough good racehorses to assure a really competitive field . . . and some owners were worried about the consequences if their horse were to outclass one owned by the royal stables.

Bob Strachan devoted much of the first half of 1977 to protracted negotiations with officials of the government of Jamaica. Moses Matalon, whose family interests included property development and heavy construction in Jamaica and the Caribbean, played a leading role as advisor to both IHC and the government in evolving a plan whereunder the government would acquire all of the shares of the Montego Bay owning company and assume that company's additional obligations to IHC for loans and advances made during the construction and operation of the hotel – a total of $4.3 million. IHC would make a further advance of $1.1 million, and would accept Jamaican medium-term 8 percent notes for a total repayment value of $7 million. The Rose Hall lease would be terminated releasing IHC from continuing obligations to absorb operating losses, provide working capital, and act as employer of the hotel staff; but IHC would continue to operate the hotel under a management agreement which could be terminated at the government's option. With the conversion of the Ocho Rios and Kingston leases to franchise agreements, Inter-Continental had neutralized a potential loss exposure of up to $8 million. The risk would be limited only to Jamaica's performance under the long-term notes, a matter of some concern to the outside auditors when certifying IHC's 1977 accounts. In the event, despite one or two late payments in the early years, the loan and interest were eventually paid in full.

Several additional U.S. air carriers had been certified to operate flights in direct competition with Pan Am on certain routes in the Atlantic and Pacific, or to open routes from newly designated U.S. cities direct to points overseas, thereby diverting traffic from Pan Am's traditional U.S. gateways. Pan Am, alone of the U.S. carriers, had no U.S. route system despite repeated applications to the regulatory authorities over the years. With an upturn in traffic already apparent in 1977, Pan Am's Chairman Seawell set access to a competitive domestic route system as a high strategic priority for the airline, even if it meant merger with a predominantly domestic carrier. In this regard it would be important for IHC to have increased visibility in the United States, particularly in New York and Washington. Although the United States had been high on IHC's destination priority list for four years, it had been

The Inter-Continental New York was acquired in 1978 as part of IHC's drive to increase its visibility in the United States. Since then the hotel has been the hub of many high-profiled events. Here excitement builds up outside the hotel during the Democratic National Convention in 1992.

difficult to close any deals without being able to make investments or to guarantee rents, both of which measures could not be considered in light of IHC's existing resources and commitments. Two attractively priced acquisitions in New York – the Mayfair and Delmonico's, both on Park Avenue – and the opportunity to acquire the operating contract on the newly opened Chicago Ritz Carlton had to be foregone for want of investment funds after unsuccessful attempts had been made to find financial partners for these projects from among IHC owning company principals in the Middle East.

By the end of the year, IHC paid a $2 million dividend to its shareholder while earning $11,382,000. Pan Am was back in the black at $45 million.

Potter and Newman were made senior vice presidents in early 1978, and the division chief executives were appointed "presidents" of their divisions. Yusuf Haroon left IHC to pursue private investment opportunities and was succeeded by Ed Trippe as vice president – development.

After a competition with Hyatt, Inter-Continental was selected by Massachusetts Mutual Life Insurance Co. to become operator of the 600-room Four Ambassadors Hotel (formerly Sheraton), which it had acquired through foreclosure, in Miami. IHC would also acquire a 14 percent equity interest in the hotel, which would be extensively remodeled. Originally built as a residential property, it consisted of four towers atop a shopping, restaurant, and banqueting podium and underground carpark; 65 percent of the rooms were suites. Martin Seibold was transferred from Montego Bay as general manager. Seibold had first worked for IHC in Salvador in 1958 after emigrating from West Germany, later working in Ponce and Bogota before his first general manager's posting in Barranquilla. Later, while in charge of Medellin, he constructed the hotel's bullring (without the benefit of the usual approval paperwork from the IHC head office – a shortcoming which proved uncomfortable when Sternik paid a visit shortly thereafter). He was sent to Columbia University as an IHC scholar and served as general manager of the Hotel Ivoire in Abidjan before taking responsibility for operating the Rose Hall Inter-Continental in Montego Bay. Traditionally the gateway to the United States from Latin America, Miami was an ideal location for a major Inter-Continental property, catering to overseas visitors who were familiar with the product.

In response to the World Bank's decision to hold its biannual overseas conference in Manila, the Marcos government in the Philippines had introduced a series of incentives to stimulate hotel investment. The response was overwhelming. More than ten new hotels with more than 3,500 rooms would come onto the market in a six-month period; three of them would be within three blocks of the Inter-Continental, the first real competition in Makati after five years of record occupancies for IHC. Anticipating the competition, general manager Pierre Martinet and his staff commissioned a detailed analysis of the hotel's principal client sources. An intensified program of recognition both of the client companies and the individual guests was implemented. Every guest was identified and afforded an amenity package reflective of the volume of business he or his company or his sponsor company regularly gave to the hotel. A staff of guest relations officers was stationed in the lobby to meet and greet. The customer base was scrutinized to determine, as far as possible, which clients could reasonably be expected to defect to one of the new hotels after they opened (because of location or company affiliation with one of the new properties), and which could be retained; the latter group would receive special attention. The top accounts were

In 1978 government incentives to stimulate investment in hotels brought the first real competition to the Inter-Continental Manila. Situated in the Makati business district it had enjoyed record occupancies during the previous five years and in 1993 underwent an extensive renovation.

regularly entertained at parties, and weekends, which were among Manila's more sought after invitations, hosted not only by the hotel's executive and marketing group, but also by senior Ayala executives. In 1975, while the hotel was turning down some 30,000 room nights in booking requests from the IHC international reservations system, it did not have to deny a single request from any of its top account client base and still achieved occupancies in the high nineties. This targeted marketing paid off: after the new hotels opened, IHC maintained its competitive lead, and earned regular profits, while virtually all of the newcomers were either bankrupted by their lenders, or financially reorganized before reaching profitability many years later.

The Manila guest relations program, while it was a preemptive reaction to a competitive challenge, was recognized as a desired ongoing management and marketing feature for IHC worldwide in hotels with a high volume of repeat customers. Manuals were produced describing the program in detail and training teams installed the system in a majority of the company's hotels. This was the first of many personalized attention, recognition and targeted marketing programs instituted in the 1970s and 1980s, which were subsequently enhanced when computerized reservations and guest bookkeeping systems made it easier to identify each guest and the source of his booking more precisely.

IHC earned a profit of $2.5 million in April 1978, a record for a single month.

Signs of a changing world: the following telex exchange between Geneva general manager Desbaillets, Division President Balas, and IHC President Sternik from early June 1978:

"BALAS. GENEVA AUTHORITIES TODAY DECLARED TOPLESS BATHING WL NO LONGER BE PROSECUTED ON PUBLIC BEACHES AND POOLS CMA KINDLY RUSH ADV IHC POLICY ON SUBJECT AS DEMAND INCREASING AT OUR POOL DESPITE COLD WEATHER END DESBAILLETS"

"STERNIK/POTTER.
AS YOU KNOW WE HAD COMMENTS REGARDING TOPLESS BATHING MONT-FLEURY LAST SEASON STP THIS CONTINUES AND NOW ALSO BEGINNING TAKE PLACE GVA STP TOPLESS BATHING BECOMING CURRENT ALL OVER EUROPE AND BLV IT HARD FOR US TO AVOID HOWEVER WUD LIKE YR COMMENT RECOMMS VIS A VIS IHC POLICY END BALAS"

"BALAS CPY POTTER.
RYT 141506 CONTENTS REFLECT EXACTLY WHY IHC DECENTRALIZED STP IN LINE WITH QTE WHEN YOU HAVE SEEN ONE YOU HAVEN'T SEEN THEM ALL UNQTE OUR GUESTS EDUCATION SHOULD NOT BE LIMITED IN THOSE PLACES WHERE SUCH EDUCATION IS ALSO OFFERED IN OTHER HOTELS OF HIGHEST REPUTE STP IF INDEED PROBLEM EXISTS CMA YOU MIGHT CONSIDER RESERVING SEPARATE AREA FOR NATURE LOVERS STP STERNIK"

"DESBAILLETS
AS LONG AS TOPLESS NOT UNLAWFUL SEE NO REASON WHY THIS SHUD NOT BE ALLOWED GVA WITH THOUGHT GIVEN TO POSSIBILITY OF SETTING ASIDE SEPA-RATE AREA FOR NATURE LOVERS IF FEASIBLE STP WE WUD NOT LIKE TO UPSET OR DISTURB OTHER PAYING GUESTS END BALAS"

A truck delivering bottled gas to the Saipan Beach Inter-Continental Island Inn dropped a liquid propane gas tank onto the pavement, cracking it near the fresh-air intake vent for the kitchen air-circulation system. The resultant explosion and flame spread immediately through the kitchen seriously injuring four employees.

Lufthansa had become less happy with its hotel investments. While DLH and IHC as equity partners had shared investment risks equally in the West German hotel development program

The Berlin Hilton became the Inter-Continental Berlin in 1978. Enlarged and re-decorated, today it is a flagship property in the company's German portfolio.

IHC, as operator, was earning management fees in some of the properties even as the property owners were being faced with losses or, worse, cash shortfalls. DLH therefore proposed that IHC sell a share – ideally 50 percent, but at least 25 percent – of its wholly owned West German management company (holder of the leases and management contracts on the West German hotels) to DLH. IHC's board reasoned that since the management systems and expertise being delivered by IHC to the West German properties were intrinsic to, and exclusive corporate property of, Inter-Continental, a sale of an interest in such assets was out of the question. However, DLH was making a unique continuing contribution of its own to the success of the West German hotels and a way should be found for DLH to be compensated therefore.

In the great era of rail passenger travel in the early 1900s, the New York Central Railroad's interests had created Park Avenue in New York by covering the tracks which led to its main terminal, Grand Central, and constructed a group of five hotels, each at a different price level, on prime blocks within walking distance of the terminal. By the 1970s the railroad was bankrupt, and a consultant was appointed by the court to recommend a plan for the sale of the hotel properties for the benefit of the creditors. Inter-Continental had prepared a bid to acquire the Barclay Hotel, a 785-room property (120 rooms were parlors in two-room suites) just off Park Avenue between 48th and

49th Streets. In the wake of the consultant's sudden announcement that it would accept only a combined offer for all three remaining properties (Roosevelt, Biltmore and Barclay), IHC entered into an arrangement with the successful tenderer, Loews Corporation, to acquire the Barclay from Loews, concurrently with Loews' closing with the railroad trustees. The $36 million transaction was completed in short order; Pan Am advanced the necessary funds, with long-term financing to be secured in the future (a mortgage loan was arranged with Connecticut General Life Insurance Co. in early 1979). IHC took possession and began work on plans for a total remodeling and rehabilitation of the property, and on an application for a property tax rebate under a city incentive scheme introduced to encourage property restorations.

The Willard Hotel in Washington, D.C., and its predecessor namesakes located on a prime Pennsylvania Avenue site, had played an important role in the political history of the United States, housing national leaders and important visitors for more than 120 years. Leading Washington property developer Oliver Carr and Inter-Continental joined in a proposal to lease, restore and operate the hotel, together with an integrated office and shopping building on an adjacent site, in response to a tender offer under the supervision of the Pennsylvania Avenue Development Commission. In December 1978, the commission announced that it would accept a submission by developer Stuart Golding and Fairmont Hotel Company (of San Francisco), leaving IHC to search for other possible Washington sites.

After a period of detailed analyses of all staff management positions within Inter-Continental, each job had been classified according to a system of salary ranges. A structured system of salary adjustments related to performance and current inflation levels was established. The corporate commitment to management by objective which had earlier been applied to the annual bonus plan for general managers was incorporated into an incentive award system covering all corporate management-grade staff, to take effect in 1979.

After a series of preliminary preparatory discussions, a senior negotiating team headed by Paul Sheeline was invited to China and initialed a comprehensive letter of intent with the Chinese Tourism & Travel Administration which envisioned joint development of hotels in five destinations. As the first such agreement reached with an American (or Western) hotel group, the event brought widespread press coverage. Pan Am was concurrently pressing its bid to be the designated U.S. carrier to open (or reopen in Pan Am's case) service between the United States and China; Seawell gave full support to the IHC effort. As it happened, Pan Am got the route and, after an extensive series of serious and complicated negotiations involving Burgund, Newman, Potter, Rufe, and Strachan, agreement was reached with the Chinese covering a multi-use hotel, office block and residence complex to be built on a prime Beijing site. At the last minute the financial partner withdrew, and the project died.

The Ivory Coast government decided to acquire IHC's and Mayer's shareholdings in the Abidjan hotels; IHC would continue to manage, and in due course would also take on management of the Ivoire Casino.

Pan Am and IHC posted record profits in 1978: $118 million and $19.5 million respectively.

After four years of severely limited funds for growth, the number of projects in the design and construction stage had reached its lowest level since the late 1950s. In neither 1978 nor 1979 did the company open a hotel which it had developed and designed. Staffing had been trimmed to fit the company's reduced requirements for architectural, interior design, and project management services. Only in the United States, where Pan Am was in the midst of a high-level lobbying campaign to win supporters in key cities for its bid to acquire National Airlines, was Inter-Continental in a position to aggressively pursue new projects.

But the rapid growth of the early part of the decade was paying off in profitability despite the pressures of rapidly rising fuel prices on the world's industrial economies. Pan Am's fuel bill doubled in 1979, just as its merger with National was about to add a collection of older, fuel-inefficient, short-range aircraft to its fleet.

In Portugal, the Ritz in Lisbon was to be returned to the private control of its original owners after a period of use as a way station for ex-residents of Portugal's newly independent African colonies. Inter-Continental was able to negotiate a contract for operation of the hotel, while the owners pledged to find the funds to restore the property physically to its former position as one of Europe's finest hotels. A performance clause set clear goals for profitability.

In Turkey, a strike and general civil unrest forced the closing of the Istanbul hotel after a bloody incident, involving a shoot-out on the hotel's lobby escalator, boiled over from a demonstration in Taksim Square which had become a favorite venue for political violence since the hotel had opened. On an earlier occasion, after a confrontation between unions and police, thirty-six bodies had been brought in from the square and dumped in the hotel's lobby. As it was impossible to operate, IHC unilaterally canceled the lease and began a long series of negotiations which would eventually lead to a withdrawal from Turkey.

The franchised Inter-Continental Belgrade and adjacent Sava Conference Center opened in time to host a major World Bank conference.

The Borobudur Inter-Continental, opened in 1974 in Jakarta, Indonesia.

At a meeting of the general managers of Europe, Middle East, Asia and Pacific, held in Frankfurt, Sternik announced the formation of a Middle East Division with Pierre Martinet as president, to be based in Athens. Martinet had joined Inter-Continental for the opening in Jerusalem and was transferred almost immediately to Karachi as chief steward for that hotel's opening. A Swiss national, he had worked for Hilton in Teheran. After assuming additional responsibilities in Karachi, he was transferred to Bangkok to take charge of the food and beverage operation. He served as general manager in Kabul, Teheran, and Manila and succeeded Lance Brokenshire at the Borobudur in Jakarta when health problems forced Brokenshire to take early retirement and seek less strenuous employment (as one of the Alcoholic Beverage Control Board Commissioners for the State of Victoria in Australia). Under Martinet's direction, the major program of construction corrections to the hotel were eventually completed. A competitive situation similar to that which he had faced in Manila had developed in Jakarta, except that the Borobudur was one of the new properties (and in this case the largest one), not the established market leader as had been the case in the Philippines.

The Mid East Division would initially include the hotels in Amman, Muscat, Riyadh, Mecca, Taif, Dubai, Teheran, and Kabul, with new hotels scheduled to be opened shortly in Bahrain, and Abu Dhabi, Al Ain, Sharjah, and Ras al Khaima in the United Arab Emirates. (The Sharjah hotel

Inter-Continental's expansion into the Middle East started in the 1970s and continued into the 1980s and 1990s. The Inter-Continental Al Ain in the United Arab Emirates (top) opened in 1981 and the Semiramis Inter-Continental in Cairo (above), overlooking the Nile, dates from 1987. The Jeddah Inter-Continental in Saudi Arabia (right) opened in 1992.

was sold just prior to completion, to be operated by the new owner without IHC, and the Ras al Khaima property was abandoned by its owner for lack of finance when it was 85 percent completed.) Construction had begun on major hotels in Cairo and Jeddah, and IHC was well advanced on negotiations in Yemen and Qatar, neither of which projects would eventually be

Signing an expanded marketing services agreement between Lufthansa and Inter-Continental are (left to right) Fred G. Peelen – Inter-Continental regional vice president, West Germany, Paul C. Sheeline – Inter-Continental chairman, Dr. Guenter Berendt – managing director, Lufthansa Commerical Holdings, Professor Guenter O. Eser – member of Lufthansa executive board, and Dr. Eric H. Bleich – Inter-Continental regional vice president – corporate relations, Europe.

built. While IHC's properties in the Middle East were the leading hotels in each location, construction was nearing completion on several competitive, top quality hotels to be operated by major international chains, some of which had little, if any, Middle East experience, but all of which had major brand recognition and strong sales forces in the United States, Europe and/or Asia. They included Hyatt, Sheraton, and Marriott; Hilton International was already well established in the area. Martinet and his newly established group faced a major task of targeted sales and product quality assurance if IHC were to maintain its long-term position as a market leader in the region.

In West Germany, DLH and IHC reached agreement on a program of joint marketing support for their hotels whereby Inter-Continental would be provided with greater access to DLH's customer base, and with prime DLH identification within West Germany. DLH would open airline check-in facilities in the hotel lobbies and IHC would expand Six Continents Club recognition to a large segment of DLH's frequent traveler clientele. IHC's German operating company would pay DLH DM 1 million per year for their services; a steering committee of senior marketing executives from each company would oversee the various agreed projects. Eventually such innovations as a reduced-fare barter arrangement for IHC business travel and DLH employee identification cards entitling holders to special rate reductions in IHC hotels were introduced. The former Berlin Hilton had been sold to a private investor with whom Bleich negotiated an Inter-Continental franchise; the hotel would be enlarged to 660 rooms by 1980, raising IHC's West German representation to 3,700 rooms in eight cities.

In the United Kingdom, Le Soufflé in the Inter-Continental London would join Hamburg's Fontenay Grill as a Michelin-starred restaurant, recognizing Peter Kromberg's achievements among the group of talented chefs who were changing England's culinary landscape. Kromberg, who had grown up on Lake Constance in West Germany, took his first apprenticeship position at the age of fourteen and a half in the Duisburgerhof. Some nine years later, he joined the Athens Hilton kitchen brigade where, with an occasional summer assignment in Davos, he remained for three years. A sous chef with whom he had worked in the Hilton had joined IHC in

Peter Kromberg, executive chef at the Inter-Continental, London. His achievements were recognized when Le Soufflé, the hotel's restaurant, received a Michelin star.

Amman and was later appointed executive chef to open the Siam Inter-Continental. He contacted Kromberg, who accepted a position in Bangkok in charge of the *garde-manger* and butcher shop. He found Inter-Continental to be less structured and regimented than Hilton, but more personal regarding its employees. Within a few months, the chef was transferred and Pierre Martinet, the hotel's acting food and beverage manager, recommended that Kromberg be appointed executive chef; at twenty-six he was the youngest in IHC to hold that position. With a huge garden on the hotel property, Kromberg raised a flock of geese, feeding them an Alsatian diet, and served some spectacular meals when the holiday season rolled around.

His plans for a transfer to New Zealand were aborted when Peter Balas, newly appointed general manager at the Portman in London, offered him the opening chef's position. Remembering Balas' roll-up-his-sleeves approach during the hectic days of the Bangkok opening, Kromberg accepted, recognizing that London would offer extraordinary challenges – it was hardly a center of culinary excellence or innovation in 1971. After his days in Athens and sunny Bangkok, London in the winter was grim and foreboding; he wondered whether he would last six months.

The Portman's Rôtisserie Normande was a modest success from the start, and within a few months was attracting the notice of serious food-lovers. Named executive chef for the Hyde Park Corner hotel during its construction, he was able to provide some input into the kitchen design, although space restrictions limited his contribution; changes would have to be made after the hotel was open and operating profitably. The hotel's culinary reputation would be made in its banquets and in Le Soufflé, a small jewel of a restaurant which offered an eclectic menu of up-to-date original dishes, featuring unusual soufflés among its various courses, and a world-class wine list. Twenty-four years later, Kromberg would still be the hotel's executive chef. Management would give him the opportunity to create and grow; he would be trusted and respected as a professional. In 1994 the Egon Ronay guide would name Le Soufflé its restaurant of the year. Earlier, Kromberg would join the United Kingdom's other pre-eminent chefs in the preparation of a spectacular banquet served in the Brighton Pavillion to honor the great continental chef Carême.

IHC began to redeem some of the off-shore debentures which had been floated in 1971 by repurchasing $2,000,000 of the securities in the open market at a price below par. And a $6 million dividend was paid to Pan Am.

The Pan Am/National Airlines merger was approved late in 1979 and made the combined airline potentially a major force in U.S. domestic travel with a hub-and-spoke system feeding traffic to and through Miami, Houston, and New Orleans on coast-to-coast routes across the southern United States, and from virtually every point in Florida to most of the major east coast population centers. The problems of integrating the two airlines' unionized workers (Pan Am's were the highest paid in the world; National had survived on a long history of fiercely fought wage battles and operated with fewer, and less well paid, staff) would substantially delay the achievement of the synergistic financial benefits which had been foreseen for the combined airline.

Pan Am's 1979 profit fell to $76 million, and Inter-Continental's to $18.4 million (the 1978 figure had included a one time only capital gain of $4 million).

Developed with Pan American Life Insurance (no relation to the airline), the Inter-Continental New Orleans opened in 1983 as part of IHC's plans to expand in the United States.

During the period leading up to and immediately following the Pan Am/National merger, IHC had successfully negotiated to acquire land for a 500-room hotel in the Galleria Post Oak section of Houston; joined with Pan American Life Insurance (no relation to the airline) to build a 500-room property in New Orleans; negotiated a lease for a new 500-room hotel and integrated shopping center in an urban renewal area of Boston; committed additional funds to the remodeling of the New York Barclay; and was working with a developer on a site in Dallas. All this created a potential funding requirement of at least $20 million over the next two to three years, even more if long-term debt could not be found for Houston on acceptable terms. IHC potentially had its financial back against the wall, but on the bright side had a reasonable expectation of strong future earnings from the existing portfolio, especially from West Germany where profitability had at last been achieved in every property.

The airline had underestimated the cost of the merger with National and was struggling to achieve any economies of scale from the combined operation. IHC was asked to lend its "surplus" cash; instead a further $5.5 million dividend was paid.

IHC's presence in the Middle East continued to expand during the late 1970s with the building of the Regency Inter-Continental Bahrain.

OPPOSITE: The Inter-Continental Abu Dhabi, United Arab Emirates. The new standards for guest-room and bath sizes reflected in this luxury hotel had been under development since the mid-1970s.

In Iran and Afghanistan, local political unrest was leading to rapidly deteriorating conditions for international business travelers. It was only a question of time before it would be impossible for Inter-Continental to continue to perform under its operating agreements. In the wake of the fall of the shah, the establishment of the Islamic Republic of Iran, and the seizure of the U.S. embassy in Teheran, the IHC hotel had become the chosen refuge for members of the foreign press visiting Iran. They had been on hand for, and had duly reported, the destruction of the hotel's wine cellar by armed fundamentalists – emptying and/or breaking thousands of bottles of vintage wines at the hotel's loading dock. Occasionally troops would attempt to raid the reporters' rooms. The two remaining expatriates tried valiantly to preserve some sort of order, but were continually vilified with posters demanding "death to foreigners." Teheran general manager Frank Mielert, a former assistant to Balas and acting general manager in Paris, rebuffed one group of marauders with the admonition that "This is an hotel, not an embassy". Unlike the other chain hotels in Teheran, which had been owned directly by the shah or his government, the Inter-Continental was 50 percent foreign-owned, a factor which probably contributed to the delay in direct seizure of the property. But by early 1990 Mielert and his successor Tony Mueller-Gebrand were faced with a de facto takeover by the workers committee. Reluctantly, but in concern for his personal safety, IHC directed Mueller-Gebrand to prepare a letter to the government and owning company stating that IHC had been forced from the property and was "turning over the key." The letter would be delivered only after he was safely out of the country. Shortly thereafter IHC began a proceeding to recover its losses under its U.S. government expropriation insurance. After a number of years, involving hearings at an international tribunal in The Hague, a settlement was finally obtained.

The opening of two major hotels expanded IHC's presence in the Persian Gulf: the Regency Inter-Continental in Bahrain and the Inter-Continental Abu Dhabi in the United Arab Emirates.

Both hotels were of a luxury standard and reflected the new corporate standards for guest-room and bath sizes which had been under development in the mid-1970s. IHC's market research had shown that while the room and bath configuration introduced in the hotels that had been opened in the 1960s and early 1970s was competitive with existing hotels in many parts of the world, most U.S. construction was featuring substantially larger guest rooms even in less than first-class properties. Frequent business travelers were growing accustomed to such accommodations in the United States and would expect to find them overseas. U.S. chains which were beginning to expand abroad were incorporating these large rooms and expanded bathroom facilities in their planning for proposed new properties, particularly in Asia. If IHC were to retain its position at the top of the first-class line, its standards would have to be upgraded. In the existing hotels where room sizes were already fixed, better quality furnishings and upgraded public spaces, together with enhanced personalized service and guest recognition programs, would have to be relied upon for competitive advantage.

The Abu Dhabi hotel, which featured a marina, beach facilities, and an auditorium as well as extensive meeting and restaurant facilities, was designed by the Cambridge, Massachusetts firm of Benjamin Thompson Associates in a striking modern style. Special floors of deluxe suites were incorporated into the plan, enabling the hotel to serve as venue for meetings of several heads of state, including particularly the periodic gatherings of the Gulf States Co-operation Council. The selection of Thompson, a very distinguished U.S. architect, who had been chairman of Harvard University's Department of Architecture, was in line with Sheeline's attempt to upgrade IHC hotel architecture.

A NEW PARENT

In 1980 the world's airlines suffered the worst decline in traffic and earnings in their history, losing more than $2.5 billion; U.S. carriers reported aggregate losses of $400 million. Pan Am's airline operations were no exception, producing operating losses, before income taxes, of $247 million. However, during the year the company sold its ownership position in the Pan Am building recording a $294.4 million gain on the sale. This gain plus IHC's pretax profit of $41.6 million resulted in an overall net profit of $80.3 million for Pan Am. IHC's results represented a 23.6 percent increase over the prior year, but included non-operating items of $8.68 million, chief among which was a $2.7 million gain on the sale of IHC's investment in the Miami hotel.

Following the Miami sale, IHC negotiated a management agreement for an expansive resort near Fort Lauderdale. Built as an adjunct to, and catalyst for, a vacation condominium development, the 500-room hotel would incorporate a world-class health spa and fitness center as well as golf, tennis, and swimming facilities. IHC became involved near the end of the construction period and was attracted by the owners' willingness for IHC to manage, without equity participation. The resort was well away from Fort Lauderdale and its signature canals and beaches, and its potential clientele would be exclusively vacation-oriented; this was not a group with whom IHC's frequent-business-traveler-directed sales force had regular contact. From the opening day the hotel floundered, and IHC would eventually be asked to lend funds to construct conference and meeting facilities in the hope that business and business-cum-pleasure corporate meetings could draw sufficient clientele to fill the guest rooms.

Texas, the traditional center of the U.S. oil industry, was a major target for IHC expansion. The state's three main metropolitan areas, Houston, Dallas, and San Antonio, were among the fastest growing anywhere in the United States. A site for a Houston Inter-Continental had been acquired, and a project in Dallas was nearly ready to be announced, when an opportunity arose to acquire and restore the historic St. Anthony Hotel in San Antonio. This seemed a perfect fit for assuring IHC a leading role in Texas. When the oil bubble burst not long thereafter, IHC's massive exposure in Texas proved to be an expensive burden. Sheeline would comment several years later that IHC's inability to find partners to share the risks in Houston and San Antonio was one of the most serious negative aspects of his administration.

A hybrid management services agreement brought the Buenos Aires Plaza Hotel into the Inter-Continental family for a short period, until remittance problems from Argentina forced IHC to withdraw. A second hotel in Abu Dhabi, at the desert oasis of Al Ain, also designed by Ben Thompson, and the 400-room Forum Budapest completed the Inter-Continental opening schedule for 1981.

Virginia Baker, who had been director – housekeeping

The magnificent Al Bustan Palace Hotel in Muscat, Oman, opened in 1985.

since 1966 and had played a leading role in the continuing development and upgrading of the company's guest room standards, became Inter-Continental's first woman general manager, with her appointment to take direct charge of the Rose Hall Inter-Continental in Montego Bay.

Shortly after the sale of the Pan Am building, IHC was requested to prepare a strategic plan for long-term growth, the notion being that Pan Am would earmark a significant portion of the profits

from the office building sale to hotel activities. Within six months it was clear that these funds would be needed to keep the airline in business. Instead IHC was encouraged to seek Eurodollar financing against its own balance sheet and credit rating. A short-term solution would be a $40 million revolving line of credit which Citibank was prepared to extend to IHC.

On April 1 1981, John Gates died at his home in Greenwich, Connecticut. Two days later, Juan Trippe died at the age of eighty-one. A Pan Am memorial tribute quoted Trippe from a 1934 speech: "By each successive step, aviation is advancing to that potential ideal of a universal service to humanity. By overcoming artificial barriers aviation can weave together, in close understanding, the nations of the world, and lift for the peoples of the world those horizons which have long limited the perspective of those who live upon this earth."

Stanley Grinstead, deputy chairman of Grand Metropolitan (above) and (right) Paul C. Sheeline, chairman of Inter-Continental, at the time of the sale of IHC to Grand Met.

Pan Am's cash situation was worsening by the day. IHC had paid a $10 million dividend to the parent in mid-April. Throughout May and June negotiations were continuing with a group of commercial banks for a renewal of Pan Am's $500 million revolving credit with IHC shares as collateral. An in-depth financial analysis of IHC had been prepared by a Wall Street investment bank to support an aggressively high valuation. In the middle of July when one of the key banks withdrew from the consortium, the negotiation collapsed and Pan Am was literally out of funds. Checks began to bounce. Without consulting IHC, Pan Am directed a transfer of $20 million from IHC's bank account to Pan Am, a transaction carried out without the signature or authorization of any IHC officer. Sheeline was facing a personal dilemma: as a Pan Am employee he was bound to follow the directives of his seniors; as chairman of IHC's board he felt he had a conflicting obligation to protect IHC's assets for the benefit of its own creditors. He sought legal advice from a friend in a Wall Street law firm, only to be advised that the firm could not help as it was representing another client which was in negotiations with Pan Am.

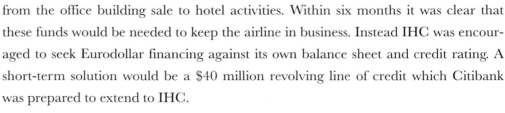

That other client turned out to be Grand Metropolitan, a major British conglomerate which in early August requested, and received, an opportunity from Pan Am to make a preemptive offer to acquire Inter-Continental. Two Grand Met board members, Stanley Grinstead, deputy chairman, and Clifford Smith, arrived in New York on a Thursday, spent all day Friday, Saturday and most of Sunday in meetings with Pan Am and IHC officers (Sheeline had been advised by Seawell of the pending transaction on Wednesday) and attorneys for both sides, and made a $500 million offer for the company late Sunday evening. Seawell called a special meeting of his board of directors to seek approval. Sheeline, who had been a member of the Pan Am board since the mid-1970s, disqualified himself from the voting but was asked whether the price was fair. Many Pan Am directors were incensed at being forced to make such a serious decision with no advanced warning. Some wondered why they should not sell the airline and keep the hotel company. All were concerned that Pan Am must get a full price for this sole remaining non-airline asset. Should there not be an open bidding opportunity to try to get a better offer? Pan Am had no cash to meet end of the month payrolls; jet fuel suppliers were demanding cash on delivery in certain airports. In the end, immediate action was required. The pain may have been somewhat reduced by Sheeline's honest judgment that, based on IHC's earnings, limited fixed assets, and future commitments, the company was worth probably very little more than $300 million to an existing hotel company with its own brand name.

Hans Sternik learned that he had been sold, when he picked up a copy of the *International Herald Tribune* at a Greek island port where he had disembarked from a holiday cruise with friends for a short shopping stop.

Grand Met moved quickly to close on the purchase which was completed on September 10 1981. As part of the settlement Pan Am repaid $41 million in advances from IHC, and Grand Met insisted that IHC's pension plan, heretofore a part of Pan Am's, be fully funded concurrent with the sale. Sheeline convinced Grand Met that the maintenance of a Pan Am association with IHC was essential, at least in the short run, and accordingly a continuing services agreement was negotiated whereby Pan Am, for a fee, would continue to provide office space and services, worldwide communications facilities, full access to the Panamac reservations system, and use of Pan Am computer hardware for various IHC accounting applications. A barter transportation

Hans G. Sternik, president of Inter-Continental (above), and (left) Sir Maxwell Joseph, chairman of Grand Metropolitan.

agreement would provide discounted positive-space- and deep-discounted-space-available Pan Am travel for IHC personnel, the cost of which could be offset by Pan Am against charges for crew accommodation or other services at IHC hotels.

Pan Am recorded a $222 million after-tax profit on the sale; the airline's record operating losses (caused to a great extent by one of the worst recessions in four decades) wiped out this one-time gain resulting in an overall $18.875 million loss. Seawell resigned shortly after the IHC sale. Sheeline would remain on the Pan Am board until the company's demise ten years later.

IHC's new parent was a rapidly growing United Kingdom publicly listed company that earned £136 million net profit in its year ended September 30 1981. It had begun as a collection of London hotels put together by Maxwell Joseph, a successful English property agent. The initial acquisitions – the Mount Royal in Oxford Street (1957) and the Grand Hotels (Mayfair) (1961) – led to the formation of a public company, Grand Metropolitan Hotels, which by 1963 was London's largest hotel group with sixteen hotels in the capital. Stanley Grinstead had been with the group since 1957. Through a steady program of acquisition and construction Grand Met expanded its hotel portfolio and entered into the catering, grocery, leisure and liquor store businesses. In 1969, in its first major move into the branded food business, Grand Met acquired Express Dairies, one of the United Kingdom's largest milk and dairy producers,

Shortly after its opening in 1927, the May Fair Hotel (inset) was honored by a visit from George V and Queen Mary. In 1982 the hotel was renamed the May Fair Inter-Continental London.

distributors and retailers, for £32 million. With the sort of speed which would characterize Grand Met's reaction to opportunities over the years, Maxwell Joseph had put an offer in place within forty-eight hours of learning that the company might be for sale. Its 1970s' acquisitions included Berni Inns, a chain of 100 inns and hotels (£14 million) and Mecca Holdings, a chain of dance halls, bingo parlors, ice-skating rinks, restaurants, betting shops, and gaming clubs (£33 million). In 1971 and 1972 Grand Met expanded into the brewery business acquiring Truman, Hanbury and Buxton, a medium-sized regional brewer with some 1,000 pubs in London and the southeast (£48 million), and later Watney Mann, one of the United Kingdom's largest brewers in a transaction of some £400 million, the largest single industrial acquisition in the country up to that time. With the takeover of the two breweries Grand Met had doubled in size, acquired a large Watney wine and spirits subsidiary, International Distillers and Vintners (IDV), and had changed the nature of the group away from the hotel and catering trade to a major food, drinks and retailing company; "Hotels" was dropped from the corporate name. The next seven years were ones of financial consolidation of the new acquisitions and product development, introducing such new brands as Malibu, Croft Sherries, Bailey's Irish Cream and Webster's Yorkshire Bitter.

With virtually all of its income production in the United Kingdom, Grand Met began to look overseas for diversification. The Liggett Group in the United States distributed several IDV products through its Paddington and Carillon subsidiaries. Rebuffed in an attempt to purchase the biggest wine and spirits subsidiaries, Grand Met mounted a successful $450 million offer for the entire Liggett Group, thereby acquiring a tobacco company with diversified investments in U.S. soft drink bottling, fitness equipment, and pet foods (the Alpo brand). Recognizing tobacco as a long-term "dying" industry, Grand Met planned to eventually dispose of the tobacco business while building on the consumer product lines, and to use Liggett as the vehicle for expansion into other branded consumer products in the United States. Within a year of the IHC acquisition Sir Maxwell Joseph would die, to be succeeded as chairman by Stanley Grinstead.

Grand Met's strategic purpose in the Inter-Continental acquisition was to expand and strengthen its hotel holdings through brand recognition. The existing portfolio of hotels, located predominantly in the United Kingdom, had no particular unifying feature of which the public might be aware. Grand Met operated every size and every class of property, only three of which (in London, Belfast, and Brussels) had the same name: Europa. The hotels were in varying states of repair and, with the exception of five deluxe properties on the Continent, all were earning room rates well below such competitors as Hilton and Inter-Continental. Virtually all were 100 percent owned by Grand Met or operated under long-term leases. A committee of John Travers Clarke, Grand Met chief executive – hotels and catering, Anthony Walford, managing director – Grand Metropolitan Hotels (GMH), Sheeline, and Sternik (known affectionately as the "Gang of Four") was appointed by Grinstead to review the GMH hotel portfolio and determine which hotels could be profitably identified with the Inter-Continental or Forum brands. The remaining properties would be sold, and the proceeds used to defray the cost of the IHC acquisition. The "gang" initially identified seventeen (eleven IHC, six Forum) properties for integration. It was decided to retain the Inter-Continental management structure and U.S. base; the existing GMH head office would be substantially downsized and converted to a Forum Division headquarters foreseen to be headed by Walford. GMH senior staff would be relocated to Inter-Continental properties, service departments or division offices, whenever possible.

Just what had Grand Met acquired for its half billion dollars? Firstly, obviously, a group of eighty-three hotels in forty-seven countries, only six of them fully owned (Vienna, Paris, Wiesbaden, Hanover, New York, San Antonio), gave Grand Met a major international presence in the hotel trade. Secondly, and from Grand Met's viewpoint perhaps more importantly, each hotel was identified with the IHC or Forum brand and each occupied a market position clearly ahead of most of its competitors in most locations. In London the Portman Inter-Continental, with a physical product no better than and a location inferior to the Grand Met Britannia and Europa Hotels, was earning an average room rate at least 50 percent higher. The Inter-Continental brand was well known and respected among international frequent travelers. In the travel trade IHC maintained a high profile among tour and incentive and retail travel agents who regularly booked clients internationally. IHC was well represented with sales outlets around the world and with hotels in most of the world's important cities except in North America and Scandinavia. A group of properties was under construction in the United States, with an active development department searching for more. The IHC name was relatively unknown among U.S. frequent travelers, unless they had traveled overseas, and the company's ability to successfully operate and market U.S. hotels catering primarily to U.S. residents was unproven and perhaps suspect. In local communities around the world IHC's restaurant and banqueting facilities were market leaders in nearly every location. Three European hotels had earned a Michelin star for their top restaurants. Food and beverage innovations had included in-room display cooking rotisseries; lavish breakfast and luncheon buffets that offered an excellent product, speeded-up service and controlled labor costs; in-room minibars (first introduced over the accountants' objections) which increased beverage sales, added to customer satisfaction, and operated in most cases with no addition to the staff; a *Food and Beverage Idea Exchange* publication, edited out of the Europe Division office; participation in the Frankfurt Culinary Olympics – thirty-six gold medals and number one among hotel chains in 1976 – organized by Harold Talalas; prepackaged foods production; and an annual joint promotion with Holland American Line, with IHC chefs joining the *Rotterdam*'s round the world cruise at IHC locations and serving local specialties aboard the ship on the cruise's next leg. Well-documented architectural standards, and product standards for all hotel furnishings and equipment, assured a certain high level of guest comfort.

The properties were managed by a seasoned group of executives; nearly all of the hotel general managers had been with the company for more than fifteen years, of which at least five years had been spent at the general manager level. Seventy-five percent of the department heads had worked in two or more different hotels, and 50 percent had worked in more than one of the company's divisions. A highly competitive salary and benefits package was in place for all staff positions. Regional training centers had been established in Hanover in West Germany and Medellin in Colombia. Departmental workshops were scheduled at least biannually. And company-provided housing, where applicable, was being consistently improved (the Duke of Wellington, while a guest in Graham Jeffrey's London Inter-Continental apartment, had described the family dining facilities as "squalid"). The company's day-to-day operations were being competently supervised by four division offices, led by and staffed with highly professional long-term IHC hotel operators. Grand Met had paid an amount equal to about twenty times earnings for this enterprise. A 5 percent return on investment was not particularly attractive; IHC would have to grow its profits and control its costs, and quickly, if its parent were to be satisfied.

OPPOSITE: The restored La Verriere restaurant and tea salon in Le Grand Hotel Paris.

The IHC board of directors would continue to function, but the Grand Met system of regular person to person "callover" sessions between Grinstead and Sheeline would assure speedy communication with the shareholder on all matters of policy and financial commitments.

In the first year of Grand Met ownership, IHC leased new office space in New York and moved to 1120 Avenue of the Americas. A joint venture was formed with COMSAT General to develop the first international two-way video conferencing system available to the general public with the first installation linking Inter-Continental London and Inter-Continental New York. A controlling interest was acquired in Scanticon International, an operator of purpose-built, top quality, conference center hotels, created and headed by Danish entrepreneur Jorgen Roed, which was soon to open its first U.S. facility in Princeton, New Jersey.

The Grand Met parentage created certain unique problems involving hotel liquor licenses. When Prohibition ended in the United States, most of the states enacted strict laws aimed at

precluding any single entity from controlling all three major elements of the alcoholic beverage trade: production, distribution and retail sale. Since Grand Met was a major producer of spirits overseas, and of wines in California, and held wholesale distribution licenses in New York State, IHC's hotel retail liquor licenses would be in jeopardy. In California and New Jersey special enabling legislation was enacted, placing restrictions on the number of IHC properties and/or the proportion of Grand Met products which could be stocked or sold. In Florida, Mississippi, Massachusetts, and Hawaii, IHC could easily comply with existing laws. Texas required the establishment of a separate company to independently operate the liquor business, an arrangement organized by a local attorney who had long experience with Texas alcoholic beverage law. In New York, special legislation was proposed, and then withdrawn when it became clear that certain Irish–American interests were prepared to fight the issue because of their dislike of all things British (despite the fact that Grand Met through its dairy and Bailey's Irish Cream business was one of the Irish Republic's leading export earners). The problem was solved by moving

The façade of the Carlton Inter-Continental dominates Cannes' elegant Croisette.

the liquor import and distribution subsidiaries out of New York State, a loss to the state of two companies' taxes and employees.

Kenneth Meinen, a former Pan Am personnel vice president, joined IHC as vice president – personnel resources, replacing Hynes who had resigned. Tony Leidner, a senior attorney in the Pan Am legal department, had transferred to IHC just prior to the Grand Met acquisition as senior vice president and general counsel. Ed Trippe had become senior vice president – development; both had been Pan Am employees.

Revolving credit agreements of $50 million each were negotiated with Morgan Guaranty and Citibank.

Michael Cairns was appointed president of the Forum Division, which had recently expanded to fourteen hotels (eleven of them in Europe) with the integration of several GMH properties. Forum would take temporary responsibility for the operation of ten other GMH properties in London and Paris, until they could be sold. New Forum hotels were under construction in Jordan and Saudi Arabia. Cairns, an Englishman, had joined IHC in 1968 as resident manager in Bangkok. He served four years as general manager in Auckland and a similar period as the

A separate Forum Hotels operating division with new graphics and logo was established with the integration of several Grand Met properties. The former London Penta became the Forum London.

FORUM HOTELS
INTERNATIONAL

Southern Cross general manager in Melbourne, transferring when that hotel was sold, to Maui where, as managing director, he also served as regional director – operations for the Pacific. During this period he played the leading operations role in a series of surveys for various hotel projects in Australia. His task at Forum would be to produce a uniform brand image and product standards for the division's hotels and to spearhead development activities, particularly in Europe, where it was believed that existing three-star hotels would be interested in a Forum affiliation supported with the full range of IHC marketing, reservations and operational services. The only real brief on what constitutes "Forum" continued to be: a good businessman's hotel, charging value for money rates at least 30 percent below an Inter-Continental in the same city.

Pete Sutherland elected to relieve himself of the stress of his division presidency and opted to serve as opening managing director of the Inter-Continental Houston (with regional responsibility for San Antonio and New Orleans), with the prospect of retiring in another five years. Mario di Genova, who had been with Grand Met in charge of its luxury properties in Europe, would now return to IHC as president of the Americas Division. During the years since his departure from IHC he had been chief executive of the Italian Ciga Group, and of Americana, and Ramada Hotels in the United States.

Two major hotels in key destinations – Singapore and Athens – opened in 1982. Both featured unique atria lobbies, inverted downward in the case of Athens, striking modern architecture (Singapore was the trendy imaginative American architect John Portman's first project out-

The De La Ville Hotel, Rome, was one of the Grand Met hotels that joined the Inter-Continental portfolio in 1982. It has a prime location near the top of the Spanish Steps.

side the United States), collections of original modern art, swimming pools and health clubs, and arcades displaying the most up-to-date international fashions. Through a franchise arrangement similar to the Keio operations in Jakarta and Saipan, the Pavilion Inter-Continental Singapore would feature a luxurious "Maxim's de Paris" restaurant modeled after the famous *Belle Époque* establishment on Paris' Rue Royale. (Maxim's had had a longstanding relationship as a cuisine advisor and wine purveyor to Pan Am; and its chairman, Louis Vaudable, was a good friend of IHC.) Most of the rooms in the Athenaeum Inter-Continental would command views of the monuments of Athens' Acropolis. The leading international designer Dale Keller was responsible for the interiors. The ballroom was Athens' largest, with Austrian crystal chandeliers, and was outfitted for simultaneous translation as well as trade-show and social functions.

Early in 1983, Anthony Tennant, a Grand Met group managing director, was given responsibility for overseeing IHC, along with the IDV wines and spirits businesses which he had directed for a number of years. He was an expert at marketing product brands (a "brands manager," he called himself) and had built IDV into one of the largest (it would soon be *the* largest) wines and spirits businesses in the world. After immersing himself in the general principles as well as the details of IHC's operation, and observing its people at work at various levels around the world, he would eventually conclude that Inter-Continental was not a brand in the classic sense since it did not offer a product which was absolutely consistent wherever it could be found, unlike a bottle of J&B whiskey, a packet of L&M cigarettes, or a tin of Alpo dog food. The consistency, if any, was in the customer's willingness to pay a certain price reflecting his belief in the brand's value. Tennant was also anxious to put his finger on the USPs (unique selling propositions) which distinguished IHC so that these could be enhanced for improved profitability. These concerns would be recurring themes in his corporate oversight of IHC for the next four years.

The program of restoration, upgrading and redecoration of most of the former GMH properties was generously funded by Grand Met and resulted in major increases in operating profit as each hotel was repositioned at the top of its appropriate market niche. Trading profit (that is, the profit from the business before deductions for interest costs and income taxes) was to grow from £22.9 million in the fiscal year 1981/82 to £37.9 million by 1986/87, after a deduction in each year of $13.5 million to amortize the cost of leases and management contracts which had been capitalized at the time of the company's acquisition from Pan Am.

An enhanced program of standards development was introduced under the full-time direction of Ed Dowling. A standards committee consisting of general managers from each operating division, together with corporate department heads, met regularly to look at and test new products, as well as to propose modifications to existing standards.

The purchasing organization was reorganized to be able to offer a wider line of products with attractive "net" prices, replacing the former purchasing commission system. Products which IHC could not offer at competitive prices would be dropped from the line; hotels would be required to use the central organization whenever, but only if, cost advantage could be proven. As an added service, hotels could be invoiced and pay in any one of five major international currencies. Sources for comparable quality goods were identified in dollar, sterling, and European currency countries for most operating equipment so that as exchange rates varied from time to time IHC could shift its orders from one manufacturer to another thereby giving the best possible price, based on its local currency, to each hotel. A program was eventually developed by Craig Finefrock, the staff vice president responsible for the department's reorganization, for central purchasing to operate on a "break even" basis and to distribute its net earnings, after a reasonable allowance for overhead costs, back to its customers in the form of an annual rebate in proportion to each hotel's gross volume of business placed with Inter-Continental Purchasing Services (IPS), the new name for the procurement department. The remodeling and upgrading programs for the GMH properties were to be managed by the technical services department augmented with a small London office of former GMH staff.

Audrey Goldberg became the first woman to be an IHC corporate officer with her election as vice president – law and company secretary in 1983.

The other shareholders' interests in the London Penta and the Portman were purchased by IHC; the Penta became the Forum London and began a program of upgrading public spaces and elevators. The leasehold on the Mark Hopkins in San Francisco was also acquired.

Problems with the Boston hotel's partner's inability to conform to a pre-agreed construction schedule led to IHC's withdrawal from the project, giving rise to a lengthy lawsuit.

Consideration was given to moving the IHC head office to the United Kingdom in the hopes of synergistic, and basic operating, cost savings which might accrue from being closer to Grand Met's base. A well-known consultant firm which specialized in international corporate moves was asked to study the matter. The resulting report, supported with detailed cost comparisons, budgets for relocation, and estimates of redundancy costs and changes in productivity levels, indicated a total expenditure which would require several years to recover in operating cost savings. Not quantified, but described in the report, were the time and money costs of retraining and the significant intangible cost of the loss of knowhow which would of necessity follow the required large-scale layoff of existing staff. All in all a bad investment; the subject was dropped.

As his first step in planning improved system-wide manpower development programs, Meinen consulted with the division chief executives to identify, by priority, those activities which the operating group needed in order to improve their hotels' profitability. He then set about locating individuals and consultants to develop the required programs, among the first of which was a structured, annual, performance-review system to be applicable at every level of management from hotel department supervisors up to the senior executives of the corporation.

Inter-Continental for years had carried out an orientation program for newly appointed general managers which involved a several-day visit to the corporate head office to meet privately for an hour or so with each of the senior officers and department heads, to learn how the various head-office-directed activities of the company intermeshed to support and oversee individual hotels' operations. Under Meinen's leadership, a program was instituted to identify outstanding potential candidates for future promotion as general managers from among those currently employed as executive assistant managers and department heads. These individuals were brought to New York and met with a presidential review board (consisting of Sternik, Potter, Meinen, and one or more other officers) to discuss the candidate's goals and objectives, and to develop together a structured plan to assure a series of future assignments, or training activities, which would broaden the candidate's experience and knowledge as his or her career progressed.

OVERLEAF: The Amstel Inter-Continental in Amsterdam, seen from the Amstel River.

In connection with the Houston opening, Joe Smyth developed an incentive scheme to encourage visitors to the city to try the hotel. Any guest who stayed in it for five nights would receive a free economy-class round-trip ticket to Europe on Pan Am. Named "Houston Plus," the program was expanded the following year as "USA Plus" to include all of IHC's U.S. hotels, and to offer American Airlines domestic flights in addition to Pan Am European travel. By this time New Orleans and a 680-room property in San Diego had been opened.

The sudden increase in the volume of U.S.-originated business had led to the establishment of an IHC-staffed stand-alone reservations facility in Houston offering toll-free connections throughout the United States. Shortly thereafter a similar unit was opened in London, offering toll-free service within the United Kingdom and direct booking services from Europe that were handled by agents fluent in the principal European languages. Both offices were equipped with electronic measuring devices which recorded the time lag before each incoming call was handled, as well as the number of "lost" calls if a caller disconnected when he was not answered

promptly, and gave management the ability to monitor these offices' efficiency, and to regularly adjust staffing levels to correspond with demonstrated demand.

Like many conglomerate companies, Grand Met applied a measure of "return on capital employed" when allocating company assets for growth and development, and by this measure its hotel activities made a poor showing, particularly when compared with marketing companies whose fixed asset investment was modest. Since it was customary under standard United Kingdom accounting practice to revalue property assets on a regular periodic basis, it was almost impossible for the wholly owned hotels to improve their return. A hotel valued at, say, $50 million might be earning a return of $5 million, or 10 percent on capital employed. If the hotel were to increase its profit annually by $1.5 million, the valuation experts in the third year would increase the asset value – based on earnings growth and inflation – to at least $80 million and more likely to $85 million. Thus a 60 percent improvement in earnings, when measured by return on capital, would show zero growth or possibly a falloff to 9.4 percent. There was no solution to this paradox so long as a major portion of the company's income was flowing from its wholly-owned hotels.

But the pressure for improved performance remained, and was intensified when profits were negatively affected by international economic jolts which curtailed international travel for whatever reason. It is a fact of hotel-operating life that in a mature hotel, in a modestly inflationary environment operating at 70 percent occupancy or better, as much as 95 percent of every dollar of increased room revenue can flow to the bottom line, since the marginal costs of servicing the room are just about equaled by the marginal income which that room's guest produces in other services (food and beverage, laundry, telephone, etc.). Thus in good times, profits can be very, very good; but in the event of a four or five point reduction in occupancy, profits will experience a comparatively precipitous fall, even when the hotel immediately reduces guest-contact and restaurant-production staffing proportionately with the fall in number of customers. Any effort to fully protect profit in such times can succeed only through drastic reductions of, say, advertising and promotion (when it is most needed) or widespread reduction in the level of guest services and comfort – possibly counterproductive in the long run, particularly for a top of the line product. Two major shocks – a worldwide inflation, and a collapse of world oil prices – occurred during the 1980s. Each forced IHC and its hotels to develop contingency operating plans which could be put into effect on short notice to minimize the negative effects on net profit.

Within two years the Europa (London) and Prince des Galles (Paris) were sold to Marriott and the Lotti (Paris) to the Italian Jolly Group.

Sheeline and Sternik continued to be troubled by the growth in corporate overhead costs. A comparison of head counts with those of one of the company's chief competitors revealed that, while the organizational set-up was different, the total overheads were almost identical. While IHC tended to perform many functions in-house, the competitor's costs for the same services purchased from outsiders were the same or higher, although the competitor could discontinue or reduce the scope of a function without the inconvenience or redundancy costs of staff cutbacks.

In 1984 Booz, Allen, Hamilton was engaged, once again, to analyze IHC's operation and its growth plan, and recommend an organizational structure which could manage the business more efficiently with, it was hoped, fewer people. Their conclusion: further decentralization together with increased accountability for the division chief executives. Taking into account the growth pattern and the location of IHC's principal assets, the world was repartitioned into four geographical areas, each headed by an area chief executive, each with sufficient staff to take complete responsibility for operations, accounting, sales, marketing, and development within his area. The head office would limit itself to policy, and those system-wide functions which could only be efficiently performed at the center: corporate planning, corporate accounting, investment planning, worldwide reservations, worldwide marketing and corporate identity, central purchasing, and standards. Development and technical services, while continuing to report to the center, would perform as service providers to the area chief executives, with one or more individuals in each department more or less exclusively assigned to projects within a specific area. The head office would be strengthened with the appointment of an executive vice president – operations. The new assignments were: executive vice president – operations, Pierre Martinet; president – Europe/Middle East, Peter Balas; president – Pacific, Asia, Latin America, Kane Rufe; president – North America, Michael Cairns; president – Forum, Edward Trippe; president – Africa, Alex Furrer; president – Latin America (reporting to Rufe), Mario di Genova.

An appetizing display of seafood at the Inter-Continental Mombasa in Kenya.

Trippe's appointment recognized that Forum's main priority was growth and development. Reynolds Burgund succeeded him as head of the development department.

While the plan established a more efficient structure for managing the business, and took into account the need for succession planning at the top, its net effect on head count was much less than hoped for. When a subsequent study of IHC's computerized management systems revealed the need for strengthening in this area, IHC was no leaner in total members of staff, a situation which was becoming of increasing concern to Sheeline and Sternik as well as to Grand Met.

In Africa a new Mount Kenya Safari Club all-suite hotel was opened in Nairobi under IHC management; the original seventy-room club at Nanyuki had been under IHC supervision since 1980. New hotels in Mombasa in Kenya, and Franceville, Gabon, would open in 1985. And the division had taken on responsibility for the construction and operation of casinos in Nairobi, Zambia, and Zaire, as adjuncts to the hotels in each location.

A hotel in Luxembourg, which was originally planned as a Forum, was changed in mid-construction to be an Inter-Continental, and enlarged in size – two decisions which increased its capital cost to a level which would make acceptable returns almost impossible when the hotel finally opened.

Many of the former GMH hotels were classic older buildings built long before the imposition of strict fire-safety construction codes. All of the older IHC-designed properties were planned according to the then-current standards applicable in the United States, or local country, whichever was the more strict, but were in many cases out of date by the 1980s. The takeover of the GMH properties was the catalyst in leading IHC to undertake a system-wide review of life-safety standards and institute a program of retrofit on all properties to assure an optimum level of safety for guests and staff. Two disastrous fires at competitive hotels which received worldwide publicity lent a sense of urgency to the project and helped to convince hotel owning companies of the absolute need to make the necessary capital expenditures.

At a meeting of all of the officers at the newly opened Inter-Continental Hilton Head Resort, a serious discussion of IHC's appropriate role in resort development led to a policy based on the company's known strengths and weaknesses in marketing such properties: Inter-Continental would develop resorts only where:

(a) The location was an established destination with the necessary air service, highways, and other infrastructure already in place. (IHC could not afford the cost of pioneering.)

(b) The "high" season was at least four months a year, with a climate which would attract shoulder-season business for at least eight additional months. (Hilton Head had already proven to be unsaleable, except at giveaway rates, for six months a year.)

(c) The property would have facilities, and be conveniently enough located, so as to be able to attract business meetings and conferences at least six, and preferably nine, months a year. (Frequent business travelers were IHC's bread and butter; its marketing people were in regular contact with them.)

(d) The proportion of strictly vacation travelers would be no more than 30 percent of total volume. (IHC had no sales organization in place to regularly reach this market segment; the hotel's own staff would have to carry the burden.)

(e) The destination was sufficiently attractive and the level of competition sufficiently balanced that room rates at least 90 percent of IHC city hotel rates – and during the high season, higher – could reasonably be expected.

Eleanor Leslie became vice president – marketing planning and research, IHC's second woman vice president, and Jack Kennedy, who had been working on the promotion of group meeting business and had served a short term as general manager in Fort Lauderdale, was elected vice president – corporate sales.

The Inter-Continental Sydney was a unique combination of

OPPOSITE: The Inter-Continental Sydney opened in 1985 in the city's historic treasury building which was converted to include shops, bars, lounges and restaurants. Its vaulted sandstone cortile is an example of the careful restoration that went into the conversion.

BELOW: Lord McAlpine of West Green, Inter-Continental's partner in the ownership of the Hotel Inter-Continental Sydney, surveys the harbor view with Stefan Bokaemper, hotel general manager.

RIGHT: An old print showing Sydney's treasury building. At one time Australia's "finance ministry," it was later restored as the Inter-Continental Sydney.

modern architecture and classic restoration. The historic treasury building was put up for tenders on a long-term lease. McAlpine and IHC through their jointly owned Apsley Hotels Ltd. (owning company of Inter-Continental London) developed a plan to restore it to include restaurants, shops, bars, and lounges, and to construct an adjacent tower containing 500 guest rooms, rooftop health club, and technical plant. Built on a high point in the central business district, guest rooms offered views of the Sydney Harbour Bridge, or the opera house, or the botanical garden with the harbor and the ocean beaches in the distance. The central cortile atrium of the treasury building, with its iron-caged elevator, would become a popular lounge and Sydney meeting place serving light meals and beverages.

The Al Bustan Palace Inter-Continental Muscat was an unusual fusion of deluxe commercial hotel and private royal guest palace. It was constructed in a record two years by a Cypriot firm which was also one of the principal owners of the Athenaeum Inter-Continental, and its lavish interiors were the creations of Rochon of Paris, the firm which had been in charge of the redesign and restoration project at the Carlton Inter-Continental in Cannes. The 300-room hotel included one floor of royal suites. Reached via private elevators, each suite was decorated to reflect the culture of one of the member states in the Gulf Cooperation Council. The opening coincided with the celebration of the fifteenth anniversary of the reign of Sultan Qabus. In Saudi Arabia, IHC opened its fourth hotel, in Abha, an agricultural area in the south of the kingdom.

A "401-K" capital accumulation plan was made available to all corporate employees and general managers whereby employee contributions, matched by company contributions, would be invested in a selection of mutual funds (unit trusts), the earnings on which would accrue tax

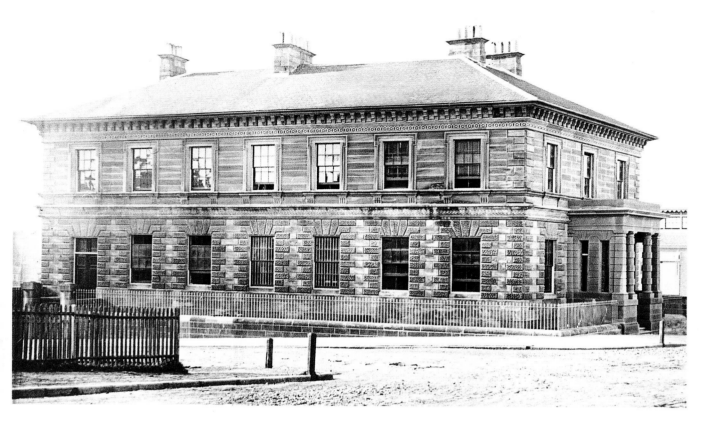

The original treasury building in Sydney was built in three stages between 1851 and 1920. Inter-Continental spent three years restoring it to its former glory.

free until such time as the balances were actually withdrawn. The contribution itself could be deductible from gross income for U.S. income tax purposes, with certain restrictions.

On October 1 1985, Hans Sternik became chief executive officer (continuing as president), with Sheeline remaining as chairman. In his nearly fifteen years as chief executive, Sheeline had presided over a hotel group which had more than doubled in size, with a fifteenfold increase in profits. The quality and consistency of the company product had been steadily improved. Within its target market, IHC had carved out a leading position in the world. Its reputation as a fair and attractive employer, offering professional growth opportunities, assured a steady flow of ambitious and talented managers at entry level positions, although wage levels were certainly not the highest in the industry. Relationships had been nurtured and strengthened with the owning companies of Inter-Continental managed hotels; Sheeline took pains that no one should forget that a hotel owner is as much Inter-Continental's customer as the guest who walks into the hotel lobby. The notion that a management contract without an equity participation was a "no risk" venture was put to rest; if IHC were to manage a given hotel, it would have to put total project profitability high on its list of goals. Perhaps the overriding characteristic of Sheeline's management style was a commitment to business integrity. No one who worked with him could ever have the slightest doubt as to where he and IHC stood on matters of professional ethics.

The Pakistan government, after several changes in policy, decided to privatize its holding in the Inter-Continental hotels. A local entrepreneur offered to purchase IHC's investment and to buy out the management agreements, subject to all accounts being settled and remittances effected. It was to be the first time in twenty years that IHC's accounts receivable from Pakistan would be anything like current.

RADICAL CHANGE

Pan Am was contracting its operations. It had sold its Pacific route system and was withdrawing from cities on routes which were consistent money-losers. Its ability to continue to provide worldwide communications services to IHC was increasingly in doubt. Badly needed enhancements to Panamac in order to improve IHC's access to a wider on-line customer base rated a low priority at Pan Am, which was itself considering a merger of Panamac into another airline's system. Clearly IHC would have to find an alternate reservations system. To lead in this undertaking, as well as an overall reappraisal of computer-based management systems, John Cahill was recruited from the Sheraton organization to be IHC vice president – management information systems. "Global II," the name given to IHC's new reservations and communications system, was given the go-ahead in October 1986, with a development budget of $8.5 million. The system would provide direct on-line connections to major airline reservations systems, and through them to at least 60,000 retail and wholesale travel agencies throughout the world, offering a "paper free" format for making bookings, whether on a travel agent's personal computer or at a reservation station in an IHC booking office. Complete data on each hotel could be called onto the user's screen, along with room availability, rate information, special promotions – everything which might be needed to fill the traveler's needs and confirm his booking. The system would also provide statistical data to track agency production and the effectiveness of individual marketing promotions. Each hotel would continue to control its own availability, with the ability to effect status changes instantaneously at any time.

Later enhancements to the system would enable the tracking of Six Continents Club members' and top client hotel usage throughout the chain.

In its initial design Global II could be programed to accommodate 200, later 300, individual hotels. After a worldwide training program at every level, involving more than 600 company employees in forty countries, the system would go into operation early in 1988 from its Stamford, Connecticut, base. Within six

With just three words you can get VIP treatment around the world… "Six Continents Club"

The Six Continents Club, a guest recognition program, started in 1966, was expanded over the years.

years, Global II would deliver bookings for more than 30 percent of IHC's room revenue (in some hotels, nearly 50 percent), with a huge growth in airline-system-generated reservations.

Peter Smith, a marketing specialist recruited from Johnson and Johnson, joined Inter-Continental as senior vice president – marketing and sales, replacing Joe Smyth, who resigned and took up a position with Hilton Hotels Corporation.

Early in 1986 it was apparent that bookings for the upcoming summer season in Europe were behind plan; dollar values were falling and worries about exchange rates made many would-be travelers wary. IHC developed a special Europe-wide summer sale offering, in most cases, substan-tially discounted rates quoted in guaranteed dollar amounts. This program, enhanced from year to year, would become a perma-nent IHC promotional feature, and would significantly reduce wide occupancy fluctua-tions which many of the commercial prop-erties had experienced during the summer months in prior years. It would be expanded to the United States and other appropriate destinations in later years.

A 650-room hotel had been built on a prime waterfront Biscayne Bay site in down-town Miami by Ted Gould, a successful property developer who was determined to create in the hotel, and adjacent office and residential blocks, a genuine monument to quality. No expense was spared: meters and meters of marble, handmade woolen rugs, 12-foot matched paneled doors, silver from Italy, china from West Germany, four restaurants each with its own kitchen area, south Florida's largest ballroom (designed to be convertible to a casino if the laws would one day be changed to permit licensed gaming), buildings designed by famed archi-tect Pietro Belluschi and a centerpiece sculpture by Sir Henry Moore. It opened with Trust House Forte management and the owner and operator immediately clashed, Forte left, and the hotel's occupancy hovered around 6 percent. The lending banks seized control of the property through foreclosure and while the case was dragging through the courts, development staff vice president John Cashman (a former area financial vice president for Europe who had joined IHC in Ireland and served in a variety of finance positions in Europe and head-quarters) negotiated an interim IHC management arrangement on the property through contacts

The Inter-Continental Miami's lobby features *The Spindle*, an 18-foot marble sculpture created by Sir Henry Moore.

which he had developed with the lead bank on another project. Although the hotel was still not totally complete, IHC was able to secure emergency funds to furnish the top suite in time for a Miami visit by President Reagan, the publicity surrounding which helped to put the hotel on the map. The occupancy was tripled in three months and by 1989 had reached 68 percent. In 1986 Chris Mander took over the property for IHC as general manager.

Mander had been a cost accountant in a paint factory in the United Kingdom, was visiting Helsinki at the time of Inter-Continental's opening there in 1972 and responded to an advertisement seeking a chief accountant. Told that his inability to speak Finnish precluded his being considered, he turned up at the hotel and was offered a job in the steward's department, with a work permit, which he accepted as he wanted to remain in Finland to pursue a romantic attachment. In three months, he moved from dishwashing to night audit to assistant chief accountant. His career took him to Kabul as chief accountant, to Istanbul as controller – only to wait for the hotel to be completed; and to Teheran in the era of 100+ percent occupancies. (A *Gourmet* travel and food article of the time noted that there were four unique restaurants in Teheran, and that if you were lucky enough to be staying at the Inter-Continental three of them were under the same roof: a French rôtisserie, a Persian cuisine jewelbox, and an Asian/Polynesian rooftop.) His next posting was to Dubai as regional operations analyst for the Middle East. He accepted an offer of a position as sales director in Dubai, commenting: "It will certainly be good experience for me, I don't know whether it will be good for IHC!" This was the time when four new hotels had opened in Dubai and Inter-Continental's occupancy had fallen to the fifties, while it maintained its leading food and beverage position in the community. He then joined the Mid East Division office in Athens taking charge of personnel while serving as Martinet's assistant. With the exception of Jordan, more than 80 percent of the Mid East hotel staff were expatriates so it was necessary to maintain and operate a full-time recruitment program attracting workers from some twenty different countries. Based on a well-structured training and executive succession program which he developed for the

Chris Mander joined Inter-Continental in 1972 in Helsinki and in 1995 became general manager – Hotel Inter-Continental Chicago and regional vice president operations – Canada.

division, Sternik selected Mander to be his assistant in the head office, with the added responsibility of preparing a hotel personnel manual for use throughout the chain. Returning to hotel operations, Mander succeeded Fred de Roode (who was being transferred to Maui) as resident manager at the Inter-Continental New York, before his assignment in Miami.

A joint venture was formed with Banamex (a Mexican banking and property group) to develop a group of top-class hotels in Mexico. While priority was to be given to a commercial property in Mexico City, the plan would involve hotels throughout the country, under a "Sierra Inter-Continental" brand name. An existing hotel in Monterey was acquired, to be rehabilitated by the group; rectifying its life-safety shortcomings consumed most of the capital budget. Construction would be undertaken on resorts in Cancun and Manzanillo, but the partners were never successful in locating a suitable site in Mexico City. Continuing disagreements over standards (IHC expected a product superior to the Hyatt and Westin properties) and adherence to engineering specifications (in the Cancun hotel local project managers authorized an air-conditioning installation which was woefully inadequate for the building and which ignored the specification provided by IHC) would result in a dissolution of the partnership four years later.

In Washington Golding, the original successful bidder for the Willard restoration, had been unable to finance his project, to the annoyance and embarrassment of the Pennsylvania Avenue Development Commission (PADC) which had set a time deadline for construction to begin. Golding eventually contacted the Oliver T. Carr Company (with whom IHC had been associated) and the two developers redesigned the project, combining Golding's tender-winning facades with Carr's proportionate hotel/commercial/retail space utilization formula, eventually receiving the necessary authorizations to proceed. IHC's technical services department, particularly architect Pat Gemma, played a key role in the complete redesign of the Golding scheme's hotel space layout, resulting in improved operating efficiency and enhanced guest convenience. Through consultation with the U.S. Secret Service, plans for elevators, suite configurations, and communications systems were adjusted to provide optimum security for visiting heads of state. The restoration process, insisted upon by PADC, was exacting and costly as most of the interiors were in derelict condition. Using old photographs as a guide, moldings, lighting fixtures, furnishings, wallcoverings, mosaic floors, woodwork paneling, and column finishes were re-created, often requiring special artisans experienced in some of the finishing styles common at the turn of the century.

The hotel reopened to the public in August 1986. The night before, the actresses Mary Martin and Carol Channing were forced to interrupt their performance of *Legends* at the nearby National Theatre because of a bomb scare; they came knocking at the Willard front door looking for safety, and were happily received.

The formal inaugural week featured a series of social events involving the various agencies which had made the restoration possible, the chief justice of the United States, and President Reagan, whose alma mater, Eureka College, gave a fund-raising benefit at the Willard. Press coverage treated the reopening as an event of historic importance.

Heading up this extraordinary Inter-Continental operation was J. T. Kuhlman, who had joined

OVERLEAF: A "Welcome Home" parade for troops returning after World War I, led by President Wilson, passed the Willard Hotel and its adjacent Occidental Restaurant on Pennsylvania Avenue. Inset: The hotel, restored to its former glory, opened as the Willard Inter-Continental in 1986.

General manager J. T. Kuhlman greets President and Mrs. Reagan during the official opening of the Willard Inter-Continental in Washington in September 1986. A fund-raising dinner for Eureka College, the president's alma mater, was held at the hotel as part of the opening festivities.

Inter-Continental in 1975 as a twenty-eight-year-old assistant food and beverage manager at the Embajador in Santo Domingo. His original ambition had been for a career in the foreign service, following in his father's footsteps, for which he studied at the Maxwell School of International Studies at Syracuse University. Upon graduation he was turned down by the U.S. State Department, whose hiring profile at the time was biased away from the traditional background from which Kuhlman had come. He took a job with Club Med as a "G.O." – very attractive and fun kind of work for a twenty-three-year-old – in Martinique and Acapulco. Returning to Miami, he visited Pete Sutherland, a close friend of the family (Kuhlman's father was stationed in Santiago when Sutherland was running the Carrera), who advised him to go to hotel school. Kuhlman enrolled at Miami's Florida International University and with credits from his Syracuse courses earned a degree in nine months. After Santo Domingo, he served as assistant food and beverage manager during the opening in Maui, and later as Pete Sutherland's administrative assistant in the America's Division office. After resident manager positions in Rio and Fort Lauderdale, he was assigned to the Castellana in Madrid as general manager, where he supervised a modest upgrading of the hotel's public spaces. A three-month assignment at the St. Anthony in San Antonio preceded his selection for the Willard.

From its earliest days, when Inter-Continental was often the most modern hotel edifice in its city or nation, the company had taken a leading role in controlling utility costs. A utilities rate consultant reviewed monthly billings for power from each hotel and negotiated with local suppliers to assure the best possible rates under existing tariffs, and frequently to introduce separate rate scales for hotels. In locations with power scarcity problems the electricity bill of the IHC hotel might be one of the highest in the city. In the late 1970s and early 1980s as energy costs were rising all over the world, Inter-Continental had undertaken an in-depth study of conservation practices which could control and reduce hotel energy consumption, and protect the environment into the bargain. Under the direction of Reiner Boehme, IHC's staff vice president – engineering, pilot studies were undertaken in several European hotels which established conclusively that a program of sub-metering to measure consumption in the various departments of the hotel would localize energy consumption data so that department heads could analyze their own departments' energy costs, and take meaningful steps to control this consumption. Boehme, with a university degree in electrical engineering, and experience in construction, had joined Inter-Continental in 1970, responding to a newspaper advertisement, and was assigned to Kabul (a city which he had visited on a hitchhiking round-the-world journey when he was fresh out of school) as assistant chief engineer. During his three and a half years in Afghanistan the hotel's engineering department undertook outside maintenance work for embassies and businesses in the city. During his assignment as chief engineer in Teheran he established engineering administrative systems which became IHC standards, and managed to reduce energy costs by 25 percent. His next posting was to Istanbul, where his detailed lists of incomplete construction and engineering facilities resulted in a two-month delay in the opening of the hotel while necessary corrective action was being taken. Next to Jakarta, where original problems with the plumbing and air-conditioning systems were still being corrected. With an engineering and maintenance crew of 130 people, later increased to 170, the hotel undertook such major improvement projects as the expansion of the hotel's sports facilities, and the conversion of one guest room floor to residential apartments (the cost of which was recovered in less than a year). By 1980, Boehme was transferred to a base in Frankfurt where he took responsibility for maintenance engineering in the European hotels, and played a leading role in the detailed study of the GMH properties which led to the selection of those to be integrated with Inter-Continental, and in the programs for their upgrading.

By December 1986, Sternik had determined to expand the pilot energy-control program to the entire chain. Its full implementation, unfortunately, would be impeded by a series of changes in corporate leadership which would begin in 1987 and continue for at least four years.

Late in 1986, Peter Balas resigned and became president of the International Hotel Association, ending an Inter-Continental career of nearly thirty years during which he had had personal hands-on involvement with the planning, opening or takeover of more than eighty hotels, no doubt some kind of record in the industry. Ed Trippe succeeded him as IHC president – Europe and Middle East, with Horst Handl, then regional vice president for West Germany, to assume additional responsibilities for European operations.

Continuing losses led to a decision to sell Houston and San Antonio; under British accounting the properties became inventory held for sale, and the losses would be charged to reserves rather than be consolidated into IHC's trading profit.

Peter Smith had conducted an advertising agency review and recommended the selection of Lois Pitts Gershon Pon/GGK to develop a new coordinated print and television campaign for use worldwide. On television the main thrust would be in the United States where IHC's brand-name recognition among domestic frequent travelers still fell far behind many of its competitors. George Lois and the agency staff studied the company, its product and its reputation and were impressed by the internationalism, the high rate of repeat business, and the level of personal service,

personified by the deep involvement and commitment of the group's general managers. The campaign would emphasize these strengths by featuring representative photographs of individual hotels, the general managers themselves, and the phrase "again and again" spoken in each hotel's local language. Print advertising, and collateral materials to be produced in the hotels, would feature a distinctive "Inter-Continental blue" background. Using telephone research IHC determined that brand awareness after three weeks of television advertising jumped 100 percent. But follow-up research three months later showed a fall back to the pre-television level, a disappointing result.

In the United Kingdom, Sir Stanley Grinstead was preparing to retire as Grand Met chairman, and Allen Sheppard, group managing director for the company's United Kingdom brewing, consumer services and foods businesses was designated as his successor, at the same time taking on responsibility for the Inter-Continental business. Sheppard, who had come to Grand Met from the automobile industry, had scored major successes in leading the restructuring of many of the United Kingdom businesses to achieve improved operating efficiencies and to concentrate on marketing strengths. In his view Inter-Continental's rate of return on capital was clearly inadequate when compared with other Grand Met core businesses. He challenged IHC senior management to "half" the company, that is: to operate with a substantially reduced corporate head count. He shortly appointed Ian Martin, former head of the breweries business and currently in charge of Grand Met's U.S. businesses, to oversee a restructuring of Inter-Continental. A survey conducted by a Grand Met brewing executive, John Jagger, produced a radical program for corporate reorganization involving additional decentralization to regional operations executives, the elimination of support staff at the area chief executive level, the consolidation of management responsibility into three geographical areas (Americas/Pacific; Middle East/Africa; Europe) and the replacement of in-house services (marketing design, for example) with outside consultants and service providers. Coming from a non-hotel background, Jagger brought no bias to his task; he was able to concentrate on the singular goal of head-count reduction. In early September 1987 Martin studied Jagger's recommendations and within days a series of reassignments and resignations was set in motion which would permanently alter the company's structure.

Sternik, Strachan, and Trippe were the first to leave. Responsibilities were changed from day to day: Martinet had three different titles in four months before he finally resigned. The board of directors ceased to meet, and Martin took full charge.

Early in 1987 international travel had begun to rebound. IHC's trading profit for the fiscal year ended September 30 1987, the last of the old regime, rose to £37.9 million, a 25 percent increase over the prior year.

Strategically, Grand Met was evolving into a group each of whose core businesses was to be among the leading players in the world marketplace. The IDV wines and spirits business was by one measure or another the world's largest. Could the hotel business fill a similar role? Certainly not with the existing portfolio and, growing at the then current rate of three or four properties a year, not in the foreseeable future. United Airlines, under pressure from Wall Street, was in the process of divesting itself of the hotel and rental car businesses which it had acquired in an effort to become a complete travel company. Hilton International which it had acquired only a few months earlier had been sold to the English Ladbroke group. Now Westin was being put on the market. Its strengths – the United States and Central America – would mesh well with Inter-Continental and result in a combined group of nearly 200 properties. In only a few cities were both companies represented, and in the event of a merger one or the other property could be sold. Westin was well experienced and successful in the United States; presumably its operating talent could add value to IHC's not yet very profitable U.S. properties. A task force was formed to make an in-depth study of Westin. Except for the numbers of staff needed to operate the central reservations offices, a number which could only be determined by experience and business volume, the task force calculated that the merged Westin/IHC could be operated with a corporate head count increase of only 35 percent above IHC's planned staffing levels, while increasing gross revenues by nearly as much as 80 percent. A bid was made for the major portion of Westin, but was passed over by United in favor of an offer for the entire group from a consortium of the Japanese Aoki interests (with hotel operations in Brazil) and the Texas Bass Brothers. Had the Grand Met bid succeeded, the merger of the two groups would have consumed the major portion of 1988.

Martin had instituted a detailed review of all development activity then in progress and canceled any projects which were not located in high visibility, strategically important major cities. In the confusion surrounding the corporate reorganization, new hotel development activity came to a near halt for almost a year. Patrick Copeland was transferred from a senior marketing position in IDV to become chief executive of Inter-Continental and John Jagger was named chief operating officer with responsibility for marketing and directing the three area chiefs: Cairns – Europe; Rufe – Americas/Pacific, to be based in the head office; and Furrer – Middle East/Africa, whose office was moved to London, sharing a space which had been rented as an IHC Europe-cum-Forum headquarters a year or so earlier with Cairns.

Grand Met USA occupied a leased building in suburban Montvale, New Jersey, which had been acquired along with Liggett. With the divesting ("decluttering" was the colorful term) of several of the U.S. businesses (tobacco was finally disposed of), Grand Met no longer needed more than 40 percent of the building. With a rental less than a third of what IHC was paying for its New York center-city office space, a move by IHC made good economic sense. An additional benefit might be the end of the Teamsters Union representation of IHC office staff, with a healthy corresponding increase in productivity.

For many in the Avenue of the Americas headquarters, changing their place of work to New Jersey was impossible because of commuting costs and family considerations; for others it was so inconvenient as to be unacceptable. The lack of public transport made commuting except by automobile exceedingly difficult. Grand Met made generous relocation allowances for those who would move and separation payments for those who could or would not. These costs, the cost of the final buy-out of the union contract, the costs of the move, and the redundancy costs for the cut heads around the world, were borne by Grand Met in its accounts, under the heading "Reorganization Costs," and are reported to have totaled nearly $20 million, the sort of one-time expenditure which a large conglomerate can swallow as an investment in future profitability. An added burden was placed on the company's pension reserves since many of those departing would do so as early retirees, in many cases some ten years ahead of normal retirement age. With completion of the move to Montvale three people remained from the head office marketing group, one from development, and not a single secretary. The learning curve was steep indeed; teaching an entire clerical staff the communication codes for 100 cities around the world – half of which they might never have heard of – was a very elementary first step in re-creating a smoothly functioning office.

Albert Pucciarelli, Inter-Continental's executive vice president, general counsel and secretary.

With the move to Montvale, and the continuing reorganization, IHC lost Martinet, Burgund, Leslie, Meinen, Leidner, Smith, and, in the field, Peter Birchall, a highly regarded general manager, who had joined IHC from Marriott and served with distinction as general manager in Rio, Lisbon, and Paris. Sheeline, who had retired in 1986, continued to be paid under a consulting arrangement, but his services were never requested. Steve Landon, who had joined IHC in 1978 and had become senior vice president – finance and controller, was transferred to Grand Met. Albert Pucciarelli, a long-time member of the Grand Met USA law department, became IHC's senior vice president and general counsel.

Several new marketing executives with experience in consumer products including, of course, United Kingdom beers were engaged by Jagger to invigorate IHC's promotional activities. The Six Continents Club was reinvented; six months earlier it had been seen as an unnecessary project for a couple of heads which had needed to be cut, and had been sent into limbo.

In the last week of March 1988, a worldwide meeting of all IHC executives and general managers (the first such in the memory of all but a handful of attendees) was staged at the May Fair

Inter-Continental London, to review the progress to date of the reorganized company and set the tone for vigorous growth and profitability. Orchestrated to the nth degree and ending up with a gala banquet (featuring an off-color after-dinner speaker), it was designed to rebuild morale and set a tone for the future. Martin expressed confidence that Inter-Continental, leaner and meaner, could now aspire to being a core business within the Grand Met scheme of things. He was honest to a fault, however, in responding to a question concerning Grand Met's long-term commitment to the hotel business: we've been offered more than a billion dollars for IHC within the past weeks and we turned it down . . . but everything has its price.

In the Middle East the Semiramis Inter-Continental Cairo, an 840-room property overlooking the Nile (whose construction had been twice delayed by financing problems and disputes with consultants) opened in 1987 with Raymond Khalifé as general manager. Ben Thompson was the architect and Dale Keller created the interiors. Having been advised in January of a July 1987 opening, Khalifé had commenced full-scale marketing, engaged 1,200 staff and begun training when the contractors announced a likely further delay. On June 1 Khalifé gathered 600 employees at the site in the hotel lobby to send a message about meeting the July date. The construction and furnishing firms took note, and moved into high gear with the result that 100 rooms were available and opened for business on July 15, and the hotel was totally completed by mid-October. By April 1988 IHC was the city leader in room rate and operating profit.

The principal Cairo shareholder – the al Suleiman group from Saudi Arabia – had also built a splendid 500-room IHC hotel in Jeddah, designed by Bill Tabler as architect. As

ABOVE: The original Semiramis in Cairo operated for more than seventy years, from 1897 to 1974.
RIGHT: The Semiramis Inter-Continental opened on the site of the original hotel in 1987.

construction neared completion, it was purchased by the royal protocol department for use as a palace guest house, and added to the group of palaces supervised by IHC.

In the fiscal year 1987 the wholly owned Inter-Continental New York, under Fred Peelen's direction, and the Inter-Continental London, in the last year under Graham Jeffrey's direction, led the group in contribution to trading profit, the more remarkable in the latter case where IHC's equity participation was but 50 percent.

The Meurice in Paris was sold to the Aga Khan for operation by the Ciga Group. Grand Met used the occasion to make a gift of an ambulance for use in one of the Aga Khan's hospitals.

A major hotel opened in Seoul in time for the 1988 Olympic Games. Inter-Continental had become involved when the hotel was already half completed, and brought the Rifenberg architecture firm (a group which had done several IHC remodeling jobs) from Bangkok to design and install the interiors in record time. With project coordination under vice president – technical services Sydney Rappoport, and preopening operating planning directed by general manager Giorgio Bagnasco, a very tight schedule was met and the property opened full to capacity.

With another new agency in place, the corporate marketing group unveiled a striking series of advertising pieces featuring drawings by the well-known artist Michel Granger showing globes of the earth in various abstract formats (a carved orange and a knife on a pewter plate; a spherical piece of luggage; a globe posed before an open door) and carrying the tag line "It's where you go when you've arrived."

In 1988, John Jagger represented IHC at the opening of the Inter-Continental Stuttgart, and a Scanticon Conference Center Hotel opened near Minneapolis, Minnesota, in the United States. Participation in the financing of a Scanticon in the south of France, near Nice, was cancelled.

The Inter-Continental Seoul opened in 1988 to house visitors and competitors for the Olympic Games in Korea and is one of the country's most successful and luxurious properties.

OPPOSITE: An exterior view of the hotel.

Whether the Martin–Copeland–Jagger reorganized, down-sized management structure could be successful in significantly improving IHC's profitability and growing the company, would never be determined.

The sales of Hilton International and Westin at high multiples of their earnings had helped to set the stage for an intense international competition for established and trophy hotel properties. Prices were rising and deals were being consummated at extraordinarily high levels. Grand Met, which now knew that there was little possibility of doubling IHC's size in short order, and aware that other more attractive investment opportunities existed for building onto other core businesses, reached a decision before the middle of 1988 to dispose of IHC. To streamline the offering, the portfolio was stripped of its two main losers – Houston and San Antonio – by selling them to a Grand Met property company, and pending commitments reduced to a minimum.

On August 8 the company was publicly announced to be for sale. A data room was established for prospective purchasers to learn about its assets and contracts. Every hotel group in the world had a look, if only to secure some insight for future competitive advantage. On September 30 it was announced that the successful bidder was the Seibu Saison Group of Japan.

No provision was made for Grand Met to fully fund the pension scheme before the closing of the sale. Saison commenced detailed engineering and architectural studies which pinpointed the status of the various upgrading works-in-progress and the deferred maintenance conditions in certain other properties. The effectiveness of the company's existing marketing staff and programs was questioned. In final negotiations a hard bargain was driven by both sides, finally settling on a purchase price of some $2.2 billion. The deal closed on December 15, 1988. To its credit, Grand Met management had seized the moment and converted the underlying value of its long-term hotel portfolio into a handsome cash infusion immediately used to fund its acquisition of the Pillsbury Company. A year later the deal would probably not have been do-able, certainly not at the price. Sheppard and Martin had pulled off one of Grand Met's greater coups.

Saison was a group of Japanese companies engaged primarily in retail trade, whose genesis was in the Seibu department stores, established in the 1940s, which had begun a major expansion in the mid-1950s. By the time of the Inter-Continental acquisition the Saison Group was not only a leader in the operation of department stores, supermarkets, generic brand retailing, and convenience stores, but also had branched into property development including residential, commercial, resort, and hotel facilities, as well as retail travel operations, helicopter transport, and food processing. It had developed and promoted a major domestic and international credit card, and in many of its businesses had established ties and franchising relationships with such overseas companies as Sears Roebuck, Dunkin Donuts, Allstate Insurance, Jaguar, and Citroën. Several of the entities in the group were listed public companies. The creator of, and driving force behind, this conglomerate was Seiji Tsutsumi, an innovative strategic visionary and well-known patron of the arts. Through its theater and museum sponsorships (and the retail galleries in its stores) Saison provided support for performing and graphic artists. Seiji Tsutsumi was himself a poet and novelist.

The Inter-Continental acquisition offered Saison an opportunity to expand its horizons beyond Japan, to become a truly international player. Recognizing the need for a partner in a successful bid for IHC, Saison worked with Baron Hilton, chairman of Hilton Hotels Corporation (the owner and/or operator of Hilton Hotels in the United States) in analyzing the IHC business; the two agreed, subject to board approval, to make a joint bid to Grand Met. At the last minute Hilton's board balked at the price which was felt would be required to succeed, and withdrew from the consortium. There would have been tremendous synergy for Hilton, and the duplication of properties in a few U.S. cities would have provided opportunities for individual divestitures.

Saison decided to go ahead on its own. John van Praag, a one-time business consultant with McKinsey and Company, who had been involved in hotel development and investment banking in Asia, was engaged by Saison as a consultant, and during the due diligence period commenced discussions with SAS, the Scandinavian airline (which had been one of the bidders for IHC, in a consortium with VMS, at the time a powerful packager of hotel investments, based in Chicago) aimed at their joining in the acquisition. In Saison's and SAS's early studies, certain wholly owned IHC properties – where there was more than one property in a given city or where a property had a high trophy value but was not essential to IHC's mainstream frequent international business traveler network – were identified for probable sale, thereby financing as much as 15 to 20 percent of the purchase price of the group. Yuji Tsutsumi was named chairman of Inter-Continental; he had been an executive of Prince Hotels, a company controlled by another branch of the Tsutsumi family, and had later spent several years in Canada running some personal businesses before returning to Japan to consult with Saison in the construction and opening of the Seiyo Ginza Hotel, a super deluxe boutique property developed by the group on a nearly priceless city center site in Tokyo.

The Inter-Continental which Grand Met had acquired was professionally staffed and capable of operating itself. The company which Saison purchased had no one in its executive committee with more than a year's seniority with the company, and no one, with the exception of Emmett Gossen (in charge of business development, he had joined from a similar position with Sheraton), who had any track record of expertise or success in any aspect of the hotel trade. Michael Stajdel, vice president corporate sales, a lone holdover from pre-reorganization days, was the only ranking head office executive with experience in marketing and selling hotels. Unlike Grand Met, Saison had no cadre of internationally experienced individuals available to transfer from other companies in the organization. Bringing hotel professionalism to the executive suite was an urgent necessity. The due diligence exercise had revealed a strong and loyal cadre of hospitality professionals at the hotel level. It was this group of general managers and regional vice presidents, through their steady hands in the individual operations, who had kept the company moving ahead during Grand Met's year of corporate reorganization turmoil, and would do so again during the first years of Saison's ownership.

On December 21 1988 Pan Am flight 103 was blown up over Scotland by international terrorists. On board were Joyce di Mauro, IHC director of marketing design, and Roger Hurst, a recent hire as staff vice president – marketing operations; their boss Steve Dunn, a former Grand Met brewing executive, had switched his booking to British Airways at the last moment. Copeland delivered the message personally to di Mauro's family. William Ferguson (then the human resources senior vice president) and Potter drove to Hurst's home to inform his wife and assure her that she and their two small children had friends available for consolation at this difficult hour.

Early in 1989 Emmett Gossen successfully negotiated leases covering the formerly franchised Inter-Continental and the Schweizerhof hotels in Berlin, both of which were to be substantially upgraded by their new owner. A Scanticon Hotel and Conference Center – a joint venture with U.S. West, a regional telephone company – opened in a business park in suburban Denver, Colorado, and the Forum Glasgow commenced operations in Scotland. The franchised Forum Bratislava would open later in the year in Slovakia's capital.

Calling on long-term friendships with certain Westin executives, Yuji Tsutsumi approached Helmut Hoermann and succeeded in engaging him as president of Inter-Continental early in

1989. Hoermann had had a long and successful career with Hilton International (HI), starting in 1964 in a training program at the Queen Elizabeth in Montreal and serving as executive assistant manager in Montreal and Düsseldorf, before being named general manager in Berlin – at twenty-nine years of age Hilton's youngest. In 1974 he was transferred to Cairo and by 1988 he was in charge of some twenty Hilton hotels in the Middle East and Africa, based in Cyprus. In 1984 he moved to HI's head office as executive vice president, becoming president three years later just as HI was being acquired by United Airlines. Six months later HI was sold to Ladbroke's for $1.07 billion, and Hoermann went to Westin as president, a position which he then left shortly after Aoki's takeover. A few months later John Calvert, long-time chief financial officer of Westin, was brought to Inter-Continental and by mid-November 1989 had been named chief executive officer.

By April 1989 negotiations with SAS had resulted in the airline acquiring a 40 percent equity participation in IHC, with an investment of $500 million. SAS, under well-known management guru and chairman, Jan Carlzon, was embarking on a program to develop a comprehensive worldwide complete travel system offering a "seamless travel experience" where air and ground bookings could be made simultaneously and revised at any point in the course of a journey. Carlzon was building a network of airline alliances (Continental in the USA; LAN Chile in South America; Thai and ANA in Asia; and British Midlands in the United Kingdom) which would extend SAS's trunk route system to a large portion of the world. Swissair and Austrian Airlines were also targets for affiliation to improve SAS access in eastern Europe, Africa and the Middle East. An essential feature was the ground base to be provided at the hotel. Future enhancements would include on-board (or en route from the airport) hotel check-in, and airline check-in in hotel lobbies. IHC, with a quality image and a presence all over the world, seemed to be a perfect fit in this SAS push for an integrated worldwide network.

SAS had clear expectations as to profits and dividends and brought a somewhat pragmatic and conservative spirit to the table regarding expenditures for operating costs and investment. Saison's apparent long-term view of the efficacy of hotel property investment would seem to preclude the disposition of any hotels. It would be difficult if not impossible for the earnings of the existing hotels to service the acquisition debt, a problem with which both shareholders would shortly have to come to grips.

SAS was anxious to formalize and publicize the airline/IHC relationship at the hotel level. The existing SAS hotels were studied to determine whether, and how, they could be more closely integrated with the Inter-Continental and Forum brands. Other airlines with whom IHC had developed close working relations perceived (without any particular evidence to support such perceptions) that the SAS connection would work to their disadvantage, leading Lufthansa (by

Count Dr. Eckener and his Zeppelin
visit our Club by air.

now the owner of Penta Hotels and deeply involved with the Kempinski group) to press for a sale of its IHC equity positions and British Airways to seek another hotel group or groups to replace IHC as their preferred travel partner throughout Europe, the Middle East and Asia.

Copeland, Hoermann and Calvert introduced a new organizational structure in September 1989 which decentralized day-to-day operating responsibility to a group of eight senior vice presidents each operating on a stand-alone (that is, without a dual appointment as a hotel general manager) basis, and responsible for ten to twelve hotels. This group represented a wealth of IHC operating experience from all over the world; all but one of these executives had been with Inter-Continental for more than fifteen years: J. T. Kuhlman – France, Iberia, Mediterranean; John Wright – United Kingdom, Benelux; Horst Handl – Central Europe; René Protto – Africa; John O'Shea – North America; Tom Krooswijk – Middle East; Marcello Pigozzo – Latin America; Stefan Bokaemper – Pacific/Asia.

Provision was made for a major expansion of the worldwide sales force, with incentives for each sales group based on preset quotas. Such a financial commitment would require continuous monitoring to be certain that each sales office was justifying its cost in actual bookings; the ability to down-size, shut down, or relocate any given office based on production was an essential feature of the plan. John Davis-Slade was hired from outside the organization to oversee this build-up.

In Chicago, a major historic restoration combined with a rehabilitation of an adjacent post-war hotel block built by Sheraton had resulted in an upmarket Inter-Continental with a Forum Hotel next door, both supported with a combined back-of-the-house engineering, housekeeping, administration, and reservations system. Sandor Stangl, who had managed Inter-Continentals in Hanover and Hamburg (after leaving Jerusalem), and had been responsible for major rehabilita-

Before and after pictures of the Spanish court in the Hotel Inter-Continental Chicago (above and opposite bottom) and its swimming pool (above right and opposite top). IHC spent four years restoring the building to its original splendor and the hotel opened in 1990.

tion programs during his tenures as general manager in Vienna and San Francisco, transferred from San Diego to be general manager of the Chicago property. The original financing plan for the hotel had collapsed in mid-construction and IHC was faced with a need to assume 100 percent of the ownership and to secure bank finance.

An opportunity arose to acquire the Miami hotel from its lenders, and the board approved the transaction. Calvert had had Westin experience in syndicating hotel ownership partnerships, and it was expected that such a route would be followed to spin off a major share of the Miami and Chicago equity.

Late in the year, the Frankfurt hotel's shareholders decided to sell their shares and appointed BHF Bank to find a purchaser. Under pressure to better an offer which the bank was negotiating with an overseas property developer, IHC received authorization to acquire 100 percent of the shares, at a full price which was justified only when taking into account the potential value of the hotel's north parcel for alternate commercial development.

At a two-day workshop/brainstorming session held in January 1990 at a rural retreat in the Kent countryside, the company's shareholders, directors and officers participated in the development of a corporate mission statement, and discussed long-term implementation goals. A marketing research firm was commissioned to conduct an in-depth study of IHC's market position as perceived by its actual and potential clientele: "Project Argonaut."

TOWARD THE FUTURE

Early in 1990, a worldwide conference of general managers and executives was convened in Maui to communicate and discuss the goals and objectives which the shareholders had adopted for guiding the newly reorganized company in its future growth. The atmosphere was mostly upbeat and a clear sense of corporate purpose and direction was beginning to emerge after two and a half years.

Van Praag was by now a member of the management board and joint managing director with Calvert. A series of executive suite political maneuvers shortly thereafter led to the appointment of an in-house study group to review once again the IHC organization structure to see whether its operating costs could be curtailed – a concern being more frequently voiced by SAS. IHC's seniormost management was excluded from the discussions. The recommendation this time: move the company's headquarters to the United Kingdom; disband the expanded sales organization – which was about 60 percent staffed at the time; abolish the senior vice president operating group; centralize in London a cadre of four senior operating executives with area responsibility; and disband the quality assurance and internal audit functions. The directors were told that this change would reduce operating overheads by $20 million annually. No quantified analyses were presented to support the $20 million figure, nor was any budget developed for pre-estimating or controlling the cost of the proposed changes. Reportedly more than $35 million was spent in redundancy, separation, early retirement, rehiring, and moving costs together with capital improvements to newly leased office facilities. The contracts of Calvert and Hoermann, and most of the other head office senior officers, were bought out as the Montvale office was abruptly closed. Van Praag became chief executive. If SAS were expecting a leaner IHC to emerge, the lavish offices created in London's Devonshire House and the purchase of such luxury amenities as a six-passenger Daimler would no doubt come as a surprise.

The net result was a move to the United Kingdom, an immense loss of knowhow, a near halt in corporate direction while new people learned their jobs, and, as it worked out, no net reduction in operating costs. In the new organization J. T. Kuhlman would be IHC president, John Wright would take charge of European Operations; Raymond Khalifé, the Middle East and Africa; Stefan Bokaemper, Pacific/Asia; and Fred Peelen, the Americas. All would relocate to London. Cairns would be executive vice president in charge of "special projects."

An attempt to form a syndicate to own a portion of the equity of the Dutch and German hotels led to the acquisition of the Hotel des Indes in The Hague and a buy-out of the other shareholders in Cologne and Düsseldorf. Van Praag, who assumed that the syndicate price would reflect the stand-alone market values of the hotels, was forced to abandon the project when the underwriters did their asset valuations based on cash flow.

By the end of 1990 the acquisition bridge financing provided by Japanese banks had been renegotiated, with help from chief financial officer Ron Gilbert, who had joined IHC from the Transamerica group in December, leading to a drastic reappraisal of proposed capital expenditure.

The moves and reorganization were to have been completed and in full effect by January 1991. Suddenly, the Iraqi invasion of Kuwait and "Operation Desert Storm" brought international travel nearly to a standstill. Airlines on some days cancelled almost 50 percent of their transatlantic flights and long haul service to Asia was curtailed and rerouted. IHC's new operating group reacted with speed and decisiveness. Emergency programs were set in place to reduce services, staff, and costs in all hotels whose business was being affected by the war.

With substantially reduced funding foreseen for new development activities, the technical services, purchasing and development departments were targeted for further staff reductions.

IHC hotel staff in Saudi Arabia and the Gulf were essentially in a war zone. Kuhlman and Khalifé flew to Saudi Arabia to take hands-on responsibility for operations. With Scud missiles targeted at Riyadh, all IHC employees in the city were called together and offered transport to Jeddah in buses already parked in the hotel's carpark. None accepted the offer and the hotel's guests continued to be attended to, although it had been necessary to set up a bomb shelter, which was furnished with oriental carpets and a soft drink and refreshment bar to alleviate as much as possible any inconvenience and discomfort.

During 1991 IHC assumed an operating relationship with the newly restored Metropole Hotel in Moscow after a long series of negotiations spearheaded by Pucciarelli, who spoke the language and had long had an interest and a graduate degree in Russian affairs. While renegotiating the Tamanaco management contract with the Venezuelan Tudela interests, then the hotel's majority shareholders, IHC and Dr. Tudela evolved a plan for a joint venture company which would develop hotel opportunities in Venezuela and the Caribbean. The assumption of the management of a hotel in Santo Domingo in 1994 would be the first result of this cooperation.

Both of IHC's shareholders had a special interest, and well-publicized track records in, matters of environmental consciousness and preservation. IHC had introduced various environmentally sound practices over the years, but had never packaged or promoted these initiatives in a systematic manner. Van Praag and Kuhlman led a special effort which culminated in the publication of a manual and the establishment of a company-wide structured awareness and action program which would set industry standards. Special attention was given to laundry operations, a prime user of

OPPOSITE: The striking architecture of the Yokohama Grand Inter-Continental, opened in 1991, makes it a landmark in the city.

Dagmar Woodward joined Inter-Continental in 1971 and became the company's first female general manager in Europe. In 1992 she received the prestigious "U.K. Hotelier of the Year" award.

energy and chemicals in the hotel. Walter Behr, IHC's staff vice president laundry operations (who had been Vienna's youngest department head in 1964), and Boehme made major contributions to the manual task force, headed by Richard Hawkes (later Manila general manager). A continuing environmental council, under the chairmanship of May Fair Inter-Continental general manager Dagmar Woodward, would develop new programs and set annual achievement targets for such quantifiable environmental matters as energy consumption. Woodward, originally from Germany's Black Forest region, had joined the Frankfurt IHC in the early 1970s as an apprentice trainee chef, direct from hotel school. After a year, she took up a cashier's position at the Bristol and George V hotels in Paris, where she was also working part-time as a model. Moving to London, she continued modeling and worked as a temporary restaurant cashier at Brown's Hotel and in the personnel department of the Hyde Park Hotel. Returning to Inter-Continental at the opening of the hotel at Hyde Park Corner, she was initially a coffee house supervisor and eventually managed this 1,000 covers a day operation. Over the next years she held food and beverage management positions in London, Paris (at the Meurice), Washington, San Diego (helping with the turnover of the property to Marriott when IHC withdrew), and again in London at the Forum. After a period as resident manager in New York, she became general manager of the Portman, transferring to the May Fair in 1991.

In 1990, the Scanticon operation had become a serious cash drain on IHC; by late 1991, shepherded by Potter and David Hom, vice president and associate general counsel, IHC completed its divestiture of the Scanticon operating company and its equity investments.

During 1991, it was becoming clearer by the day that SAS and Saison interests were too far apart to assure consensus on basic issues of company control and direction. Van Praag attempted to identify potential investors to purchase or dilute the SAS interest and nearly reached an agreement with the Dieter Bock organization from Germany.

The Yokohama Grand Inter-Continental opened in 1991, the first hotel to be operated by IHC in Japan, with leading fashion designer Hanae Mori as its first guest. Gerhard Schmidt returned to Inter-Continental as general manager. Yokohama is a very popular weekend destination and,

unlike many city center hotels, had no difficulty filling its rooms on Fridays and Saturdays. Except when events were taking place in the contiguous convention center, the hotel faced low weekday occupancies. One promotion aimed at senior citizens offered an "age" discount for weekday visits: a sixty-five-year-old guest would qualify for a 65 percent discount. To introduce the promotion a famous pair of 120-year-old twins were invited and publicized while checking into the hotel. Their 120 percent discount resulted in a 20 percent payment to them by the hotel.

Sueaki Takoaka, chairman of Inter-Continental, 1992 – 96.

The Yokohama property also presented a classic example of controlling energy consumption. In the opening weeks, staff went about their work following their usual habits; and the first month's utility bills exceeded anything ever before experienced in Inter-Continental. A task force of senior hotel executives, with assistance from Boehme, analyzed the operation, comparing Yokohama consumption against IHC benchmarks, and pinpointed wasteful practices throughout the hotel. These included excessive use of water by room maids and cooks who would turn on spigots and leave them running; a tendency for cooks to light up all the ovens and burners on ranges and under woks when coming on duty and leaving them lit whether actually cooking or not; pumping heated and chilled water through the air-conditioning system pipes throughout the year, rather than chilled water exclusively in summer, and heated exclusively in winter months; and supplying 100 percent outside air to the ventilation system, rather than a mixture based on demand peaks and valleys during the day, particularly in kitchens and banqueting rooms. By installing submetering to identify departmental responsibility and instilling a sense of energy consumption and environmental awareness among the entire staff, energy cost reductions of $1 million were achieved in the fifteen months from June 1992 through September 1993.

In the first weeks of 1992 Saison began a reorganization of its management of the hotel business. The Seiyu Ltd., a Saison Group company engaged in a wide range of retail, publishing, financial, and entertainment activities, was to become the chief shareholder of IHC and to direct its future growth. Sueaki Takaoka, Seiyu's chairman, became IHC's chairman. Van Praag would shortly leave the company and Yuji Tsutsumi assumed other responsibilities in the Saison Group.

Takaoka, who died shortly before the publication of this book, was a Tokyo University graduate, and had taken an active part in journalism at the Chunichi Shimbun Newspaper Publishing and the Nippon Broadcasting System. In 1963, he joined the Seibu department stores and after this performed various important roles in the Saison Group, as well as in the retail industry in Japan. Appointed the chairman of the Japan Chain Stores Association in 1988, he became vice chairman of the Japanese Federation of Economic Organizations. He has published a number of books on the retail industry.

Celebrated for his profound knowledge of the arts, Takaoka, as the director of the Saison Museum of Arts and the president of the Ginza Saison Theatre in Tokyo, made great contributions in the introduction of modern arts, especially in Japanese films and plays. Several of his outstanding screen achievements, in which he participated as the executive producer, won prestigious prizes and are highly appreciated in Japan and elsewhere.

It should be noted that Takaoka also played an important role in some of the greatest court functions, as a nobleman descended from one of the Japanese royal families. He acted as a leader of the traditional recitation of Japanese poems at the New Year poetry party held in the imperial court.

Takaoka's urgent priorities were to buy out the SAS position, and to achieve an organizational and financial restructuring of the hotel group. A series of negotiations led by Gilbert and Sir Nicholas Pearson resulted in a SAS withdrawal in April 1992, involving a sale of IHC's ownership interests in the London Portman, and the Cologne and Düsseldorf hotels to SAS.

At Takaoka's insistence the senior operations executives were decentralized once again in September 1992, with Kuhlman taking over the western hemisphere from a Miami base, Bokaemper moving to Hong Kong to supervise Pacific and Asian operations under newly appointed area president Adachi; and Michael Cairns in London in charge of Europe and the Middle East. Peelen and Pigozzo would take responsibility for North and South America, respectively, under Kuhlman, while Khalifé would supervise the Middle East and Africa under Cairns. Cairns would resign a few months later to be replaced by John Wright. Wright had joined Grand Met in the late 1970s to operate two resorts in the north of Greece, having earlier led the operations of an English group with some twenty hotels in the Caribbean, Africa, and the Middle East. Later in charge of the Amra and Petra Forums when they opened, he was moved by IHC to London as general manager to oversee the conversion of the Penta London to the Forum London and the attendant £7 million upgrading program. Transferred to the United States to be general manager of the Inter-Continental Atlanta while it was under construction, he had been recalled to London to take regional responsibility for the United Kingdom hotels during the Martin/Jagger 1987–8 reorganization.

Robert B. Collier, joint managing director.

Each of the three operating divisions was to operate in many ways like a separate company with corporate support through a "services company" headed by Robert Collier. In the Van Praag 1990 reorganization Collier had been recruited away from Sheraton to head IHC's marketing and sales organization, the same position which he had held with ITT Sheraton and, before that, with Trust House Forte. Collier's degree in history from Cambridge University had led him initially into an entry-level position with a leading advertising agency. As a founding member of the International Hotels Environmental Initiative, born under the aegis of the Prince of Wales' Business Leader's Forum, Collier has played a leading role in Inter-Continental's, and the world hotel industry's, enhanced environmental awareness and performance.

After a comprehensive study of various applicable international tax aspects, carried out by IHC's long-time taxation vice president, John Tibbs, a financial restructuring was put in hand in 1993 to create an operating company which would hold and service hotel leases and management and franchise agreements. This company is foreseen to be listed on a major stock exchange some time in the future. Most of the group's property assets would continue to be held by property companies to be owned by various member companies in the Saison Group.

With the announcement of these major reorganizations, Collier was named

Gavin N. Simonds, joint managing director.

OVERLEAF: The Bali Inter-Continental Resort opened in 1993 and set new standards of luxury for future company resort developments.

Yuji Tsutsumi, chaiman of Inter-Continental's Asia/Pacific Division, 1995.

joint managing director responsible for the hotel operating side of the company early in 1994. Gavin Simonds was hired from the London investment banking firm Kleinwort Benson to be joint managing director responsible for finance, legal, property management, and corporate planning activities. His expertise would be called upon to instill the sort of discipline which would be required for a successful relationship with the investor public when IHC goes public.

The privatization of the former East German hotel company gave Hans Worms, newly appointed IHC senior vice president – business development, an opportunity to conclude leases and management contracts for Forum hotels in Berlin and Hamburg, and an Inter-Continental standard hotel in Leipzig. Contracts were also secured for an existing Forum class hotel in Geneva, and the Churchill, a first-class luxury property on Portman Square in London.

Shortly after the Saison acquisition, Steve Fukuda, a Cornell graduate who had worked with Yuji Tsutsumi in Canada, had joined the IHC development department from Saison and had negotiated a long-term management agreement for a top-class resort in Bali. Designed by the well-known, environmentally super-sensitive, Indonesian architect Hadi Prana, the completed hotel would feature an extraordinary variety of materials, finishes, graphic art, pools, plantings, statuary, waterfalls, and lagoons, creating an experience of a new vista at every turn of a corner all unified into a setting emphasizing closeness to nature. President Suharto presided at a simultaneous 1993 opening of a group of new Bali hotels and made a personal visit to the Inter-Continental thereafter.

A new program of Global Partner Hotels and Resorts was introduced to offer IHC's customers a wider selection of destinations, and to offer owners of quality hotels an opportunity to benefit from IHC's marketing and sales power and travel industry alliances through a representation agreement involving a base fee supplemented with charges for bookings actually produced. This program, headed up by Charles E. Brownfield III, proved particularly attractive in the United States and expanded rapidly from 1993 onward.

John Wright became area president – Europe for Inter-Continental in 1993.

With the operating divisions in place, projects to update IHC's product and service standards were undertaken. A structured quality assurance inspection program was developed with an outside contractor, and a statistically valid system for measuring guest satisfaction was introduced.

In 1994 a joint venture arrangement with the Presidente group of hotels in Mexico brought six prestigious properties into the Inter-Continental and Forum family, in Mexico City, Cancun, Ixtapa, Puerto Vallarta, Cozumel, and Los Cabos.

Marcello Pigozzo became president of the Asia/Pacific area where Yuji Tsutsumi would become chairman; Alvaro Diago, with experience in IHC hotels in Colombia, Brazil, Argentina, New York, and Miami replaced Pigozzo in Latin America. A graduate of the Glion hotel school, Pigozzo had joined Inter-Continental in 1970 as a management trainee at the Tamanaco, after completing a one year's contract with London's Savoy Group. Promoted to front office manager in the Embajador in Santo Domingo, he was one of the department heads who served as "extras" in some of the scenes of *The Godfather*, the "Cuban" sequences of which were filmed at the Embajador. Pigozzo's first general manager posting was in Managua where he was sent to reassert IHC's operating control of the property after the overthrow of Somoza. Upon arrival, he discovered that the hotel was fully occupied with troops and the various victorious Sandinista *comandantes* (who were not paying for their rooms or meals) and the international press, who paid daily in cash, which was promptly used to buy the next day's food in the open market. General manager assignments in Valencia, Quito, the Tamanaco, and Miami preceded his election as senior vice president – Latin America.

"Inter-Continental Hotels and Resorts" was introduced as the company's new corporate name, recognizing the increasing role which resort operations would play in IHC's future.

In Buenos Aires, early in 1995, IHC opened its first new hotel in South America in twenty-one years, highlighting a revitalized program of Latin American development led by Kuhlman and area development vice president Bill Bagwill, a University of Washington and Cornell graduate. Construction was under way on hotels in São Paulo, Brazil, and Cartagena, Colombia, and agreements for new properties were concluded in Panama and Guatemala.

Joint venture operating companies would be established in 1995 to bring existing hotels in South Africa and new and remodeled properties in Turkey into the Inter-Continental group.

In Asia, a unique multipurpose development of shops, offices, departmental store, and an Inter-Continental Hotel opened in 1995 on a site in the old city center, Bugis Street district of Singapore. The hotel and shopping arcade would

Marcello Pigozzo became Inter-Continental's area president, Asia/Pacific in January 1995.

INTER·CONTINENTAL®
HOTELS AND RESORTS

The Inter-Continental Buenos Aires was IHC's first new hotel in South America in more than twenty years.

The Sandton Sun & Towers Inter-Continental Johannesburg. IHC entered South Africa through an agreement with the Southern Sun Hotel Group, making it the first luxury hotel group to have a presence in South Africa for 20 years.

incorporate restored and reproduced shophouse façades, preserving a portion of the colonial "look" of old Singapore for future generations. Seiyo Corporation, another Saison Group company, would be responsible for the retail activity in "Bugis Junction" as the center would be known. Later in the year, the Inter-Continental Tokyo Bay, built on a bay-front location as part of a major urban renewal effort, would open in Japan.

Singapore general manager Daniel Desbaillets, who had held similar positions in Colombo, Bangkok, and Montreal, was a second generation IHC general manager; his father had led the

Inter-continental Genève for many years. Another two-generation combination was José Lovaton, long-time chief of the Santo Domingo Embajador, and son José who was appointed general manager of Inter-Continental Medellin early in 1994.

The Inter-Continental Tokyo Bay, opened in 1995.

Terje Myklebust, former head of SAS Hotels, who had joined IHC's development organization in 1990, and development officer Nihal Sirisena were working to enhance IHC's partnerships with existing hotels in eastern Europe, and concluded agreements for new hotels, or conversions of existing properties, in Tirana, Albania; Sofia, Bulgaria; and Ljubljana, Slovenia.

Khalifé and Middle East development vice president Georges Bekhazi had expanded IHC's resort portfolio with contracts for hotels in Luxor, Sharm-el-Sheikh, and Hurghada in Egypt, and completed negotiations for IHC's involvement with the reopening of Le Vendôme and the rebuilding of the Phoenicia Inter-Continental in Beirut.

A company-wide review of the way it was conducting its business was undertaken late in 1994. This re-engineering-style reappraisal of operating systems would be tackled by task forces staffed from among company executives at all levels, with assistance, in some cases, from outside consultants.

Initiatives begun in individual hotels and regions – notably North America – would be examined to determine their applicability system-wide. The uniform goal would be to serve the group's customers more effectively and efficiently, at optimum – hopefully lower – costs to the hotels and the organization. As an outgrowth of the hotel level analyses and changes, head office support activities could logically be tailored to more precisely support hotel operating needs and goals.

The Inter-Continental New York would host twenty heads of state during the commemoration of the United Nation's fiftieth anniversary, and the Inter-Continental Los Angeles, which had opened in 1992, would achieve a certain measure of fame, after the fact, when it was revealed that it had housed the sequestered jury from the O. J. Simpson trial for several months.

To assure a steady supply of top-quality management talent, the company introduced a fast-track corporate management development program, which identified promising young university graduates and enrolled them in a structured program of work experience combined with formal continuing education, leading to a graduate degree in business administration. Successful completion would lead to an appointment as a general manager within ten years.

LEFT: Presidente Inter-Continental Mexico was the company's first joint venture agreement, adding six hotels and resorts to the group in 1994.

Frederik de Roode (right), vice president and general manager of the Inter-Continental New York, with President Chirac of France.

As the company approached its fiftieth anniversary, it had emerged from a seven-year period of never-ending organizational change and could face its future with a measure of financial confidence. Its property assets were continuing to be improved through carefully controlled upgrading and remodeling projects.

The organizational stability and business disciplines introduced under Sueaki Takaoka's leadership had resulted in greatly increased profitability and unprecedented development.

In March 1996, Seiji Tsutsumi assumed the position of Chairman and Chief Executive Officer of Inter-Continental Hotels and Resorts after Takaoka's untimely death.

Shortly after graduating from the economics department of Tokyo University in 1951, Tsutsumi joined his family run department store, taking the reins of management as Store Director the following year, and ultimately as President of the rapidly growing Seibu Department Stores in 1961. Over the course of the next three decades Tsutsumi turned a small department store on the edge of Tokyo into a dynamic conglomerate of roughly 200 companies and over 125,000 employees worldwide with a total revenue of US$ 40 billion by 1995. While Seibu Department Stores is still one of the group's anchor companies, Saison has widened its family business into the areas of finance, real estate development, and travel and tourism, with Inter-Continental Hotels as a core member.

Internationally, Tsutsumi pursues a broad spectrum of activities, including those that call on his experience as a corporate executive, as well as others that reflect his personal interest. In the area of international political economics, he is an active member of both the Trilateral Commission and the Japan-US Business Council. Tsutsumi has written extensively on the topic of the ex-Soviet economy, and has been a Guest Professor at Moscow University since 1982. He is also a board member of the International Council of the Museum of Modern Art in New York, a trustee of the Royal Academy of Arts in the UK, and is part of the committee working to restore and preserve the Angkor Wat Temple in Cambodia. For Tsutsumi's outstanding achievements in letters and in business, he was awarded the French Officier de l'Ordre de la Légion d'Honneur, as well as the

The Inter-Continental Los Angeles opened in 1992. The hotel was "home" to the O. J. Simpson jury for several months during 1995.

Commander's Cross 1st Class for Services to the Republic of Austria in the area of culture.

Under the pen name of *Takashi Tsujii*, Tsutsumi is an acclaimed author of a number of novels, short stories, poetry collections and essays. Both as a businessman and as an international man of letters, Seiji Tsutsumi, recognizing the unique quality and global nature of Inter-Continental and its people, is determined to ensure that the company maintains its global leadership role into the 21st century.

What had begun of necessity half a century earlier when hotel managers had been recruited from a variety of backgrounds, and been installed to run individual hotels almost as independent

entrepreneurs, had consciously evolved over the years into an operating style which emphasized the individual nature of each hotel and its role as a good citizen and leading local business entity, sensitive and responsive to its own unique environment. Within the framework of an approved business plan and budget, hotel management teams took charge of the business and delivered a product consistent with standards which evolved for the entire group, but which wherever possible were enhanced to emphasize the local culture and assure competitive leadership in the local market-place. Lessons learned in one part of Inter-Continental's world would be shared through regular structured and informal meetings of groups of managers and functional department heads. A worldwide monitoring of key personnel assured opportunities for career growth. Inter-Continental would flourish as an international collection of hotels, each highly competitive in its individual market, reflecting no uniform, specific national origin or style. The group would be consistently marketed worldwide as a quality product. Worldwide communications and booking systems would support the individual hotels. Managers who could grow in such an environment would become the strength of the company; those who needed a textbook set of instructions from above would be unhappy and probably fail. Inter-Continental's reputation and strength reflect the success of this management style, and the commitment of those individuals who have been its implementers, even through periods of extreme adversity, for half a century.

HOTEL	LOCATION	IHC AFFILIATION Commenced	Terminated
Grande	Belém, Brazil	1949	1966
Carrera	Santiago, Chile	1950	1960
El Prado Inter-Continental	Barranquilla, Colombia	1950	1977
Reform Inter-Continental	Mexico City, Mexico	1952	1970
Victoria Plaza	Montevideo, Uruguay	1953	1968
Princess	Hamilton, Bermuda	1953	1955
Tequendama	Bogotá, Colombia	1953	–
Del Lago Inter-Continental	Maracaibo, Venezuela	1953	–
Tamanaco Inter-Continental	Caracas, Venezuela	1953	–
Nacional de Cuba	Havana, Cuba	1956	1960
Jaragua Inter-Continental	Santo Domingo, Dominican Republic	1957	1960
Embajador Inter-Continental	Santo Domingo, Dominican Republic	1957	1977
Curaçao Inter-Continental	Curaçao, Netherlands Antilles	1957	1976
Varadero Oasis	Varadero Beach, Cuba	1957	1959
El Salvador Inter-Continental	San Salvador, El Salvador	1958	1975
El San Juan Inter-Continental	San Juan, Puerto Rico	1958	1961
El Ponce Inter-Continental	Ponce, Puerto Rico	1960	1975
Phoenicia Inter-Continental	Beirut, Lebanon	1961	1976
Ducor Inter-Continental	Monrovia, Liberia	1962	1987
Hotel Indonesia	Jakarta, Indonesia	1962	1974
Southern Cross Inter-Continental	Melbourne, Australia	1962	1977
Dublin Inter-Continental	Dublin, Ireland	1963	1972
Cork Inter-Continental	Cork, Ireland	1963	1972
Limerick Inter-Continental	Limerick, Ireland	1963	1972
Frankfurt Intercontinental	Frankfurt, Germany	1963	–
Ivoire Inter-Continental	Abidjan, Ivory Coast	1963	–
Singapura Inter-Continental/Forum	Singapore	1963	1983
Mandarin	Hong Kong	1963	1974
Inter-Continental Jordan	Amman, Jordan	1964	–
Inter-Continental Wien	Vienna, Austria	1964	–
Intercontinental Genève	Geneva, Switzerland	1964	–
Inter-Continental Jerusalem	Jerusalem	1964	1988
Karachi Inter-Continental	Karachi, Pakistan	1964	1985
Okura	Tokyo, Japan	1964	1972
Esplanade Inter-Continental	Zagreb, Yugoslavia	1964	1975
Inter-Continental Hannover	Hanover, Germany	1965	1994
Oberoi Inter-Continental	New Delhi, India	1965	1985
Pago Pago Inter-Continental	Pago Pago, American Samoa	1965	1973
Siam Inter-Continental	Bangkok, Thailand	1966	–
Inter-Continental Dacca	Dacca, Bangladesh	1966	1983
Bali Beach	Sanur, Bali, Indonesia	1966	1983
Continental	Accra, Ghana	1967	1969
Ambassador Inter-Continental	Accra, Ghana	1967	1969
Inter-Continental Quito	Quito, Ecuador	1967	1988
Inter-Continental Lahore	Lahore, Pakistan	1967	1985
Inter-Continental Rawalpindi	Rawalpindi, Pakistan	1967	1985
Inter-Continental Auckland	Auckland, New Zealand	1968	1983
Inter-Continental Lusaka	Lusaka, Zambia	1968	–
Musi-o-Tunya Inter-Continental	Livingstone, Zambia	1968	–
Tahara'a Inter-Continental	Pape'éte, Tahiti, French Polynesia	1968	1974
Delmon Inter-Continental	Manama, Bahrain	1969	1970
Inter-Continental Düsseldorf	Düsseldorf, Germany	1969	1992
Inter-Continental Manila	Makati, Philippines	1969	–
Inter-Continental Paris	Paris, France	1969	–
Bristol Kempinski	Berlin, Germany	1969	1974
Inter-Continental Managua	Managua, Nicaragua	1969	–
Inter-Continental Nairobi	Nairobi, Kenya	1969	–
Inter-Continental Kabul	Kabul, Afghanistan	1969	1984
Duna Inter-Continental	Budapest, Hungary	1969	1993
Inter-Continental Medellín	Medellín, Colombia	1970	–
Vier Jahreszeiten Kempinski	Munich, Germany	1970	1994
Inter-Continental Cali	Cali, Colombia	1971	–
Inter-Continental Teheran	Teheran, Iran	1971	1980
Okura Inter-Continental Amsterdam	Amsterdam, The Netherlands	1971	1982
Inter-Continental Kinshasa	Kinshasa, Zaire	1971	–
Cyrus Inter-Continental	Shiraz, Iran	1971	1973
Darius Inter-Continental	Persepolis, Iran	1971	1973
Portman Inter-Continental	London, United Kingdom	1971	1992
Inter-Continental Cologne	Cologne, Germany	1971	1992
Inter-Continental Valencia	Valencia, Venezuela	1971	–
Inter-Continental Guyana	Ciudad Guyana, Venezuela	1971	–
Inter-Continental Bucharest	Bucharest, Romania	1971	–
Inter-Continental Helsinki	Helsinki, Finland	1972	–
Keio Plaza Inter-Continental	Tokyo, Japan	1972	–
Inter-Continental Hamburg	Hamburg, Germany	1972	–
Taj Mahal Inter-Continental	Bombay, India	1972	1995
Lee Gardens Forum	Hong Kong	1972	1976
Okoume Palace Inter-Continental	Libreville, Gabon	1972	–
Ceylon Inter-Continental	Colombo, Sri Lanka	1973	–
Munich Penta Forum	Munich, Germany	1973	–
Forum Jamaica	Kingston, Jamaica	1973	1975
Mark Hopkins Inter-Continental	San Francisco, California, U.S.A.	1973	–
Furama Inter-Continental	Hong Kong	1974	1990
Inter-Continental Prague	Prague, Czech Republic	1974	–
Borobudur Inter-Continental	Jakarta, Indonesia	1974	–
Forum Wiesbaden	Wiesbaden, Germany	1974	1991
Rose Hall Inter-Continental Hotel/ Country Club	Montego Bay, Jamaica	1974	1982
Inter-Continental Rio	Rio de Janeiro, Brazil	1974	–
Emir du Liban	Beit-ed-Din, Lebanon	1974	1976
Forum Warsaw	Warsaw, Poland	1974	–
Inter-Continental Dubai	Dubai, United Arab Emirates	1975	–
Inter-Continental Ocho Rios	Ocho Rios, Jamaica	1975	1982
Inter-Continental London	London, United Kingdom	1975	–
Riyadh Inter-Continental	Riyadh, Saudi Arabia	1975	–
Makkah Inter-Continental	Makkah, Saudi Arabia	1975	–
Inter-Continental Zagreb	Zagreb, Croatia	1975	–
Khyber Inter-Continental	Peshawar, Pakistan	1975	1985
Port Vila Inter-Continental Island Inn	Vila, Vanuatu	1975	1989
Victoria Inter-Continental	Warsaw, Poland	1976	–
Inter-Continental Maui	Maui, Hawaii, U.S.A.	1976	1996
Golf Forum/Inter-Continental	Abidjan, Ivory Coast	1976	–
Inter-Continental Istanbul	Istanbul, Turkey	1976	1979
Saipan Beach Inter-Continental Inn	Saipan, Marianas	1976	1984
Muscat Inter-Continental	Muscat, Oman	1977	–
Inter-Continental Kingston	Kingston, Jamaica	1977	1982
Ritz Carlton	Montreal, Quebec, Canada	1977	1991
Le Vendôme	Beirut, Lebanon	1977	1978
Davao Insular Inter-Continental Inn	Davao, Philippines	1977	1992
Punta Baluarte Inter-Continental	Calatagan, Philippines	1977	1989
Massarah Inter-Continental	Taif, Saudi Arabia	1977	–
Montfleury Inter-Continental	Cannes, France	1977	1982
Inter-Continental New York	New York, New York, U.S.A.	1978	–
Four Ambassadors Inter-Continental	Miami, Florida, U.S.A.	1978	1981
Forum Tel Aviv	Tel Aviv, Israel	1978	1979
Inter-Continental Berlin	Berlin, Germany	1978	–
Ritz Inter-Continental Lisbon	Lisbon, Portugal	1979	–
Inter-Continental Beograd	Belgrade, Serbia	1979	–
Regency Inter-Continental Bahrain	Manama, Bahrain	1980	–
Abu Dhabi Inter-Continental	Abu Dhabi, United Arab Emirates	1980	–
Mount Kenya Safari Club	Nanyuki, Kenya	1980	1986
Bonaventure Inter-Continental Hotel & Spa	Fort Lauderdale, Florida, U.S.A.	1981	1984
Plaza Inter-Continental	Buenos Aires, Argentina	1981	1982

HOTEL	LOCATION	IHC Affiliation Commenced	Terminated
St. Anthony Inter-Continental	San Antonio, Texas, U.S.A.	1981	1988
Forum Budapest	Budapest, Hungary	1981	–
Al Ain Inter-Continental	Al Ain, Abu Dhabi, United Arab Emirates	1981	–
Pavilion Inter-Continental Singapore	Singapore	1982	1988
Athenaeum Inter-Continental Athens	Athens, Greece	1982	–
Britannia Inter-Continental London	London, United Kingdom	1982	–
Forum London	London, United Kingdom	1982	–
May Fair Inter-Continental	London, United Kingdom	1982	–
Amstel Inter-Continental	Amsterdam, The Netherlands	1982	–
American	Amsterdam, The Netherlands	1982	–
Europa Belfast	Belfast, Northern Ireland, United Kingdom	1982	1986
Brussels Europa	Brussels, Belgium	1982	–
Le Grand Hotel Inter-Continental	Paris, France	1982	–
Prince des Galles	Paris, France	1982	1984
Meurice Inter-Continental	Paris, France	1982	1988
Lotti	Paris, France	1982	1984
Paris Penta	Paris, France	1982	1983
Europa Inter-Continental	London, United Kingdom	1982	1983
Carlton Inter-Continental	Cannes, France	1982	–
George Forum/Inter-Continental	Edinburgh, Scotland, United Kingdom	1982	–
Castellana Madrid	Madrid, Spain	1982	–
De La Ville Forum/ Inter-Continental	Rome, Italy	1982	–
D'Angleterre Inter-Continental	Copenhagen, Denmark	1982	1984
Dhahran Algosaibi	Dhahran, Saudi Arabia	1982	1985
Victoria	Amsterdam, The Netherlands	1982	1985
Mount Royal	London, United Kingdom	1982	1983
Piccadilly	London, United Kingdom	1982	1983
Kennedy	London, United Kingdom	1982	1983
St. Ermin's	London, United Kingdom	1982	1983
Chesterfield	London, United Kingdom	1982	1984
Clifton-Ford	London, United Kingdom	1982	1983
Savoy	Rome, Italy	1982	1984
Amra Forum	Amman, Jordan	1982	–
Scanticon Princeton	Princeton, New Jersey, U.S.A.	1982	1991
Drury Lane	London, United Kingdom	1983	1983
Petra Forum	Petra, Jordan	1983	–
Inter-Continental New Orleans	New Orleans, Louisiana, U.S.A.	1983	–
Inter-Continental Houston	Houston, Texas, U.S.A.	1984	1988
Inter-Continental San Diego	San Diego, California, U.S.A.	1984	1987
Nairobi Safari Club	Nairobi, Kenya	1984	1991
Inter-Continental Luxembourg	Grand Duchy of Luxembourg	1985	–
Abha Inter-Continental	Abha, Saudi Arabia	1985	–
Inter-Continental Hilton Head	Hilton Head, South Carolina, U.S.A.	1985	1988
Inter-Continental Sydney	Sydney, Australia	1985	–
Leconi Palace Inter-Continental	Franceville, Gabon	1985	–
Inter-Continental Mombasa	Mombasa, Kenya	1985	–
Al Bustan Palace Inter-Continental	Muscat, Oman	1985	–
Inter-Continental Miami	Miami, Florida, U.S.A.	1986	–
Willard Inter-Continental	Washington, D.C., U.S.A.	1986	–
Sorrento Palace	Sorrento, Italy	1986	–
Ancira Sierra Inter-Continental	Monterrey, Mexico	1986	1991
Semiramis Inter-Continental	Cairo, Egypt	1987	–
Scanticon Minneapolis	Minneapolis, Minnesota, U.S.A.	1987	1991
Strand Inter-Continental	Helsinki, Finland	1988	–
Forum Cracow	Cracow, Poland	1988	–
Taj Palace Inter-Continental	New Delhi, India	1988	–
Forum Prague	Prague, Czech Republic	1988	–
Inter-Continental Stuttgart	Stuttgart, Germany	1988	–
Inter-Continental Cancun	Cancun, Mexico	1988	1991

HOTEL	LOCATION	IHC Affiliation Commenced	Terminated
Inter-Continental Seoul	Seoul, Korea	1988	–
Schweizerhof Inter-Continental	Berlin, Germany	1989	–
Scanticon Denver	Denver, Colorado, U.S.A.	1989	1992
Forum Glasgow	Glasgow, Scotland, United Kingdom	1989	1990
Inter-Continental Chicago	Chicago, Illinois, U.S.A.	1989	–
Forum Bratislava	Bratislava, Slovakia	1989	–
Forum Shenzen	Shenzen, China	1990	–
Des Indes Inter-Continental	The Hague, The Netherlands	1990	–
Inter-Continental Toronto	Toronto, Ontario, Canada	1990	–
Hotel Metropol Moscow	Moscow, Russia	1991	–
Yokohama Grand Inter-Continental	Yokohama, Japan	1991	–
Forum Berlin	Berlin, Germany	1992	–
Inter-Continental Montreal	Montreal, Quebec, Canada	1992	–
Forum Genève	Geneva, Switzerland	1992	–
Inter-Continental Los Angeles	Los Angeles, California, U.S.A.	1992	–
Jeddah Inter-Continental	Jeddah, Saudi Arabia	1992	–
Inter-Continental Leipzig	Leipzig, Germany	1992	–
Yamoussoukro Palace	Yamoussoukro, Ivory Coast	1992	–
Las Lomas Forum	Rionegro, Colombia	1993	–
Churchill Inter-Continental	London, United Kingdom	1993	–
Bali Inter-Continental Resort	Jimbaran, Bali, Indonesia	1993	–
Terrace Inter-Continental	Adelaide, Australia	1993	1996
Hurghada Inter-Continental Resort & Casino	Hurghada, Egypt	1994	–
V Centenario Inter-Continental	Santo Domingo, Dominican Republic	1994	–
Presidente Los Cabos Forum Resort	San José del Cabo, Mexico	1994	–
Presidente Inter-Continental Cancun	Cancun, Mexico	1994	–
Presidente Inter-Continental Cozumel	Cozumel, Mexico	1994	–
Presidente Inter-Continental Mexico City	Mexico City, Mexico	1994	–
Presidente Ixtapa Forum Resort	Ixtapa, Guerrero, Mexico	1994	–
Presidente Inter-Continental Puerto Vallarta	Puerto Vallarta, Mexico	1994	–
Inter-Continental Buenos Aires	Buenos Aires, Argentina	1995	–
Royal Plaza Inter-Continental Montreux	Montreux, Switzerland	1995	–
Forum Hamburg	Hamburg, Germany	1995	–
Inter-Continental Singapore	Singapore	1995	–
Inter-Continental Tokyo Bay	Tokyo, Japan	1995	–
Cape Sun Inter-Continental Cape Town	Cape Town, South Africa	1995	–
Sandton Sun & Towers Inter-Continental Johannesburg	Johannesburg, South Africa	1995	–
Beverly Hills Sun Inter-Continental Durban	Durban, South Africa	1995	–
Forum Schweizerhof Hannover	Hanover, Germany	1995	–
Inter-Continental Sofia	Sofia, Bulgaria	1995	–
Forum Nicosia	Nicosia, Cyprus	1995	–
Lev Inter-Continental Ljubljana	Ljubljana, Slovenia	1995	–
Ceylan Inter-Continental Istanbul	Istanbul, Turkey	1996	–
Le Vendôme Inter-Continental Beirut	Beirut, Lebanon	1996	–

Global portfolio as at 1 March 1996

INDEX

PICTURE CREDITS
We would like to thank the following for providing pictures and for permission to reproduce copyright material.
Hulton Deutsch Collection pages 11, 14, 15, 19, 27; The Image Bank pages 56, 63 (Hans Wolf), 68 (M. Beebe), 85 (Clark Weinburg), 80 (John Banagan); MAGNUM pages 52, 67, 89 (Burt Glinn), 66 (Marilyn Silverston); Miami Historical Museum pages 10, 15; Pan Am Historical Foundation page 9; Robert Harding Picture Library pages 44, 45 (Adam Woolfitt), 104 (Malcolm Robertson), 72, 77, 107; Scopell Photoshop pages 150, 151 (Ary Diesendruck); Zefa Pictures pages 55, 69, 75, 97, 116. 121.

COVER

Paper sculpture created by Ann Whiting. Commissioned by Inter-Continental Hotels & Resorts in commemoration of its 50th Anniversary